THE
GUY
ON
THE
LEFT

THE
GUY
ON
THE
LEFT

Sports Stories from
the Best Seat in the House

JAMES DUTHIE

PENGUIN

an imprint of Penguin Canada, a division of Penguin Random House Canada Limited

Published by the Penguin Group
Penguin Canada Books, Inc., 320 Front Street West, Suite 1400,
Toronto, Ontario M5V 3B6, Canada

First published in Viking hardcover by Penguin Canada, 2015
Published in this edition, 2017

1 2 3 4 5 6 7 8 9 10 (RRD)

Manufactured in the U.S.A.

Cover photograph by Darren Goldstein

Library and Archives Canada Cataloguing in Publication data is available upon request

eBook ISBN 978-0-14-319618-1

www.penguinrandomhouse.ca

Penguin
Random House
PENGUIN CANADA

For my favourite sportscaster,
Jonathan Pitre

CONTENTS

prologue

GOLDEN SUNDAY

He's dead.

I say this only to myself. Can't say it out loud, because the young woman behind the wheel beside me is already redlining towards hysteria. And if I even bring up the possibility that we killed him, she will most likely spontaneously combust. So I just keep telling her he's fine. But really, I think he might be dead.

So this is how the 2010 Olympic Games, the best days of my career—heck, 17 of the best days in the history of our country— are going to end? With a body on the street in front of our car? It's at that moment, somewhere between the driver's sobs and the sirens, that I briefly have one of the coldest, most selfish thoughts of my existence.

Crap, I'm going to miss the after-party.

Not quite sure how I got here. Wait, that sounds like I'm drunk. By "here," I don't mean this intersection in Vancouver, with the ambulance, the sobbing driver, and the maybe dead guy. I mean "here" in that larger, life-retrospective sense.

I was supposed to be a gym teacher. That was the plan. Can you imagine getting to climb the rope every day? Even when you are ... like ... 50? And if that didn't fly, well, then I'd join the RCMP like my dad. Though as a kid, I'd try on his Mountie Stetson in front of the mirror, and think, dude, you look like a cartoon character. This hat was not made for your protruding ears and sizable melon. You are Dudley Do-Wrong.

I never dreamt big. Even when I stumbled into TV (not to be confused with stumbling into *my* TV, which I have also done), my only goal was to anchor the local sports in Ottawa. If I could somehow score a sideline pass for Ottawa Rough Riders games, I could die happy. I know what you're thinking: What kind of sick freak would want to watch that team up close? (Or I suppose, if you are under 30, you're thinking: What the hell are the Ottawa Rough Riders? Google them. There is some solid comedy in there.)

But here I wake up 20 years later, and it's the last day of the 2010 Olympic Games. And somehow all sorts of important people have screwed up because they've let me be a host on national television. Not only that, they let me host hockey games as my real job. Buffoons.

On this morning, though, I don't have time to go all Bryzgalov and try to figure out my place in this twisted universe. The little alarm clock in my hotel room on West Hastings Street is blinking 4:00 A.M. Gotta roll. This is about to be the longest day of my career. It will make NHL Trade Deadline seem brief. Plus, we never killed a guy on *TradeCentre*. Though Darren Pang and Pierre McGuire went at it pretty good once over whether Tomas Fleischmann was a winger or a centre. (I know. We care about hockey just a little too much. Pray for us.)

I make the short walk through the dark, mostly empty streets of Vancouver to the International Broadcast Centre (IBC). This, by the way, is the only six-hour window where the streets have been empty these last two weeks. From roughly 8 A.M. till 2 A.M., they have been packed. Mardi Gras, in February, in British Columbia, just without as many breasts being flashed. Lots of man boobs, though. Give Brian Williams a few vodka shots and the dress shirt always becomes a bandana!*

*Note: to my knowledge, multiple award-winning Olympic host Brian Williams has never done shots and taken his shirt off in public.**

**My lawyers made me add that sentence.

It's true. Canadian men (not named Brian Williams) generally love to go shirtless and paint flags on their chest when our country wins a medal. This is one of my key Olympic takeaways.

Today will be my ultimate tripleheader. I will anchor Olympic coverage on CTV in the morning, sprint to the rink to host the gold medal hockey game between Canada and the U.S., then bolt a few blocks to BC Place to commentate the closing ceremony with my Olympic co-host, Lisa LaFlamme. "No biggie," one of the bosses tells me as he passes me in the hall that morning. "Probably only be about 35 million people total watching those three shows. Don't blow it."

Great. Thanks.

The morning shift is like a house party. Athletes are being paraded through the studio for one giant Canadian victory lap. It has been the best Olympics ever for our country, and a gold medal win in hockey would give Canada the most golds ever by a host nation at a Winter Games. Our polite, over-apologetic nation has developed a swagger over the last 16 days. You can see it in the faces of some of the proud athletes coming through our studio. "Yeah, we're Canadian. We're badass now. Deal with it."

This is the last shift Lisa and I will work together in Vancouver. Some people thought it was an odd combo, the sports guy and the serious newscaster, but we've had a blast together. Lisa probably doesn't want people to know this since she is now the serious, credible host of the *CTV National News*, but she is actually an IDIOT. That's in all-caps because it's the official nickname for my group of high school buddies: IDIOTS. It's an extremely complimentary, loving term for me. IDIOTS have deranged, warped senses of humour. No joke is too dumb. Lisa quickly becomes an honorary IDIOT in Vancouver. On air: smart, polished, with a news sense that is off the charts. Off air: IDIOT. When she replaces Lloyd Robertson at CTV later that year, I give her mock grief for not bringing me with her. Because the national news clearly needs more hockey highlights and Will Ferrell movie lines. Which, in essence, is all I do.

Mid-morning, I leave for the gold medal hockey game. It resembles a scene from *The Amazing Race*: scramble out of the IBC, grab a waiting car, bail after three blocks because of the traffic, jog the couple of kilometres to the rink, just in time to host a two-hour pre-game show.

Steve Yzerman, Team Canada's general manager, drops by the set. I find Steve struggles at times in interviews since he became a GM, because he is too careful with his words, trying not to say the wrong thing, instead of just answering the questions. But today, just minutes before the biggest Canadian hockey game since '72, he is cool and smooth. Stevie Y is always clutch in the big games, I think to myself. Brian Burke, GM of the American team, also stops by. It has been just a few weeks since the death of his son Brendan, in a car accident. He tells me before we go on air he hasn't slept since the accident. Burke is a hard-ass, and we've clashed countless times on air. But we're friends when the cameras are off. When I interview him, he usually shoots down all my questions and makes an "I want to rip your head off" face for the entire segment. Then, when the cameras go off, he smiles and winks ("Gave you some good TV there, didn't I?"). He's a good man with a soft side he tries too hard to keep hidden. And on this, what should be one of the proudest days of his career, he looks broken. As he leaves the set, I have the most unpatriotic of thoughts. Part of me hopes the U.S. wins, just to give him … something.

Our set is right on top of the Zamboni entrance at the Canadian team's end of the rink (for the first and third periods). During the game, we sit in seats with the fans. When a period ends, the set pops out like a jack-in-the-box. It's a great spot to do TV, right in the thick of the crowd. In fact, fans are so close, they can actually reach over and touch us while we're doing our panels. Which is awesome, when the fans are, say, the Swedish Women's Alpine Skiing Team. But not quite as good when they are, say, the Hammered Angry Dudes after Their Side Loses Team. During one post-game show, a large well-lubricated meathead reaches over the railing and unplugs my headset, leaving me with no communication with the producer. So I just keep talking. I almost blow off an entire commercial break, which would only cost the network, oh, a couple hundred grand or so. But it gets Meathead a high-five from his equally sloshed buddy. So it's worth it, I suppose.

There have been better panel invasions by fans. During the first NHL outdoor game in Edmonton in 2003, a blitzed wannabe stuntman dove onto the set as Gord Miller, Bob McKenzie, and Pierre McGuire were on live. The set collapsed. (Temporary TV desks aren't exactly built to hurricane-proof standards.) The guy rolled off and was gone before Bob could hurt him. And make no mistake, Bob would have hurt him. In Carolina at the 2006 Stanley Cup final, a fan jumped a fence and ran across our set. We weren't on air at the time, but a tape of the moment still exists, and it is pure gold. He bumps into a startled Bob, who gives him a hard elbow as he runs away, and then yells, "I'll kill you, you f&%$ing &%$#!"

Bob is one of the best men I know. He will do anything for you. Unless you run on his set while he's working. Then all bets are off. Kevin Pratt, one of our long-time *NHL on TSN* videotape wizards and the official collector of our many bloopers, plays the tape for us every few months for kicks while we're killing time before a game. I always watch Bob and howl, and Bob always chuckles at me. Because while he is threatening to kill the guy, I don't even bother to look up from my notes, pressing the talk-back button to our production truck to calmly say, "We might want to get some security." By now, I'm used to drunken fools who want to be on TV, and Bob's readiness to pummel them. I still expect to look at Twitter one day and see a tweet from Bob that reads something like, "Stamkos signs eight-year extension in Tampa. Oh, and I just beat a man to death with my iPad. Confirmed."

For the gold medal game, two of Vancouver's finest are flanking the panel, ostensibly to protect us from the drunks. Reality is, they're protecting the drunks from Bob.

The atmosphere in the building that Sunday is equal parts electricity and anxiety. This historic, euphoric time for our country feels like it hinges on 60 minutes of hockey. Yes, it has been an incredible Olympics for Canada, but if there is no gold today, it still will feel like a failure. That isn't fair to all the other athletes who have done the country so proud, but it is reality here in Canada.

I spend a great deal of time trying to decide what to say in the opening 30 seconds I get at the top of the show, just before puck drop. You'd like to be deep and eloquent and poetic before this kind of moment. Steve Dryden, TSN's managing editor of hockey and the brains behind much of what we do on the panel, sends me a few thoughts about how rare it is for a country's culture to be so intertwined with a singular sport. I put some of that into my own words and use it ... but I decide halfway through the intro that all this deep thinking really isn't me. So I cut it short and end with three simple sentences.

"This is Canada. This is hockey. This is for gold."

A 2–0 Canada lead halfway through the game temporarily eases the national anxiety, but shift by shift, the Americans chip away at Team Canada's (and the country's) confidence. When Zach Parise scores with 24 seconds left to tie it 2–2, 18,000 fans, and about 25 million more at home, primed for the party of their lives, sit in stunned silence instead.

During the commercial break before the overtime intermission, it hits me. Pretty much every person in the country is watching us right now. I turn to the panel (Bob, Darren Pang, and Nick

Kypreos from Sportsnet—remember this was the CTV/Rogers Olympic Broadcast Consortium) and say, "Well, boys, we probably should try not to screw this one up."

We don't. And neither does Canada in overtime. They dominate play early, but the game falls into a bit of a conservative lull a few minutes in. So much so that my eyes drift to my phone. My 10-year-old son has a big playoff game back home (the minor hockey scheduler who picked that time should be fired), and I'm eager for updates. As I'm quickly scrolling through texts, I hear the one word that will become synonymous with this moment:

"Iggy!"

The building is so nervous, so quiet, that from our seats right behind the U.S. net, I can clearly hear Sidney Crosby call for the puck from Jarome Iginla, who has dug it out of the corner. I look up from my phone just in time to see Crosby, maybe 30 feet away from me, slide the puck under Ryan Miller, and into … history.

Bedlam.

Sorry, Mom, but I believe the only two words that come out of my mouth are "holy shit." (Thankfully, Chris Cuthbert, the guy calling the game, has a slightly better choice of words with his historic, perfect "golden goal" call.) I'm not sure if mine is a primal reaction to the weight of the moment, or because I almost missed it trying to get an atom hockey score.

I was in grade 1 in 1972, and only have faint recollections of watching TV in our school gymnasium when Henderson scored against the Russians. Not even sure if that memory is real. I might have been making caterpillars out of egg cartons at the time in art class. We did that a lot. So I am instantly determined to soak up every second of our generation's version of "The Goal." I just stand and watch. Those "no cheering from the press box" lessons are too ingrained. But this is one of those few times you wish you could suspend those rules. My old journalism profs will wince when I say this, but I want to go nuts like everyone else. I want to jump on backs and pour beer over my head and generally be … Canadian. You can't live in this country and not be bursting. But instead, I just soak it up for about 30 seconds and then start getting ready for the post-game. That is the thing about our business. There is no savouring. You watch history happen and then almost instantly start trying to figure out what you are going to say about it.

I'm not sure what I said. I still have never watched the tape. I'd just get mad about some dumb comment I made, or some smart one I didn't. Doesn't matter anyway. I could have read my grade 12 trigonometry textbook aloud and no one would have minded. Canada was in the best mood of its collective life.

We do about an hour of post-game, and then it's time for more wind sprints. I have about 10 minutes to get over to BC Place for a live shot with Lisa to preview the closing ceremony.

Until Crosby's goal, I was concerned about the way the Games were going to end. Lisa and I attended a top-secret dress rehearsal the night before, and it is … strange. The producer is an Australian who thought it would be funny to just throw every Canadian stereotype into his production. So the program is full of giant inflatable moose and beavers, and Mounties and hockey players. While watching the rehearsal, I think to myself: If Canada wins, this will be fine. Everybody will be in a great mood and ready to laugh (plus, the nation will be half in the bag). But if Canada loses that hockey game, this could be a disaster. We know our comedy in Canada, and nothing is funny when you lose to the U.S. in hockey.

The bosses seem a little nervous about me hosting this show. They warn me several times to "resist the smartass" in my commentary. To which my comeback is, "So you want me to play giant inflatable beavers … err … straight?"

At every Olympic opening and closing ceremony, the organizers hand out a booklet that explains each element of the show, so the commentators from every country can explain it to their viewers. But for this show, the notes don't really let people know this is a tongue-in-cheek celebration of Canada. So while these giant beavers are flying around BC Place, this is the sentence commentators are supposed to read for their viewers: "There are six million beavers in Canada, more than any other country in the world." So in places like Japan, Chile, and Estonia, I'm guessing the commentators deliver that line as straight as Walter Cronkite. Which is pretty embarrassing. Except Canada won hockey. So now it's pretty freaking funny.

When the closing ceremony ends, Lisa and I fight through the massive crowd to a car waiting to take us back to the hotel. Lisa jumps in the back, and I, always the gentleman, call shotgun and grab the front. There is a sweet young woman volunteer behind the wheel. As the car takes off, I close my eyes and take a long, deep breath. This has been the craziest, longest, best day of my 20 years in this business. I'm exhausted, exhilarated, and can't wait to crack open a beer at the after—

WHAM!

He comes out of nowhere. We are going through an intersection on a green light, and he just sprints into our path. We hit him head-on and he flies over the hood and onto the pavement. The driver screams. I'm not sure what I say. Probably "holy shit" again.

This is not happening. The one black eye, the one horrific moment of these otherwise spectacular Games, was the tragic death of Georgian luger Nodar Kumaritashvili in a training run just hours before the opening ceremony. Please don't tell me we've killed another guy 10 minutes after the closing ceremony.

Police and paramedics are literally parked at the intersection when the accident happens. They are sprinting towards us within seconds. After we make sure everyone in the car is okay, I get out to check on the guy we just hit. He's down and not moving, with a paramedic already over him. A police officer tells me to go back to the car. Lisa is comforting our driver, who is a mess. She has done nothing wrong. This guy ran into us like he was on a kickoff team and the car was the returner.

For the next ten minutes or so, we sit. Our driver sobs quietly as paramedics surround the victim. And that selfish part of me imagines what the morning tabloid headline will be: "DOUBLE MURDER! CROSBY KILLS USA, CTV CO-HOSTS KILL TOURIST!" (Though it probably would have been singular—HOST—as I would have undoubtedly blamed Lisa, and copped a plea.)

But then, like some bizarre SNL sketch, he suddenly gets up. Not even gingerly. He pops up like a wide receiver trying to show the defensive back he didn't hurt him (a lot of football metaphors in this story ... odd). The paramedics try to lay him back down, but he wants no part of it. He runs over to the driver's side window of our car and yells, in what I believe is a hammered Irish accent, "So sorry, my bad!" And he's gone! Sprint-limping (limp-sprinting?) down the street, with a paramedic giving fruitless chase.

Just like that, this movie I'm playing a bit part in goes from tragic ending to Seth MacFarlane script. I'm laughing. The poor driver is in shocked silence. Which sure beats the "I just killed a guy" sobs of the last 10 minutes. And Lisa is being a pro, trying to figure out what we do next. Turns out a police officer just asks a few questions, then gives the driver a number she has to call for an insurance report. And it's done. No corpse, no headlines, and crucially ... no missed beer.

I end up going straight from the CTV after-party to the airport, where I pass out on a row of chairs, about 24 hours from the time I woke up. I toss my jacket over my head, but still hear the guy sitting across from me say to his buddy, "Hey, I think that's James Duthie. He looks ... homeless." Solid analysis, frankly.

chapter 1

THE GUY ON THE LEFT

I'm at a hockey tournament in Pittsburgh with my son, doing what parents do at minor hockey tournaments: drinking beer while sitting on a highly contaminated carpet in a hotel hallway, watching the kids play mini-sticks.

This woman, a mom from another team staying on the same floor, is staring at me. It's a stare we Canadian broadcasters get a lot. The "I know you, but can't freakin' remember your name" stare. Sure, most sports fans know us (and we have a few of those in our country). But the rest of the population can be just a little off with the names. Over the years, strangers have greeted me with various forms of the following:

"Hey, it's ... TSN guy!"

"Hey ... Quiz guy!"

"Dude from the Olympics!"

"It's the guy with the monkey!"

"Don't you work at my Starbucks?"

"Hey, it's James ... Cybulski!"

"Cory Woron!"

"Darren Dreger!"

"Dutchy!"

"James Dutchy!"

"James Duffy!"

"Mike Duffy!"

"Farhan Lalji!" (That guy was really drunk.)

"Seth Meyers!"

"Ben Stiller!"

"Ed Helms!"

"Channing Tatum!" (Okay, that one never happened.)

I don't mind. I've always felt that Canadian TV sportscaster is an ideal level of celebrity (somewhere between U and Y on the "A-lister" scale). Think about the benefits:

- No paparazzi (except for Gino Reda).
- No mob scenes outside your hotel (except for Gino Reda).
- No paternity suits from South American housekeepers (look, Gino, it was bound to come out eventually).

And yet, there are so many positives:

- Always given the best tables (at Tim Hortons).
- No problematic excess wealth to blow on drugs and bling.
- Complimentary powder puffs.

And, perhaps most importantly, you get to meet literary agents and publishers who ask you to write books that will almost certainly be used as goalposts for basement ball hockey within weeks of purchase.

I didn't really want to write this one. It's hard to write about yourself when you have spent your career telling other people's stories. And I much prefer the weekly columns I've done about important, pressing issues like how my dog could swing a five iron with his mouth and hit a ball off a tee. (True. See last book.) But I do have tales. And best to get them told before it's too late. I have this theory that once you hit 40 or so, your brain feels like it just finished five plates at a buffet. It's stuffed. So from that moment on, every time you create a new memory, an old one falls out the opposite ear. When my youngest daughter was born, I lost the entire second half of the '81 Super Bowl. So better to get everything on record now.

I do have a request for librarians and shelf stockers at Chapters: don't stick this book in the autobiography section. Not. Worthy. Autobiographies should really only be written by presidents, astronauts, and Nobel Prize winners. Oh, and swimsuit models. I will cozy up by the fire to read about Kate Upton's "magical summer by the lake" any day. But besides Kate, they should really make a rule that you have to be minimum age 60 before you write your life story. Even worthy, relevant autobiographies are silly sometimes, especially the early chapters. No matter what wondrous things you have accomplished in life, we don't really need to hear every single detail of your childhood. We don't care about how you skipped school when you were 10 and got the belt from the headmaster. Just skip to the part where you are fighting off sharks on the life raft with your dead sergeant's wooden leg. That does not happen in this book, by the way. Sadly. This book will follow the usual story-of-my-life timeline, but I'll try to skip most of the boring junk and just share the humiliating stories that you will mock me for on Twitter for the next decade. Least I could do. And if you start to nod off, just skip to the chapter where Aaron Ward attacks me with a knife on the streets of Boston.

Back at that hockey tournament in Pittsburgh, a smile finally comes across the face of the woman staring me down. "I know you!" she exclaims, while wagging her finger like I'm guilty of something. Why do people always do that when they say, "I know you"? I always worry that I kicked them in the shins in kindergarten and they have come back to seek bloody vengeance. "I know you!" she repeats. "You're ... you're ... the guy on the left!"

Err ... Sorry?

"When I watch TSN ... the panel ... you're the guy on the left!"

Why, yes, I am, I suppose. Proud to be him. So I guess that is what this book will be. How I got to be the guy on the left. And the weird and wonderful characters I've met on the way there.

These are my memories, my interpretation of events, and all errors are mine. Though wherever necessary, I've checked with others who were there to make sure things happened the way I recall. And when they disagreed with my version, I had them killed.

chapter 2

THE SECRET LIFE OF LITTLE JIMMY

The daydreams are always worst in the morning. I am 12 years old, and lost in space. My brain is always aimed anywhere except the direction it is supposed to be. One of my chores is to walk our dog, a miniature poodle named Thumper (after the rabbit in *Bambi*—back off, I didn't get a vote) every morning before school. For years, I take the exact same rectangular route: down Valewood Crescent, left into The Greenbelt (the massive forest behind our neighbourhood), through the woods, left at the path by the McMurrays' house, and back up the street to home. I can do it in my sleep, so my mind meanders endlessly.

Blackburn Hamlet is a typical suburb 20 minutes east of downtown Ottawa, where many of the houses are virtually identical, including ours and the McKinnons' place next door. This particular morning, I stumble back from the walk, open the side door, let Thumper off his leash, and slump up the stairs towards my parents' en suite bathroom, where I shower every morning. Half-asleep and mind wandering, I ditch clothes as I walk: sweatpants on stairs, T-shirt on railing, Speed Racer underwear wherever it may fall. (I know you should probably give up cartoon underwear by the time you hit double digits, but I really love Speed Racer.) I open Mom and Dad's bedroom door, and stagger in ...

... And run right into Mrs. McKinnon, my lovely neighbour, in her bra and undies (definitely not Speed Racer). She doesn't scream, though I believe I let out a brief high-pitched yelp, like a kitten when you step on it.

Little did I know Mr. McKinnon was away at a conference in Regina. So Mrs. McKinnon kinda bit her lip, gave me a knowing smile, extended her hand, and led me towards the bed. I never thought this would happen to me ...

Stop it! See, this is what I mean about the daydreaming. It's problematic. No, this did not turn out like the *Penthouse Forum*s we would read in my friend Tom's basement. (Tom's dad had the greatest stash of *Penthouse* and *Playboy* in all of Blackburn. Tom was a great friend to me.) I turn and bolt from the house in a panic, before Mr. McKinnon can beat me with a bat, not even bothering to fetch Thumper. It's "leave no MAN behind." Doesn't say anything about dog. My mom makes me go back and get him a few minutes later—the most awkward doorbell ring and greeting ever—as a kind and understanding Mrs. McKinnon, now in housecoat, hands Thumper back to me, smiling that sympathetic "I always knew you weren't quite right so I won't press charges" smile.

And sadly—no wait—pathetically, this is not my worst Daydreaming Dog Walk story.

Within weeks of the McKinnon Incident, I grab the leash, do the same 15-minute route, and this time walk in the door of the proper house, where I find my father waiting for me, wearing a deeply troubled look on his face as he stands there, holding ... THE DOG!

So yeah. I took the leash for a walk.

My childhood is too happy to merit many more minutes of your time. There aren't enough skeletons. I really could have used a psychopathic uncle with a dungeon under the cornfield behind his farmhouse, where he kept my entire Little League team for one torturous summer. No such luck. Instead, I get two amazing parents, two nurturing older sisters (except for when I'm little and they pin me down and dangle their long hair in my mouth to torment me ... sickos), and a normal, *Wonder Years*–like suburban upbringing. (Alison White was my Winnie Cooper, just in case she doesn't come up again. She lives in Seattle I believe, so if someone there reads this, look her up, and tell her she rocked my grade 7–8 world.) But I suppose later in the book, when I'm getting NHL stars to run over each other with Zambonis, you might need a little context. You know, that typical autobiographical "how his childhood shaped him" stuff. Hence the daydream dog-walking stories. I figure they shed a little early light on why eventually I would end up making ridiculous music videos about delay-of-game penalties instead of having a legitimate, grown-up job.

I am born James Forbes Ryeburn Duthie (my closest friends still call me Forbes) in Ottawa in 1966. I am a giant freakin' baby, "biggest in the hospital," Mom still says proudly. Dad figured he had himself a nose tackle. But by about 14, it was pretty clear he had, at best, a kicker. Living almost entirely off Pop-Tarts and lime Jell-O for most of my youth likely stunted my growth. A lawsuit is still being contemplated, though if I have to give up the cinnamon-frosted Pop-Tarts to proceed, I will drop it immediately.

My dad is also James Forbes, as were the three fathers before us. He is a young, freshly minted RCMP officer from Kamloops when he marries his first love, a beautiful, soon-to-be schoolteacher from Ottawa named Sheila Code. They have two beautiful little girls, Merydee and Kristy. Then after waiting a few years, produce yet another child who would eventually wear makeup.

Dad is good at the whole cop thing. He gets promoted quickly and often, and we spend the early years of my life moving back and forth across the country. Oops, I'm already getting bogged down with those childhood details I promised not to bore you with. So I'll point-form my movements and memories for my first decade or so:

Birth to six weeks old, Ottawa: Just a lot of Mom's breast in my face is all I really recall. (Sorry Mom. I love you.)

Six weeks to eighteen months old, Edmonton: We live next door to the brother of Chicago Blackhawks player Cliff Koroll. I am way too young to register this, but my parents remind me later, and he becomes my first sports idol. When I get old enough to read (roughly 17), the first thing I do every morning is check the box scores to see if the Hawks have won, and if Cliff has any points. This is probably the genesis of my infatuation with sports.

Eighteen months to five years old, Halifax: I have only one vivid memory of Halifax. And it's dark. One Halloween, Mom makes me a bunny costume. (Back off. Bunny costumes are cute when you're four.) A neighbour makes the bunny's tail, and a couple of hours before trick-or-treating, I have to walk a block or so to her house to pick it up. I am already wearing the costume and get jumped by a bunch of thugs. They taunt me, beat me, and leave me bruised and muddied in the park.* This scars me for life. Still terrified of Halloween. And bunnies. It is also why, along with the sexist nature of the phrase, I never used the term "get some tail." Just a whole different meaning for me.

*Since I was four at the time, this memory may possibly be somewhat distorted. My mom insists she never would have let me walk the mean streets of Halifax alone in a bunny costume at four. It's also possible the "bunch of thugs" might have been two ... maybe one ... six- or seven-year-old kid. And the beating may have just been a trip or shove to the ground. Okay, it's possible he just said, "Nice bunny costume," and I panicked, ran, and fell. But I did get my fur muddy. Of this, there is no doubt.

Five to eight years old, Victoria: At five, I take my first step into organized sports, as my parents sign me up for soccer. The first night does not go so well. It is rainy, and at some point, I fall and get my hands dirty. I run off the field, sobbing, showing my horrified father, and every other parent on the sidelines, my muddied hands, as if they have been severed by a machete. Mom still gleefully tells this story to anyone who will listen. I maintain the tears are brought on by post-traumatic stress from the whole bunny costume assault. My dad is so disturbed by his son's early wimpish tendencies that he signs up to coach the next year, to make sure I have no out. He will coach me in rep for the next decade, and we win multiple city championships in Victoria (Gordon Head) and Ottawa (Gloucester Hornets). I get muddy hands a lot during that time and don't scream even once. Just muffled sobs, mostly. Progress.

Eight to adulthood, Ottawa: We move back to my birthplace the summer before grade 3. If *Lion King* had been out when I was eight, I would have sung "Circle of Life." It would have sounded horrible. We settle in Blackburn Hamlet in the east end. It's a tough hood on the wrong side of the tracks. By this I mean there is no Dairy Queen. I know. No child should grow up in that kind of environment. I use my street smarts to adapt and survive (two words: Dickie Dee).

Somewhere during this time, I begin my foray into fantasy sports. I don't mean the current version, where you spend your entire week trying to decide if you'll play Alex Smith on the road against the Seahawks D. No, I create my own fantasy sports world. My sisters are four and six years older than me, so I have a lot of time to play on my own. Some kids have imaginary friends. I create entire teams in multiple sports. You know *The Secret Life of Walter Mitty*? This is *The Secret Life of Little Jimmy*.

It is beyond elaborate. I play entire 80 game NHL seasons on my driveway with stick, net, and tennis ball. I play full baseball seasons in the basement with a drumstick and ping-pong ball (hit the far couch—single; above the lamp—double; ceiling trim—home run!). I invent an imaginary quarterback named T.J. (don't even give him a last name—it was the Prince/Madonna generation) and play his *entire career* out, almost 20 seasons' worth of games, with stops in San Francisco, New Orleans, and San Diego, and a still-record 10 Super Bowl wins. His stats are kept meticulously on lined paper in a binder—far neater than any of my school notebooks. (Priorities—never a strength.) The football games are split between the basement and the front yard, where T.J.'s star receiver (actually every one of his receivers) is the one birch tree in the middle of our lawn. For the better part of two years, my father can't figure out why half the branches are breaking off his otherwise healthy tree. Until he catches me one day firing J5V spirals at it from 15 yards away. Front Lawn Memorial Stadium closes that afternoon. All further games are moved to our climate-controlled Basement Dome.

My own personal fantasy leagues end around the time I notice Alison White at Emily Carr Middle School. I would create other imaginary friends well into my late teens and twenties. But they are all supermodels.

As host of *NHL on TSN*, I would often get asked what kind of hockey player I was. I have two answers. The first is, "Amazing." Then I add, "If you mean floor hockey."

In Victoria, my soccer season runs from October to April. I never see the inside of a rink. When we move to Ottawa, my dad and I decide it is time for me to become a real Canadian boy and play hockey. It doesn't go so well.

Equipment is my first problem. Dad doesn't buy me a jock, figuring no one in atom house league can raise the puck high enough, or fire it hard enough, to hurt little Jamie and his two pals. So I play my first two years of organized hockey jockless. (All children are miracles—my three, doubly so.) This is also the era just before full cages become mandatory. And the face mask Dad chooses for me is the strangest thing in the history of hockey gear—worse than Cooperalls. It is an inch-wide piece of plastic that starts in the middle of the helmet, extends past my nose, and then widens to cover my mouth. Basically, an upside-down T. How this passes safety (and aesthetic) standards, I have no idea. When I take to the ice, I quickly realize I am the only kid in house league with this bizarre headgear. Since I have never skated before, the guy at the skate exchange talks Dad into a used pair of Lange moulded boots (the precursor to Micron Mascots) to help my weak ankles. So to summarize: no jock, no mask, ski-boot skates … and questionable talent.

Still, I just love it. I may look like a cartoon character on the ice, but I fall hard for the game. I play for the next six years, and though my skating never really catches up, the one thing I can do is score. At the end of my last season of peewee, the coach announces he will give out trophies for most goals, most assists, most points, and MVP. I know I have the first three wrapped up, and figure the fourth is a lock. I tell Dad to clear some serious space on my trophy shelf. He replies that it shouldn't be a problem, because it's empty.

That team party, in our coach's basement, still haunts me. The coach, a non-parent named Johnny, decides to morph my goal, assist, and point trophies into one "Top Scorer" award, one of those cheap plastic six-inch trophies with the hockey player on top. Then he gets to MVP and pulls out a trophy only slightly smaller than the Stanley Cup. Now we're talking. "And the Blackburn Stingers Peewee Meadow Team MVP goes to …"—I am already halfway off the couch—"Our goalie, Andrew Bush!"

WTF?!? Andrew Bush only played goalie that season because no one else would. And his save percentage was, by my calculations, somewhere around .347. Oh sure, he is probably the nicest kid I know, and I've still never seen a guy try harder—sprawling all over the ice trying to make saves (while I was cherry-picking around centre ice)—but I still decide at that moment, the hand holding my can of Grape Crush shaking angrily, that giving Andrew Bush MVP over me is the greatest travesty in the history of awards:

3. Jose Theodore over Jarome Iginla for the Hart.
2. *Shakespeare in Love* beating *Saving Private Ryan* for Best Picture.
1. Andrew Bush over Jamie Duthie for Blackburn Stingers Peewee MVP.

I had been Bush-whacked! Then, as Andrew sits there beaming, holding a trophy a foot taller than him, Coach says, "I decided to add a separate award for Most Outstanding Player!"

Okay Coach, you moron, there really is no difference when between MVP and MOP when the awards are for the same team, but since this one is clearly going to me, thank you for realizing your ridiculous mistake on the MVP.

"And the Most Outstanding Player is … also Andrew Bush!"

What kind of sick joke is this, Coach?

"And for this award, Andrew, you get these brand-new goalie pads!"

Just kill me now. Andrew Flippin' Bush has just won the house league hockey equivalent of both showcases on *The Price Is Right*, and my record-smashing Gretzky-like offensive season is rewarded with one little piece of plastic.

My NHL dream dies that day. (Okay, it was probably dead the day I put on the Langes and the funny face mask, but play along.) Sure, I toil around in bantam for a couple more years, even moving up two levels, where we win my one and only hockey championship. But we never got trophies for titles back then, just medals. This teaches me very early that individual honours clearly mean more than team success. Never forget that, kids.

So to summarize, I spend my childhood hockey career as a selfish, me-first, ankle-skating floater. And just as I'm finally getting decent at 14, I quit for downhill skiing, joining Bobby Orr on the list of legendary hockey careers cut short.

Football soon takes over as my passion. My parents have season tickets to the Ottawa Rough Riders, and we go to every game together, for oh, 20 years. I don't think you could have chosen a worse period to love a professional sports franchise. Over that time, the best the Riders do is two 9–9 seasons. Or as we called it, the Dynasty Years. It's almost mathematically impossible to be that bad for that long in a nine- (sometimes eight-) team league. My Riders pull it off.

I worship the Montreal Expos too, and often bring my Sony Walkman (stop giggling, under-30 generation) to the Riders games to listen to baseball while my football team takes another thumping.

On the last Saturday of the 1981 baseball season, the Expos have a chance to clinch their first-ever pennant against the New York Mets. I seem to be the only one in section G of Frank Clair Stadium with a radio. And no, kids, there was no live streaming or TSN iPhone app back then to keep you updated. Before long, I am a live echo for Expos play-by-play guy Dave Van Horne, repeating every gut-wrenching ball and strike call to all those sitting around us. When I describe Wallace Johnson tripling home the winning run, section G goes ballistic.

I decide then and there that if I can't make it as a pro athlete, I want to be a sports broadcaster.

chapter 3

LAST CHANCE U

If this book were turned into a movie (pause for uproarious laughter), the last scene in the previous chapter—the one about me deciding in the stands of a football stadium to become a sportscaster—would fade to black, the screen would read "20 YEARS LATER," and it would flash forward to me holding an *Anchorman*-style party at my mansion. "*I don't know how to put this ... but I'm kind of a big deal. People know me.*" (I actually do say that quite often ... just ask the interns. And the parties are spectacular. Vic Rauter doing cannonballs off the roof with a martini in his hand. Magic.)

Problem is, movies skip all the years of roadblocks, gut punches, and self-doubt that come before you get to that place you dreamt of. Teenage career aspirations are no different from teenage crushes. You get obsessed for a while, then fear of rejection takes over and you move on to something else (yeah, I have scars). So while I really want to be a sportscaster at 15, I soon decide it is a corny, impossible notion. So as high school nears an end, I revert to my backup plan: gym teacher. I will go to McGill and take physical education. And climb the rope in perpetuity.

Football dominates my last year at Gloucester High School. It's pretty much all I think about (okay, along with Lesley Grignon—my high school sweetheart—who has the best dimples east of Winnipeg). I play cornerback and wide receiver for the

Gators, as well as backup quarterback. In fact (brag coming), I still hold the North American high school football record for all-time completion percentage: 100 percent. One for one. For four yards. Take that, Manning and Brady. I get into one series in a lopsided win over Osgoode High. On the first play, I complete a four-yard pass to our tight end, my good buddy Jimmy Aw (now Dr. James Aw, a wildly successful Toronto doctor). On the second play, we run a QB sweep left, where I keep the ball. The play goes nowhere (substandard blocking), and I get knocked out of bounds for no gain. I believe the tackler hits me late, so I respond in a mature, sensible fashion. I toss the ball at his head. One 15-yard unsportsmanlike conduct penalty later, my high school quarterbacking career is over.

My kicking career lasts about as long. Our regular place-kicker, Ben Charles, is injured for a key game against J.S. Woodsworth. The game is a disaster, as our previously undefeated Gators squad trails 20–0 by the third quarter. I'm playing wide receiver when we get stopped on second down at their 40, and I hear the coach yell, "Field goal!" Seriously? First of all, we need three touchdowns. Second of all, that field goal will be 47 yards. My range is 40, tops. At elevation … with a hurricane behind me … after three years working with A-Rod's "doctors."

As we set up for the attempt, I panic. Instead of using the proper three steps back, two steps sideways technique I've been using in practice all week, I decide to go old-school Tom Dempsey and kick straight on. The snap is perfect, the hold is ideal, the kick … goes about five feet off the ground and is blocked by a leaping defensive lineman's groin.

I feign anger ("C'mon, block would ya?!?"), but I'm awash with relief. My fear was that the kick would clear the line and land 20 yards short, leading to an appearance on the old Bob Saget version of *America's Funniest Home Videos*. *"Tonight's finalists for the ten-thousand-dollar prize: Dog on Fire! Baby with a Nail Gun! And Wimpy Field Goal Fail!"*

Instead, the block is so quick that no one really knows how bad my trajectory was. It gets tossed off as O-line error. We lose 20–0. I never kick again.

Still, I luck into enough interceptions that a McGill University recruiter comes to visit Gloucester, and the coach ends up sending me a bunch of letters asking me to come play there. I'd like to think he scouted me and was blown away by my Richard Sherman–like shutdown abilities. But truth is, our coach likely recommended the few of us who had the marks to get into McGill and could run without falling down.

My dad and I go down for a visit and get a full tour of the campus from one of the assistant football coaches. It's impressive, a great school in a great city, with an excellent football team (they would win the Vanier Cup the next year). But on the drive home, I have a minor epiphany. I am a 5'10", 160-pound defensive back with average speed. I don't think the Niners are really looking for that. I would undoubtedly have four or five amazing frat-boy football years at McGill, then teach gym for the next three decades. And all of a sudden, that terrifies me. Maybe it's an ambition to do something bigger that takes over. Maybe deep down, it's just a wussy Mama's boy scared of being too far from home. Either way, I decide I'm not going to McGill.

I had applied to Carleton for journalism as a backup plan. And when I get the letter of acceptance and a partial scholarship, the decision is done. I am off to the school that, at the time, everyone who couldn't get into Queen's/Western/McGill would go to. They called it "Last Chance U" (an unfair label long since shaken by the school). Cruel Queen's jerks. But Carleton had several programs that were second to none in the country. And journalism was one.

From day one, it feels like a mistake. First-year journalism at Carleton (in 1985, anyway) is a weighty, theory-heavy exploration of what the media is. And frankly, I'm not really into Marshall McLuhan. I just want to go around campus carrying a TV camera to meet girls. Plus, J-school is extremely competitive. Some three hundred students are admitted into first year. Around ninety will make it to second.

I somehow survive the cut, mostly out of fear of letting down my parents—probably the single-greatest motivator of my life. My two older sisters are ridiculously smart and had aced their way through programs at Ottawa U and Queen's. I am terrified of becoming the Paul Rudd character in *Our Idiot Brother*. (Yes, I know that movie wasn't made until 20 years after I graduated. I'm trying to update my references for the kids, so play along.)

When we finally get to do television in second year, they separate us into groups of four to do our reports. The three girls in my group are extremely intense, strong-minded young women who want to change the world in one 90-second school TV report. In retrospect, they are exactly what I want my daughters to be like. But in the moment, they are, in my embarrassingly immature mind, not fun enough. They want to have regular three-hour brainstorming meetings for story topics. I want to go to Oliver's Pub and do shots. So I quit the group and go out on my own, much like my idol, Hermey the Elf, from the Rudolph Christmas special.

You know that whole misfit/nitwit thing? That was me. Love that little elf-dentist.

I decide to stick with what I know and do my first story on the Carleton Ravens star running back Mark Brown, who has been getting national attention. I arrange for an interview with Mark at the athletic centre. When I get there, a crew from TSN is already there, doing their own story on Brown. I am solo, with camera, tripod, and a giant three-quarter-inch tape deck, roughly the size of a suitcase, which has to be plugged into the camera. (I know … I am ancient.)

When Brown arrives, the TSN crew tells him they are set up and ready to go, but he sees me and tells them, "You'll have to wait. He set up an interview with me before you guys." I will never forget that. Here is a 21-year-old, finally about to make it big

(Canada-big anyway), and he makes the national TV crew wait because I had asked him first. That day, Mark Brown teaches me a critical lesson in How to Be Classy 101.

I carry the 50 pounds or so of gear to the field that Saturday to get tape of Mark in action against Queen's. I'm a lousy cameraman, but get just enough footage to work with. In the edit suite, I add Bruce Springsteen's "Born to Run" behind the shots of Brown carrying the ball—something that would get me sued in the real world but is okay in a never-to-be-seen-by-anyone-but-my-class world.

When my professor, Ron Thibault, a producer at the local CTV station, hands out the marks, my Brown feature gets an A. And under the grade, Thibault writes, "Loved 'The Boss' as your soundtrack. I think TV is something you might want to pursue."

Professor Thibault isn't exactly my Richard Dreyfuss as Mr. Holland, but his words resonate. For the first time, I think a career in television might actually be doable.

The next year, we have an extremely intense TV professor named George Frajkor. He is tough and demanding, but also a fan of creative, outside-the-box thinking. For one of our weekly newscasts, I am assigned to be the weatherman. This does not mean standing in front of a green screen pointing at fancy Doppler radar maps. We are ultra-low tech. Our news graphics (what you see over the anchor's shoulder) are pictures cut out from magazines and taped to a piece of bristol board, then chroma keyed on the screen. Several times during our newscasts, the magazine pics fall off, leaving the anchor to introduce a story about higher tuition fees with a wad of masking tape over his or her shoulder.

For our weather, we have to do a 60- to 90-second forecast on tape. George tells us we can deliver it anyway we like, as long as it contains the correct weather information. My favourite group of the moment is Run-D.M.C., the forefathers of rap/hip hop. So clearly there is only one choice. I will do a rap weather. I rope in Boris Gomez, my best buddy in J-school, to be the D.M.C. to my Run. We dress in all black, with shades and rapper hats (not easy to find in Ottawa). In a video that, if ever discovered (and transferred—it's on beta; like I said, I'm old) and YouTubed, would likely end my career. We perform the following rap:

> We're Run 320C and we're here to say,
> listen up homeboy, it's cold today!
> 10 is the high, low tonight is 2.
> Wake up, George, we be rappin' to you!
> It's cloudy right now, might rain tonight,
> moderate winds till the morning light.
> Tomorrow gonna be much the same,
> cloudy and cool, less chance of rain!

It goes on for another verse, but I'll grant you clemency. Look, it's 1988. Rap weather seems very funny in 1988. We get an A+ on the assignment, which is better than I get on any boring paper I would write in my four years at Carleton. This proves to me that if you can do something this idiotic and get actual grades for it (and thus, by extension, make money doing it in the real world), television is the career for me!

Though my first appearance on real television makes me want to move to a cave and never come near a TV again.

chapter 4

CENTRAL ... PART? (OR HOW I BLEW 20 GRAND ON A GAME SHOW)

I make my television debut the true North American way: on a game show.

During my years at Carleton, my buddies and I often gather at my place after class and watch meaningless, generally awful afternoon TV. For some unexplainable reason, we are drawn to a game show called *The New Chain Reaction*. It's a word game where contestants in teams of two are given one word at the top of a chain and another at the bottom, with a handful of blank spaces in between. They ask for letters and try to guess the rest of the words in the chain. Each word is linked with the one below it and above it.

Here's a sample chain from an actual show (thanks, YouTube):

BACK
PACK
PARACHUTE
JUMP
SUIT
DIAMOND
SHAPE

Within a few weeks, we are so good, we can do entire chains without a single letter. And yet the vast majority of contestants seem to struggle with the most obvious words:

DRUNK

HANG_ _ _ _

"Umm ... hang glider?"

One day, we notice during the closing credits that the phone number for contestants to apply is a Montreal area code. Yes, it's a Canadian-made game show. Which usually means:

• *Up to $25 in cash prizes up for grabs!*

• *And today's bonus round grand prize ... a brand-new ... boat! (remote control, batteries not included, new from Fisher-Price).*

• *You've won a weekend for two at the luxurious Motel 6 in Cornwall!**

*For five-time champions only.

But *The New Chain Reaction* is no *Bumper Stumpers*. It also airs in the United States, and the prize money is decent. So we call. Because that is what wacky university students do. And a few weeks later, my friend Mark Ward and I are at the CTV Montreal (CFCF then) studios auditioning. We dominate. We are the '72 Dolphins, the '80s Oilers, the '90s Bulls, the 2010s Emily Blunts. We are perfection. On the way home, we are already counting our money before we have even been picked for the show. Later that summer, the phone rings, and it's one of the show producers.

"Congratulations, you've been chosen to be on *The New Chain Reaction!*" she tells me as if I've won $500 million in the Powerball. "But we've changed the show to be a one-on-one game, so unfortunately, your friend Mark didn't make it."

This may have been the worst decision in game-show-casting history, seeing that Mark is better looking and funnier than me and could have probably hosted the show, let alone be a contestant. I feel bad for him. But whatever. I'm in, baby! There isn't going to be any selfless "It's either both of us or none of us" stance here. There may be no "I" in team, but there is one in Duthie! It's always free money over friendship in the poor student years.

I spend the next month or so watching every episode to practice, and by the day of my taping, I believe I am the single-best *Chain Reaction* player on the planet. I'm cockier than Kanye.

We arrive at the studios in Montreal early in the morning, and they usher all of the prospective contestants into a room to practise the game together. I am the only male and the youngest in the group by a solid decade. This only makes me more confident. I am like the annoying smart kid in the class who puts his hand up for every answer. I am killing it. And I can see the housewives I'm competing with are rattled. There is only one woman I'm worried about. Her name (if memory serves correct … I have spent 25 years trying to black this day out of my memory, and thankfully, no tape seems to exist) is Robin, and she is the only other contestant getting a lot of words right. I try to stare her down. But then I remember my face is as intimidating as a puppy. So I back off, and instead just pray quietly that I don't draw her on the show.

The producer tells us they will be taping eight to ten shows that day, and there is no guarantee we'll be chosen. We will sit in the crowd, acting as a studio audience, and we'll only find out we're on a couple of minutes before the taping begins. And there is good news. The most money you can win on *Chain Reaction* comes in the bonus round. The pot begins at $1,000 and goes up by $1,000 every day that no one wins. Well, apparently, the last group wasn't exactly Mensa because the pot is at $8,000.

Watching the first couple of shows is painful. These particular contestants rate somewhere between dumb and hamster. The only upside is that they have zero chance in the bonus round and the pot continues to climb.

Then Robin gets chosen. When the host interviews her off the top of the show, she reveals she is the Scrabble champion of North America. This makes me throw up a little. Robin is some wordplay Rain Man. She is in my head. And apparently, everybody else's. Robin destroys three straight opponents. And stares me down in the audience with an evil grin each time. Okay, it's possible she is just giving everyone in the audience a friendly smile, but like I say, I'm shaken, so I see her as Khan to my Captain Kirk. (Note: This is the first time I have made a Star Trek metaphor. Ever. I had never even watched a Star Trek movie until I got bored on a plane recently and watched *Into Darkness*. Pretty solid work there, J.J. Abrams. I mean I'm not showing up at Comic-Con in full costume next year or anything, but it kept me awake back in 21C.)

Then suddenly, I get the tap. One of the show staffers is kneeling beside me, whispering, "Come with me, you're up next." Why do I feel like the skinny kid with no archery skills who is going to get killed first in *The Hunger Games*? The cockiness from the morning is gone, swagger-jacked by nerves and Robin—The Satan of Scrabble—cleverly disguised as a sweet woman in glasses and a sweater set. Somehow, she has stumbled in the bonus round, so the pot is now $13,000. I'm a wreck.

I go to the bathroom to give myself a quick Eminem in *8 Mile* pep talk. I stare myself down in the mirror, trying to get psyched up. I look full late '80s dork in a tweed jacket, one of my dad's clip-on ties, and my Corey Hart "Never Surrender" spiked hair. But I fight through that.

You can do this, kid. You're a journalism student. You got a respectable A– in grade 13 English. Might have been a B+. Whatever. And you have likely watched way more game shows than Robin ever has. She was too busy with those lame Scrabble tournaments ... LEARNING EVERY WORD KNOWN TO MAN SO SHE CAN KICK YOUR SKINNY ASS!

Yeah, so the pep talk didn't really go so well. I'm nervous to the point of catatonic when they bring me out on the set and the ultra-cheese disco theme music rolls. Game shows always start with the host having a short chat with the contestants to introduce them to the audience. Host Geoff Edwards strolls up to my podium and says, "Let's meet James, a journalism student who wants to be a sportscaster someday. Hey, James, all the good baseball play-by-play guys have signature home run calls. What would yours be?" WTF? Seriously Geoff, I feel like passing out right now, and you hit me with that? What happened to the simple "Where you from?" or "What school do you go to?" or ... "Would you like me to put Robin in a sleeper hold for you?" I hesitate for a second, and say, in the saddest, meekest little squirrel voice, "Uhhh … Goodbye … Mr. Spalding?" It isn't a horrible answer, but it is delivered with the confidence of a man who should never ever get the chance to call a home run, even for the Moose Jaw Little League finals on community cable.

"Goodbye, Mr. Spalding, sure … that's a good one," Geoff says, already treating me like a wounded kitten.

Game time. The first chain begins with the word CENTRAL. Robin, defending champion and evil sorceress, gets to go first.

"I'll take a letter under CENTRAL, please Geoff."

A P pops up. Somewhat oddly, Robin is stumped. Buzzer goes. The champ with a rare stumble. Geoff turns to me for my official game-show competitive debut.

"I'll take a letter under CENTRAL as well, Geoff."

PA. This, I believe, is one of the few moments in my life when my obsession with sports hurts me. The word that pops into my mind is PACIFIC. Heck, almost every sport has a CENTRAL and PACIFIC division. Plus, they are both time zones. It makes perfect sense. Has to be right. Yeah, baby. I'm about to take the lead.

"Pacific?" Cue sad game-show buzzer sound.

"Oooh, sorry, not pacific. Good try," says Geoff, gently stroking his wounded kitty. Robin is ready to pounce now.

"Another letter under CENTRAL, Geoff."

PAR. For one of the few times all morning, I see confusion and doubt in Robin's eyes. She shakes her head side to side, and right at the buzzer, mutters, "Pacific?" What the? First of all Robin, I just guessed that. Second, unless you are so smart you know some funky nouveau English, pacific is not spelled PARCIFIC. One word in, and this epic battle of morning practice-round titans is starting to look like that SNL *Jeopardy* skit. Over at the challenger's podium, I still have no clue what this word is, and I am getting more nervous by the second, but surely the fourth letter will snap my brain out of hyper-sleep.

"Well, let's try another letter under CENTRAL, Geoff." Cue game-show bell sound.

"Sorry, James, that sound means there is only one more letter in the word, and we can't give it to you."

So, just to refresh. Two words that somehow go together: CENTRAL PAR_. After a second, it hits me. Of course! How could I have missed that? Finally, that confident smile returns. The swagger is back! And so I proudly answer, "PART, Geoff!"

Well, that's odd. No instant happy bell. Instead, Geoff is just looking at me funny, like I have a booger on my lip or something.

"Did you say PARK?" Geoff inquires. What's your problem, Geoff? Hearing issues? I snap back firmly:

"No Geoff, I said PART."

Buzz.

It takes me about a millisecond post-buzzer to realize what I have just done. Once again, if this had been the YouTube era, I would be an instant idiot legend, right up there with the woman on *Wheel of Fortune* who had E_CLUSI_E NIGHTCLUB and asked for a G. (Look it up. She is my kindred.)

Central Freaking Park. Only the most famous park in the world, probably. Had already been there three times. Skated on the rink. Central Part?!? What even … is … that?

Strange thing is, my Mother of All Brain Farts calms me down a little. I figure I'm screwed already, so might as well just play. In *Chain Reaction*, you also have the option of giving your opponent a letter, if you believe they are essentially a chimp and will have no chance to get the word, thus giving you an extra letter to figure it out. Having just witnessed my brilliant work with CENTRAL PART, Robin decides this is a smart option.

"I'll give him a letter under PARK, Geoff."

B. Miraculously the kid in the clip-on tie, flatlining mere moments ago, gets a pulse.

"Bench?"

Ding! I'm back baby! I take a letter under BENCH.

P.

"Press, Geoff?"

Ding! En fuego. I soooo want to taunt Robin right now.

Give ME a letter?!? See what you get, Scrabble Bee-otch? I'm going to make it RAIN words now! And end your REIGN! See what I did there Robin? See? (I could use some work on my game-show trash talking. Strong decision to keep it to myself.)

"I'll take a letter under PRESS, Geoff."

R. I'm not even hesitating anymore, now.

"Release."

Ding ding ding!!! Robin is in a full sweat now. Reeling. It's on. I roll through the next two rounds and build a meaty lead before the final chain. But it's called a game *show*, where building drama (at least as much drama as one can expect from a Canadian-made afternoon word game) is what sells. So the last round is worth as much as all of the others combined. Robin rallies for a few words in a row, and suddenly, it is down to one word for the title. LUXURY.

Gulp. "I'll take a letter under LUXURY, please."

L.

My brain is all over the place. Luxury LIFE? Luxury LAMP? (I love lamp.) Luxury LAPDANCE? Wait, what? I am so screwed. I have to throw something out there.

"Linen, Geoff?" It's not the worst answer ever. It's no Central Part. But it still gets the loser buzzer. Robin:

"I'll take a letter under LUXURY, Geoff."

LI. The next moment still ranks in the top-10 most devastating of my life.

"LIMOSINE?"

Ding, ding, ding! Applause track. Victorious Scrabble Satan jumping up and down. And kid with bad suit and spiked hair dies a little, right there on camera. I smile the worst fake smile ever as Geoff politely says get lost, and some staffer in a headset ushers me offstage. During the commercial break, one of the cameramen comes over and, trying to be sympathetic—but failing miserably—says (direct quote—I will never forget it), "Man, I feel bad for you. That was one of the most painful losses I have ever seen. You were actually really good, but that first word … man, that'll haunt you."

Thanks for that. I hope a light stand falls and crushes your spine. From just offstage, I watch Robin win the easiest bonus round I'd ever seen on *Chain Reaction*, winning the $13,000. She would win one more game to become a five-time champion, and earn $21,000 before lunch. Tax free. Meanwhile, I am told I will be sent a lovely parting gift. I'm guessing it will be a T-shirt that says DUMBER THAN CHIMP.

On the drive home from Montreal (and then for the next, oh, seven years), I contemplate what a 20-year-old student with about $300 in the bank could have done with $21,000. It is not constructive therapy.

Robin returns the next season for the tournament of champions. I don't watch because I fear it will crush the tiny pieces of my soul that remain. My buddies tell me she wins another $40,000 or something ludicrous like that. And of course, buddies being buddies, the whole Central Part thing only comes up about a dozen times a night for the next few years.

"Hey, James, want to go to New York and go skating in Central Part?"

"I hear Central Part is beautiful in the fall!"

"Hey, Duth, you should nickname your penis your Central Part!"

Hilarious. Just frickin' hilarious.

I figure once the show airs, it will be over and gone. But I soon realize reruns and syndication are not going to be my friends here. A few years later, I'm working as a news reporter at CJOH-TV in Ottawa, a large newsroom full of cubicles, when suddenly, a producer stands up and screams, "Everybody, turn to Channel 13 right now!"

I flick my own set over. Oh, God. There I am, forced to live the nightmare over in front of my co-workers, giving them the same fodder my buddies had. And even that isn't the end. A full 12 years after the show is taped, I'm on my honeymoon on the Greek island of Rhodes when my wife gets me out of the shower to come see the TV.

Yup. Not my episode this time, but it is Robin, my apparent eternal nemesis, devouring another helpless soul in syndication. What kind of evil Japanese horror film curse haunts you on your honeymoon?

Oh, I did get the lovely parting gift. The box arrives in the mail a few weeks after the show taping. It is a cheap pink clock radio. I sob briefly, then re-gift it to my sister for Christmas. Small victories.

chapter 5

THE BURGUNDY YEARS

The newsroom at CJOH-TV in Ottawa is empty, except for me. It's 11:40 P.M. on a weeknight, and I'm packing up after filing another story on some city council meeting I napped through, when the phone rings at my desk. This is rare, as I'm still the new cub reporter at the station, so no one ever calls me, unless it's to ask me to get coffee. And they usually just scream that across the newsroom. I pick up and hear the frantic voice of Leigh Chapple, our late-news anchor. "James, they taped over J.J.'s weather forecast by mistake! We have no weather! You need to get me the weather. We have a four-minute hole in the show, and it's up in two minutes! I don't care where you get it from, just get me weather!"

Oopsie. One of our little secrets at CJOH is that J.J. Clarke, our affable and extremely popular weatherman, sometimes tapes the weather for the late show. J.J. has a complicated shift as he has to be on the noon news, the main 6 P.M. show, and at 11:30 P.M. So some nights, when there are no major snowstorms or heat waves or Rideau Canal tsunamis bearing down on the nation's capital, J.J. will tape the late weather forecast as soon as the 6 P.M. show is over so he doesn't have to stick around all night. No one at home would ever guess it isn't live. Unless of course, an editor mistakenly tapes over his forecast, and J.J. disappears forever into the Matrix.

It is the spring of 1989, when most things on TV are still recorded and played off videotape. When you tape over something, it is gone forever. There is no hard drive backup. Hard drive in 1989 is what Michael Jordan does to get to the basket. It has no other meaning to us. Likewise, I have no iPhone to look up the weather in one touch. Al Gore hasn't even invented The Internet yet. We don't have a single computer in our newsroom. All our scripts are written on typewriters with carbon paper. The only source of news is the old-fashioned wire service, a printer in the corner of the newsroom that spews out endless typed pages of information from news agencies like Canadian Press or Reuters. (Yes, this is yet another "Damn, you're old, dude" chapter.)

I sprint over to the wire, but can't find one word of weather info. I try to turn on one of the handful of TVs in the newsroom, but someone has already turned them all off using some main power switch I can't seem to find. Like I said, I'm new. I run back to the phone to tell Leigh I'm struggling. She is quickly approaching panic mode. "We have two minutes ... I need weather!" This is the single-greatest test of my entire television career so far. (I'm only three weeks in, but play along.) Think kid, think. What do you always do in an emergency situation when you are lost and have no idea where to turn? Wait, that's it! Call Mommy!

"Hello?" she says in a groggy, half-asleep voice.

"Mom, it's me. Listen I need a huge favour. Get out of bed right now, turn on your TV to Skyline Cable 22." Skyline is the local cable company in east Ottawa. Channel 22 is a 24-hour scroll of news, a wire service on TV. At the bottom of the screen is a ticker that constantly shows the weather.

"Okay, sweetie. I'm on that channel," Mom says a few seconds later. "What is going on?"

"Tell you later ... just read me the weather word for word."

So with Mom on one phone in my left ear, and Leigh on another in the right, we do an emergency weather relay.

"Okay, son. Cloudy and cool tonight with a low of 10 ... the words are moving very slowly ... did you eat all your dinner?"

"Yes, Mom ... Just the weather, please!!"

"Okay, here comes some more. Fog in the morning, with some showers. Ooh, that's not good, I'm supposed to be helping Diane Anderson with her garden ..."

"Mom ... No ad-libs! Faster!"

It goes this way for the next minute until Leigh hangs up in mid-sentence. She is back on the air, delivering Ottawa its weather forecast, courtesy of my mom in her nightie, stolen word for word from the ticker on Skyline Cable 22.

"Welcome back to *Nightline*. Sorry, J.J. Clarke couldn't be with us tonight, but here is your detailed forecast for Ottawa and the Valley. Cloudy and cool tonight with a low of ten. Fog in the morning, with some showers ..."

Not a detail missed. Mom has always loved J.J., so she is pretty proud to have been his kindred for a moment, saving her favourite TV station's ass in the process. And I have been baptized into the strange and wonderful world that is local TV news.

As a little schmuck growing up in suburban Ottawa, years before TSN and eons before the instant information of Twitter, local TV news is THE show. I've always argued that *Anchorman: The Legend of Ron Burgundy* is part documentary. The local TV newscast is basically your only place to get sports highlights, and thus it is the one program my parents watch religiously. Every night at 6 P.M., we sit down for CJOH News (Channel 7) with Max Keeping and _____ (Max went through a slew of extremely talented female co-anchors—sending one after another to bigger jobs elsewhere), J.J. Clarke with weather, and Brian Smith on sports. Those guys own Ottawa.

The concept of 24-hour all-sports networks would have seemed ludicrous back then. So when I first start thinking I might like to be a sportscaster as a teenager, CJOH is where my ambition begins and ends. In my mind, if I could someday be Brian Smith doing the local sports in Ottawa, I'd be the most successful person in the history of ever.

As part of fourth-year Carleton journalism, you have to do an internship at a media outlet. In typical lazy-me fashion, I put this off until well into my final term, and end up getting one of the very last slots of the year at CJOH. It's a one-week internship, where they sometimes let students do on-air reports, usually fluff pieces tucked in the last segment of the 11:30 P.M. news.

The first day and a half, I sit in a cubicle staring at a wall. Again, it's 1989. There isn't a web to surf. I think they legitimately forget I am there. But on the afternoon of the second day, someone finds the body of a dolphin on the shore of the Ottawa River. It is the perfect local news item: a fish—sorry, mammal—out of water story. With reporter Mike O'Byrne out interviewing some marine biologist about how this is possible, they send me out to get an interview clip with the guy who found Flipper. This becomes my first hard-hitting TV interview.

Me: So ... tell me, what were you thinking when you found the dolphin?

Dolphin-Finder Dude: I was thinking, "Hey, that's a dolphin!"

Me: Any idea how a dolphin got in the Ottawa River?

Dolphin-Finder Dude: No clue, bro.

Take that Mike Wallace. I believe the marine biology experts concluded there is no way a dolphin could survive in the Ottawa River and it must have been dumped on the shore by ... I don't know ... some Mafia dolphin hit man. Whatever. My clip makes the story. I am officially in the news business.

The next day, I am sent back to Carleton to do a story on Disability Awareness Week at the university. I end the piece with my very first on-camera "stand-up." It is beyond cringe-worthy. It features me in a blindfold walking a guide dog saying, "Most of us won't get this involved in Disability Awareness Week, but hopefully everyone who takes part will leave with a better understanding of what it is like to be disabled." Then I take off the blindfold, smile, and pet the dog. Ron Burgundy himself would have giggled at the thickness of my cheese. It really should have ended my career before it started. Luckily, they ran the piece at the very end of the late news, and the station bosses must have been deep into the scotch or already asleep, because the next day, no one told me I should change my major.

I do a better story later in the week on a group trying to salvage an old steam train in Wakefield, Quebec. The editor, an older gentleman named Alastair Young, happens to love steam trains and edits the piece like he's Michelangelo finishing off the Sistine Chapel. So it looks great, and I get several compliments from Max Keeping and the other reporters.

My internship ends, and I figure I've done okay but don't have much of a shot of getting a job there anytime soon. In fact, I'm advised by the assignment editor to try to get a summer gig in Timmins or North Bay or somewhere remote, as CJOH is only for reporters with "years of experience."

But odd things happen. In life and in news. Breaks come in the strangest of ways. On that weekend after my internship, a reporter named Guy Lepage goes skiing, falls, and breaks a rib. And apparently, they can't find anyone to cover his Monday night reporting shift. I guess the peach-fuzzed kid who got that tanta-lizing dolphin clip is still fresh in someone's head, because they call and ask if I can do the shift.

I do. And then they ask if I can do Tuesday. And then Wednesday and Thursday. And then all of the next week. With two months left in university, I'm working full-time hours in the country's fourth-largest TV market. Guy's skiing accident soon turns into a summer job offer, and when summer is over, it becomes a full-time job offer. Screw Timmins (sorry Shania). I'm not going anywhere.

I owe all of this to Max Keeping. Though most of the station's news bosses believe I'm too young and green, and need to cut my teeth in some small-town market, Max sees something in me and convinces them to keep me around. I spend the next five years as a local TV news reporter for CJOH. I had never really wanted to do news. I generally hate politics and murder and fires and ridiculous advice stories like "Tonight at six, we'll tell you how to stay in shape this holiday season by exercising and eating fewer pies!" Thanks tips. But local TV news is also wonderful in its wackiness.

One weekend evening shift, they send me to a town called Almonte, where a group of amateur astronomer super-geeks are getting together to watch a lunar eclipse. Since the best views of the eclipse don't happen until it's completely dark, we don't get back to the station until 11:20 P.M., ten minutes before the story is due to lead the newscast. (There are a lot of slow news nights in local TV.) So I sprint into the editing suite with the tape, only to find the editor, Rollie Duval, tossing his cookies every 30 seconds. And I mean cookies by the dozens. It is like the scene in *Stand By Me* where the bullied overweight kid eats all the pies and cod liver oil, and stages a barf-a-rama. But Rollie is the only editor working that night, so he is either going to edit this piece, or it isn't going to make it to air. And in news, you HAVE to make it to air.

I have structured the piece in a pretty simple, linear fashion. We show the astronomy club arriving at their hill, excited about the big event, and run interview clips with them as the eclipse approaches, cutting to shots of the sky here and there to show the moon slowly disappearing from sight. Rollie presses the buttons to make an edit, pukes, presses some more buttons, and pukes again. I am like a desperate coach, trying to egg on his athlete to the finish line.

Me: C'mon, Rollie, just 30 more seconds to cut! Two minutes to air! You can do this, Rollie!

Rollie: [Barf. Barf. BAAAAARRRRFFFFF!!!]

Me: Hey, is that … risotto?

The last 20 seconds of the story consists of a voice-over by me, showing our dramatic (by local news standards) shots of the full eclipse. Rollie has already put my voice down on the tape, but needs to cover the words with video. For now, the tape is black. But now it's 11:29, and it's clear we aren't going to finish. I am about to miss deadline, which for a summer student two months into his career, probably means I'll be working a drive-thru by next week.

But here's the rub. During this eclipse, the sky is basically dark. Sure, there's a lunar aura, but it's essentially black. So I figure, what the heck. Let's just run it like this, and pray no one notices. So I pop the tape out of the machine, leave Rollie to his trash can, and sprint downstairs to the tape room, like Holly Hunter in *Broadcast News*, handing the story to the tape operator who pops it in just as anchor Leigh Chapple is saying, "Here's James Duthie with the story …"

It looks great for the first 1:20 or so, and then comes my final cheesy voice-over, something along the lines of, "And finally, there it is! After months of buildup, and these final hours of excitement, the astronomers get to witness perfection: a cloudless, complete, cosmic miracle. A full lunar eclipse! Darkness falls every night in our world … but it only looks like this once in a blue—I mean black—moon. In Almonte, Ontario, James Duthie … CJOH News."

And the video that runs over every word of that voice-over? Black, unedited tape.

I run back upstairs to a) see if Rollie is still with us, and b) make him pinky-swear he'll never tell a soul about this.

I sneak out of the building before the show is over, figuring they all know we hadn't finished the story and just went to black for 20 seconds. I go to bed pondering, McDonald's or Burger King? Which place has the least embarrassing hats? Sure enough, Max Keeping calls me up to his desk when I arrive at work the next afternoon.

"Saw your piece on the eclipse last night, James."

"Uhh … yeah … about that … Rollie was really sick and …"

"Loved it. Great stuff. Pictures looked amazing."

"Oh. Uhh. Thanks. Yeah. It worked out … really … well."

Local news screw-ups take on legendary status. They become stories that are laughed about repeatedly for decades over beers. A couple of years into my stint at CJOH, another young summer reporter is doing a piece on a robbery. In his report, he says, "The robber was seen fleeing the scene with a baklava on his head."

Well, that's odd. Shouldn't have been hard to miss a guy running through the streets with a Lebanese pastry on his melon. I find him in the newsroom just after the piece airs and say, "Umm … Matt … I think you meant balaclava." You have never seen a face go so white, so fast.

Having your first job in local news is baptism by five-alarm fire. Which is great. I learn more in five years at CJOH doing news reporting than I do the rest of my career combined.

I am still a newbie trying to figure out the business when the Gulf War breaks out. Prime Minister Brian Mulroney calls an emergency cabinet meeting. Our excellent Parliament Hill reporter, Norman Fetterley, happens to be away, and all of our other senior reporters are on other stories, so they send Jimmy Olson (me) up there to do a live report into the 6 P.M. newscast. Max loves to test his people. And since he is the one who stuck his neck out to get me hired, he wants to test me to make sure I can handle it. So he opens our live report with (roughly) this: "So James, what is Canada's next move likely to be?" At this time in my life, I know as much about politics as Paris Hilton knows about quantum physics. I'm 23. And an immature 23. My primary focus in life is getting the number of the waitress at Maxwell's in the market. So when Max throws that one at me, the little voice in my brain responds: *Uhh Max, I have no freakin' clue. We might go to war, might not. Send some ships, maybe? Maybe go air force instead? Wait, do we have an air force? Can I go back to covering the cow-milking contests? I'm so screwed.*

Fortunately, my actual voice edits that out and does what well-trained broadcasters do when they don't know an answer: deliver a few lines of smooth, confident, pretend-you-know-what-you-are-talking-about ... BS. "Well, Max, at this point, Cabinet has several options they are carefully considering. This is a complicated and critical issue that will involve policy decision-makers at the highest levels. All indications are, it could really go either way at this point. [Dramatic reporter pause.] Only time will tell. Back to you, Max."

A whole lot a nothin'. Somehow I avoid getting fired (again). Then I start watching CNN and realize that half of all political analysis is just like that. People trying to sound smart, and saying sweet-eff-all.

I don't end up back on The Hill often. Most of my years are spent covering local stories: court cases, community events, and A LOT of city council meetings—listening to debates over whether to put a traffic light or a flashing yellow at some intersection. Painful. So I spend most of them daydreaming about covering sports. But still, these years are invaluable. To this day, I tell aspiring sports-casters, "Be a news reporter first." Sports is easy. You go to the rink (field, court, whatever) and everything is on a platter for you. You shoot your video of the game or practice and then wait to interview the athletes afterwards. Usually, they are hand-delivered by a public relations person. When you do news, every day is completely different: politics, crime, economy, health, entertainment, fluffy local fair stories—and often, you have to work very hard to get your interviews. Every day your job is to learn as much as you can about one subject and explain it to your audience in 90 seconds. It is the best TV writing class in the universe. I learn a ton from experienced reporters like Terry Marcotte and Colleen McKernan.

It's also enough to make me have brief second thoughts about leaving news when my chance to do sports first comes up. After all, in one shift my first summer at CJOH, I get to interview the prime minister, Bon Jovi, and the *Penthouse* playmate of the year. And they are all completely hammered. Kidding! (The playmate was sober.)

Then again, I also almost die doing news. Twice. The first happens after a visit to Joyceville penitentiary near Kingston, a rare media open house where they let us tour the prison and interact with some of the prisoners. No, I do not get stabbed by gang members in the exercise yard using a handmade shiv they smuggled out of the wood shop. Though that would have been a better story. It actually happens on the way home. We are tight to deadline, so I am screening the footage in the passenger seat of the car, looking through the viewfinder of cameraman Paul Wing's camera and listening on headphones. Paul is one of the best cameramen I have ever worked with—an artist. And his footage from Joyceville is no exception. But it's been a long day. We left from Ottawa around 5 A.M., shot all day in the prison, and now are racing back to try to make the 6 P.M. newscast. As I'm watching the video, I start to feel the car drift. I look up, and Paul is sound asleep, in full snore as we slide gently into oncoming traffic on the highway.

"PAUL!!" I scream, as the pickup truck coming the other way closes to about, oh, lob-wedge distance. I'm so loud and terrifying that Paul wakes up and screams too, swerving to avoid death by, oh, gimme putt distance.

I don't screen any more footage on the way home. Instead, I stare at Paul's eyes the entire way, like the creepiest of creepers, looking for the slightest hint of dozing. Paul will not fall asleep again. For about a week. Near-death experiences have a way of keeping you alert. Years later in bars, I'll tell strangers how I once almost died right after I got out of prison, like Brooks in *Shawshank*. I feel it helps my street cred.

But the other time I almost die covering news, in an attack by grandmothers with baseball bats, doesn't help my street cred at all.

chapter 6

WHEN GRANDMOTHERS ATTACK

Every young local broadcaster wonders when they'll get their big break and go national. I would make my debut on the *CTV National News* with two broken ribs, a concussion, and half my dress shirt ripped off.

It is August of 1989. I am three months out of journalism school and still as green as a TV reporter can be. I arrive for a Saturday shift at CJOH-TV, primed to cover another major local weekend news story. *"I'm James Duthie, reporting live from the Lanark Ploughing Final."* Or Kemptville Pie-Eating Competition. Or Osgoode Cow-Milking Contest. Local fairs are my beat that summer. And I own it.

But that sunny morning, a major story is developing on the Akwesasne Mohawk reserve near Cornwall, Ontario (about an hour southeast of Ottawa). I had been to Akwesasne a few weeks before, to do a piece on the emerging gambling controversy. The residents were divided over a new casino on the reserve. Half were in favour, excited by the busloads of tourists and boatloads of money it was bringing in. The other half wanted to preserve the traditional Mohawk way of life, and wanted no part of slot machines and the other baggage casinos can bring to a town.

I am proud of that initial story. We'd gotten to Akwesasne before most other media had picked up on the controversy. We'd interviewed residents on both sides of the issue, meeting some really good people who cared deeply about their reserve. It was an important, meaty story, unlike the fluff I was doing most shifts. *"And so, Max, Peggy the Pig has her third straight Lanark Hog Queen title. One for the ages. Back to you."*

But in the time since we'd been to Akwesasne, the gambling debate had gotten nasty. And on this sunny August Saturday, it is about to explode.

Ron Thibault (my old Carleton journalism professor who first told me I should pursue a career in TV) is producing the 6 P.M. newscast that night. I am sitting in my little newsroom cubicle when Ron yells something along the lines of "Duthie, there's a gunfight at Akwesasne. Get there now!"

He isn't exaggerating. Pro- and anti-gambling forces are shooting at each other. By all accounts, it is Wild Wild West near the usually Not-So-Wild East Ontario town of Cornwall. By the time cameraman Ron McKay and I arrive at the scene, there are already a dozen other reporters there, mostly from local papers and radio stations. No one is exactly clear what is happening because they can't get anywhere near the gunfight.

The Akwesasne reserve straddles Ontario, Quebec, and New York State. Police jurisdiction is muddy. So, in a scene I have trouble comprehending (then, and still), the New York State Police have set up a roadblock about a kilometre away from the gunfight and are standing there, doing nothing except keeping the media away, while the Mohawks are shooting at each other.

Surveying this odd scene, we see that about three hundred metres down the road from the police, the Mohawks have set up their own roadblock. The message is clear: This is their fight. Nobody else's business.

Except mine. Or so I have it figured. I am young, keen, and cocky. So I say to Ron, "We have to get down there." We sweet-talk one of the police officers for a while, saying we just need to get a little closer so Ron can get some video of the Mohawks behind their roadblock. (We aren't close enough to see the buildings where the shots are being fired.) The officer finally says, "Go ahead, but you're on your own."

We come up with a simple TV 101 plan. We'll walk towards their roadblock with Ron holding his camera lazily at his side, as if he is just carrying it, but really he'll be rolling the whole time. We aren't expecting much. Maybe just some B-roll (video) of the Mohawks and a sound bite or two if we ask a couple of questions politely. It won't be much, but it will give me something to use as cover video when we cut the story back in Ottawa.

As we approach the Mohawk roadblock, we realize it is manned entirely by women (wo-manned?). Akwesasne apparently isn't exactly progressive in matters of gunfight equality. The women start yelling at us to turn around "or else," at which point, I decide to say something completely idiotic like, "We mean no harm here." (I watched a lot of bad movies when I was young. Ron actually giggles a little when he hears it.)

Somewhere in the midst of this ridiculous spaghetti-western dialogue, one of the women yells, "That camera is rolling! They're filming us! Get them!"

Dang. I think I must have missed the journalism class where they teach you what to do when 15 women, all wielding baseball bats, are running at you, screaming for blood. Actually, running is a stretch. Not sure of the polite way to describe this scene, but let's just say most of the women aren't in game shape. So they aren't exactly charging at me *Braveheart*-style. To those back at the police roadblock, it surely must look like something from a Coen brothers' film. I'm not going to run away from this silliness, so I just keep using little head-fakes to deke out my attackers as they swing their bats in my direction. (Don't tell me beer-league touch football has no value.)

Ron is older, nearing retirement, and is one of the gentlest men I've ever met. Once, during an interview with an Alzheimer's patient for another story, Ron tilted down the camera away from the man's face when he started to cry. I was initially upset, because the emotion was an important part of the story. News reporters love tears (and I hated being one of those guys—one of the reasons I left for sports). Ron explained that this was a cameraman's way of showing his sensitivity. Frankly, it wasn't great for my story, but I respected the hell out of it.

Ron wants no part of this or any other conflict, and he doesn't believe they are actually going to hit him, so he just stands there, calmly. They want his camera, and begin to grab it and smack it with their bats. I am too busy doing my best Barry Sanders to really notice—until I glance over and see Ron down on his knees in a ditch, with two women grabbing at his camera and another poised to hit him over the head with a bat. So I sprint over, shove the woman who is about to try to Home-Run-Derby Ron's head, and help him to his feet.

And that is when chaos turns to sheer madness. They had already bashed the camera and ripped out the videotape, so they turn on me, screaming, "You hit a woman!" I try to calm them down, while fending off some fairly meagre bat swings, when out of the corner of my eye, I catch a blur running towards me. My brain doesn't have time to register much more than that before The Blur clotheslines me at full speed with what feels like a metal pipe.

And now, I am flying. I'm not sure how far. But visualize sling-shotting a frog, and you'll have a fair depiction. I land headfirst on the concrete, and The Blur is on me in a nanosecond. The metal pipe, it turns out, is an AK-47. And now, it's pushed hard up against my throat, choking me. Good times.

It's all happening fast, and my head is in a dense fog, but I believe my thought process goes something like this: *Well, that was a pretty good life while it lasted. Wish I'd eaten more Twinkies. Oh well. Least I got to see the Niners win a few Super Bowls. Love you, Mom and Dad. Take care of my guinea pig, Phyllis.* (I didn't actually have a guinea pig named Phyllis, so that's probably the brain injury talking.)

Turns out someone had alerted the men shooting at each other down the road that a camera crew was stirring up trouble. (Apparently, standing in the middle of the road asking harmless questions constitutes "trouble.") So my would-be manslaughterer left the gunfight, sprinted the few hundred metres up the road, and Ray-Lewised my ass halfway to Vermont.

I don't die. (Sorry, probably should have spoiler-alerted that.) The New York State Police had been watching all this from afar, somewhat bemused, I'm guessing. *(You wanna talk your way past the roadblock, kid, that's what you get.)* But the whole violent assault and choking-with-the-gun thing seems to wake them up. A couple of them run up the road yelling something I am far too concussed and oxygen-deprived to understand, and my armed choker simply gets off me and walks away.

The cops do nothing. No guns drawn. No arrests. No "Bring in the dogs to hunt this guy down!" Not even a "Hey, that wasn't nice!" The New York State Police apparently take their no-jurisdiction-on-the-reserve thing seriously. They simply tell the Mohawks to go back behind their roadblock, and they escort us back behind the police line.

Ron and I take stock of our war wounds and try to figure out what just happened. He's fine, though his camera is badly dented. So is my head. My dress shirt is ripped open, my brain is muddy (okay, muddier than usual), and my side is killing me (x-rays would later confirm the broken ribs).

And then we are swarmed. The pack of bored reporters at the police roadblock, frustrated by getting nowhere near the scene of the gunfight, suddenly has something to report on. TV crew assaulted!

It still stands as one of the strangest media moments of my career. I've never been "scrummed" like that, let alone when my head feels like it had just been on a three-day bender with the Lohans. I am trying to look cool and unfazed, with a bunch of microphones stuck in my face and cameras clicking away at the exposed welt on my side and red marks on my neck.

And what I feel, more than anything else, is guilt. In my mind, at least in those first few minutes, this is all my fault. I shouldn't have gone past the police roadblock, shouldn't have engaged the Mohawks. It was brash and stupid, and I deserve what I got. The reporters looking for the angry assault victim ready to lash out are disappointed.

I just keep quietly saying things like, "They just wanted our videotape and it got a little out of hand. It's really no big deal." Then they all run off to file their stories, leaving Ron and me alone, with no video of the incident. Every reporter has a story. Except me.

Our producer is on the phone within five minutes. Someone had filed a report and it moved on the national wire. "What the f*%& just happened? Are you guys okay?"

I don't really have a good answer to either.

Ron's banged-up camera still works, so we tape a double-ender with our news anchor, Suhana Meharchand, and race back to Ottawa. Quick TV news lesson: A double-ender is an interview done by an anchor with a person at a different location. The interviewer often asks the questions over the phone. I've done them from my kids' hockey games, from the golf course, from outside a bar (hey, at least I went outside). The interviewee has an earpiece to hear the questions, and answers them looking directly into the camera. The tape then gets shipped (or nowadays, fed digitally) back to the station, and the anchor re-asks the questions from the set, so it looks seamless and live.

Double-enders are usually put together well before a show starts. But this time, we don't get back to the station in Ottawa until seconds before the newscast begins. So we sprint the tape down the hall to the tape room, and Suhana has to re-ask her questions live. This is tricky. Suhana has to ask everything the exact same way, in the exact same amount of time, as she asked me over the phone.

She is a pro and pulls it off remarkably well, nailing every question in the perfect time frame so that the interview looks live.

Until the very end, that is. Suhana's list of questions is missing one that she had originally asked me over the phone about whether the police were going to lay charges. So when she thinks the interview is over, I still have one more answer on the videotape. So this is what goes to air:

Suhana: Well, James, we're glad you are okay. Thanks for this.

Me: No idea, Suhana. The police aren't commenting right now.

My friends and family members who see this are immediately concerned the brain injury is far worse than first believed.

Back in the newsroom, *CTV National* is all over the story. They decide to lead the 11 P.M. newscast with a report on the gunfight and an interview with me. I don't even bother to change out of the ripped shirt. I do a two-minute interview with CTV weekend anchor Terilyn Joe from our newsroom, still somewhat embarrassed and downplaying the incident.

And that is my national TV debut. My big break. Two ribs. *"Hey, Mom, make sure you watch* CTV National *tonight, I finally made it! Oh ya, and I thought I was going to die today, too!"*

The cover of the *Ottawa Sun* the next morning reads in big black Sun-ish letters "WAR ON THE RESERVE." Beneath it is a photo of bullet holes in a window from the gunfight (no one was actually shot, apparently) and an insert photo of Ron and me, with Ron picking up his battered camera, and me trying fruitlessly to button up my ripped shirt. The sub-caption on the photo would give my buddies enough material for years of ribbing: "CJOH reporter James Duthie was attacked by a group of women." Thanks for that, photo headline copy jerk.

There are stories in all the other papers too, including the *Akwesasne Times*. Though its take is a little different from the rest. I tell this story whenever I'm talking to journalism students about slanted media coverage. Its headline reads: "CJOH CAMERAMAN ASSAULTS AKWESASNE GRANDMOTHER." (They got

Ron and me mixed up—the story refers to "cameraman James Duthie" as the "assailant.") The rest of the story makes no reference to the gunfight that led to all this. If you read only this article, you would assume I drove to the reserve, got out of the car, assaulted Grandma, and drove back.

CJOH wants to go hard after the guy who took me down. They are demanding assault charges and a full police investigation into the entire incident. But I am still feeling shame and ask that they just let it go. (Ron is much angrier but also lets it fade away.)

I do finally get mad a couple of weeks later (mostly because the linebacker with the AK-47 made me miss eight weeks of touch football), but by then, it is old news. Akwesasne would explode into a major news story over the following months, with several violent incidents including the murder of two Mohawk men. Our incident quickly becomes a tiny forgotten postscript.

It would be a stretch so say the Mohawk Mauling launches my TV career. (I am back to the cow-milking contests and suburban town-council meetings the next week.) What it does do is reaffirm that news isn't where I really want to be. I would spend the next few years begging and pleading for a chance to do sports.

A few weeks later, I go back to Akwesasne. At the height of the trouble, when the entire reserve is closed off to all outsiders, we return with a crew from Mike Duffy's CTV show *Sunday Edition* to do a longer feature. (Duffy was a respected broadcaster not a disgraced senator back then.) We are smuggled across the river from Cornwall and onto the reserve on the bottom of a small boat with a blanket covering us. It feels very *20/20*.

This time, there is no violence. We get on and off the reserve without incident. And the Mohawks who help us with our story that day are kind, wonderful people.

Even the grandmothers.

chapter 7

YOU WEARIN' YOUR RUBBER BOOTS TONIGHT?

I get my first big break in sportscasting because an Olympic gold medalist made love.

Not to me. I mean, let's be realistic here. To her husband. As in sweet, successful, baby-makin' love. This isn't really coming across the way I'd hoped. Let's start over.

CJOH Sports is a three-man team when I arrive. Brian Smith, Bill Patterson, and Dan Seguin. But shortly after I get hired to do news in 1989, Dan leaves to be the main anchor at rival CBC-Ottawa. Eager to add some star athlete appeal to the station, CJOH hires Carolyn Waldo, a double Olympic gold medalist synchronized swimmer from Seoul the year before. Carolyn has zero experience, little knowledge about pro sports, and pretty much no higher education. She is only weeks into her first year at Ryerson University when she gets the job.

The bosses assign me to train her, their odd way of tossing me a bone after refuting all my attempts to weasel my way into the sports department. I should resent them hiring her, but I can't. Carolyn is kind, self-deprecating, and hilarious.

"I have no frigging clue what I'm doing," is one of the first things she says to me. "I'm not all there. I've been under water too long."

Truth is, I don't really know what I'm doing either, as I've never produced a sportscast before. But I've watched Billy and Smitty enough that I figure I can pull it off. For Carolyn's first sportscast on a November Saturday, I put everything on tape. I write all her highlight scripts and have her voice them in advance so that they look perfect on air. The only thing she does live is the on-camera intros I have written for her. The show goes perfectly. Carolyn kills it.

The next day, I get cocky. I try to fit a ton of highlights in the show and decide she will voice all of them, all live. Big mistake. I am still too inexperienced and unorganized to get everything done on time. Our one tape editor on duty is busy with news and doesn't have time for sports until the last couple of minutes before Carolyn goes on. It is the day of the CFL East and West final, and a ton of NFL games. I get the East final highlights done but don't have time to finish the West or any of the NFL. The editor promises he'll try to finish what he can as I sprint to the control room to tell the director and Carolyn to buckle up.

The first highlight pack goes well. Then Carolyn starts her West script, which has about 10 different plays on it. Unfortunately, the editor has only cut two. So after the second play, a bunch of cows in a barn appear on the tape. Carolyn is carefully reading from her script and doesn't even notice. After about 10 painful seconds, the director cuts back to her on camera and tells her to go to the next story—a Giants vs. Cowboys NFL game.

Carolyn is a little rattled, but she calmly moves on to the NFL intro. Sadly, those highlights aren't done either, so as she's describing a Troy Aikman touchdown pass, the tape is showing an elderly man jogging. The director quickly bails out of the tape again. When Carolyn realizes she's back on camera, she panics a little, and flips past a few pages of script to the last page.

"And the Ottawa 67s won 3–2 today in Sudbury. That's sports, I'm Carolyn Waldo."

And with that, our seven-minute sportscast, the last seven minutes of the 6 P.M. news, is over in about 1:15.

Usually when the sportscast wraps, there is a shot of the three anchors (news, weather, sports) and a quick goodbye. This time, there are still more than six minutes left in the show, thanks to my screw-ups. Thankfully, we have a talented weekend weather anchor named Kathie Donovan who calmly recaps her entire forecast while the news producer scrambles to find another taped story to fill the end of the newscast.

I am devastated. My only job is to ease Carolyn in and make her look good, and instead, I have just produced the worst (and maybe shortest) sportscast in the history of television. I am the producing equivalent of the "boom goes the dynamite" guy. I wait for her in the hallway as she returns from the studio.

"That didn't seem to go so well," she says in the understate-ment of the decade. "Oh well, we'll do better on the 11."

The fact that she doesn't scream at me or curl into the fetal position and weep makes me love her instantly. She remains one of the nicest people I've met in the business. And when she gets pregnant twice in the next four years, it opens the door for me to fill her maternity leave and finally become a sportscaster—albeit a temp.

My very first sportscast is a 6 P.M. show on a Saturday. It goes okay, except for the minor detail of me looking at the wrong camera the entire time, giving the budding artists in our audience more than enough time to draw my profile (not much chin, big schnozz).

One of the awkward challenges of local newscasts is "happy talk," the fake smiley chatter between the news anchor, sports anchor, and weatherperson between their segments. I am initially terrible at it, too nervous to think on my feet and generally bad at dumb, awkward segues. On one of my first shows, Kathie finishes her weather report on a hot summer Ottawa day and anchor Leigh Chapple turns to me and segues with, "So, James, how were the football fans keeping cool today at Frank Clair Stadium for the Rough Riders game?"

I freeze. I got nothin'. *Mommy.*

Finally, after a painful, seemingly eternal pause, I come up with the following, spoken in the meekest voice in the history of local TV happy talk:

"Hats?"

Leigh stifles her giggles and recovers like the happy talk vet she is, saying, "Yes, hats would work … James will tell you if the Riders were hot themselves against the Argos, coming next on sports!" Ad-libbing. Not an early strength.

A few nights later, I'm doing one of my first late-weeknight sportscasts when my microphone falls off my lapel and onto my lap. I realize something is amiss, but I am too green and nervous to react. My director is yelling, "No mic! No mic!" in my earpiece, but it still doesn't really register. So I forge on through my baseball highlights, terrified to get behind on the script and just wanting this nightmare to end.

At this point our floor director, Paul Faubert, realizes I am not mentally capable of recovering my own mic, so he climbs under the desk and up between my legs to find the mic and try to clip it back on my suit. If the moment I'm about to describe had happened today, I would have gotten more YouTube hits than *Cat Falls Off TV*. At the very moment Paul is trying to reattach my mic, my baseball highlights end and I am back on camera, where you briefly see the top of a man's head moving around between my legs.

That's right. I make my sportscasting and gay porn debuts the same month.

I'm still too scared to react. So I just read the teleprompter and try to survive with a shred of dignity left. Paul waits for the next tape to run before reaching up and getting the mic reattached. When we go to commercial, the studio and control rooms burst into uncontrollable laughter. Viewers could probably only see Paul's head for a second, and since it was 11:50 at night, they were likely either sleepy or wasted and probably didn't notice. Since there is no such thing as a viral video yet, Paul's bobbing head in my crotch just becomes one of those stories we still laugh about over beers.

But the strangest part of being a local sportscaster has nothing to do with the odd embarrassments on air. It is the weirdos who call you off air. Long before tickers, instant alerts on your phone, and apps with every stat imaginable in real time, the local sportscaster was every fan's number-one source for information. I spend half my shifts answering the phone to give out scores. (Our number is listed in the phone book—hey, anyone remember phone books?) People call every couple of minutes looking for details of games not on TV. And not many games are on TV in 1994.

Most of the callers are polite strangers, though there are about a dozen regulars. My two most frequent phone pals are the Brick brothers, John and Tom, who both work as trainers and equipment guys with various Ottawa sports teams. The Bricks call me, separately, almost every night, just to talk about sports and life, occasionally giving me tips about what is happening behind the scenes on the Ottawa 67s (junior hockey) or Lynx (Ottawa's long-since-dead Triple-A baseball team). At one point, they get in a massive fight and stop speaking to each other for months. So they call me, each asking how the other is doing, while pretending not to care. They really should offer a family therapy course in broadcasting school.

But at least the Bricks are fairly normal, nice guys. Unlike my most frequent phone-friend. I take his first call early in my tenure in the sports department:

Me: CJOH Sports, what can I do for you?

Caller (in an Elmer Fudd crossed with Joe Pesci voice): Heyyyy, how are ya? You wearin' ya rubba boots tonight?

Me: Sorry, what? My rubber boots?

Caller: Yeah, you wearin' ya rubba boots?

Me: Listen buddy, I have work to do. Do you want a score?

Caller: Heyyyy, you like da dunk tank?

Me: The ... wha?

Caller: Da dunk tank. You know, at da fay-er.

Me: The dunk tank ... at the fair? Listen pal, unless you want a score, I'm hanging up.

Caller: Okkayy ... uhhh (panicking) ... Da Cubs, how da Cubs doin'?

Me: The Cubs aren't playing tonight. Later.

Click.

"Freak," I chuckle to myself, and go back to prepping my sportscast. The next night, he calls again. Same question. "Hey! How are ya! You wearin' ya rubba boots tonight?"

This time, I just hang up. Something I continue to do for the next couple of weeks. But kids, there are some light nights in local sports when there isn't much to do in my little cubicle at the back of the newsroom. So out of pure boredom, I start to engage my new friend.

Me: Hello, CJOH Sports.

Caller: Heyyyy! How are ya? You wearin' ya rubba boots tonight?

Me: Well, as a matter of fact, yes I am!

Caller: Ooooh! What culah?

Me: I have my red ones on tonight.

Caller: Oooohhh ... Could ya put 'em up on da desk for me doorin' da show?

Me: I sure will. Right when I'm introducing the hockey high-lights, I'll throw my red boots right on the desk. And by the way, I LOVE the dunk tank.

Caller: Ooooh, I knew it!

peppermint as the months roll by

(NOTE: I would tell this story on Jay Onrait and Dan O'Toole's popular podcast 20 years later. Now, I get at least a half dozen people tweeting me every day: "Hey, you wearing your rubber boots tonight?" My old CJOH phone-a-friend, if he's still alive, doesn't realize he's a legend.)

We strike up quite a friendship, me and the Rubber Boots Guy, though I disappoint him frequently when my rainbow collection of rubber boots—I start telling him I have colours like fuchsia and peppermint as the months roll by—never actually make it on the sportscast. I try to find out who he is, but don't get very far.

Me: What do you do, anyway, bud?

Rubber Boots Guy: I work at a factowee.

Me: What do you make at the factory?

Rubber Boots Guy (panicky): Uhh … cawrs … I mean … boats … err … lawnmowa-type wheel … parts … I gotta go. Don't forget da boots!

I kind of miss the Rubber Boots Guy each time Carolyn comes back from maternity leave and I return to my regular job as a news reporter. But he's always there when I come back. And the next time I come back to sports, it will be permanent. And it will happen the worst possible way.

chapter 8

SMITTY AND BILLY

She shakes me awake. I'm a groggy mess, having crashed on the couch only three hours or so earlier. I'm not sure of her name, having only met her briefly last night, a roommate of the friend we are staying with in Halifax. She's the only one up in the house, off to work while the rest of us sleep off a night at The Liquor Dome, a trio of attached bars in the city's downtown.

"Do you know Brian Smith?" she says in a serious tone that immediately clears my morning fog. I pause for a second before answering. My initial, ridiculous thought is that Brian must have done her wrong somehow—dated her and not called back or something. Maybe she just realized Brian and I worked at the same Ottawa TV station and I was about to get a lecture by association. To this day, I wish that's all it was.

"Yes, I know him," I say, hesitantly. "I work with him. He's my bud." Her face turns ash. "You need to turn the TV on right now."

From day one, the best part about working at CJOH is getting to hang out with two of my boyhood idols. Brian Smith and Bill Patterson have been Ottawa's favourite local sportscasters forever. I grew up with them on my TV every night. Now I'm working at their station. For a 22-year-old fresh out of university, it's a little surreal.

Every shift in my early years as a news reporter, I hustle to get my report done quickly so I can hang out with Smitty and Billy in the sports department at the back of the newsroom. The months I replace Carolyn while she is on maternity are heaven, as I get to listen to their stories every day.

Brian is a former NHL journeyman and the brother of Gary "The Suitcase" Smith, one of the great characters (and nicknames) of the NHL in the 1970s. Brian has endless tales about the game. One of his favourites is about a time when Gordie Howe came to town for a function. Everyone at the event had to wear name tags, and so Gordie, being Gordie, just wrote "Mr. Hockey" on his. Well, one of the event organizers was clearly not a hockey fan, because as she introduced a group of people to each other, she looked at Gordie's name tag and said, "Mr. Hockey? What an interesting name. What's your first name, sir?"

"Gordie," Howe replies with a wry smile.

"Okay, thanks. So, ladies and gentlemen, I'd like to introduce you to Gordie Hockey!"

Though Brian is already almost 50 when I start at CJOH, he is in great shape and looks much younger. Lives much younger, too. I run into him often in the Byward Market bars, and while still at Carleton, I find out he is dating a girl just a year ahead of me in journalism school, Alana Kainz. They would be married a few years later.

Brian's greatest moment as a broadcaster comes in Florida in 1993, when the NHL is about to announce expansion franchises. Ottawa is in the running but is considered an extreme long shot. But Smitty thinks otherwise and convinces Max and the bosses to send our new live satellite truck down to Florida to cover the event. I am sitting at my cubicle in the middle of the afternoon when Lucie de Varennes, our production coordinator, takes a call, and then stands up and screams, "We got the team!"

Brian is on the air live in minutes, telling the shocking story of how Bruce Firestone somehow convinced the NHL to give the

Ottawa Senators a franchise (even though he had virtually no money). Brian stays on for several hours, interviewing all the key players in the deal. It is the signature work of his career.

Billy, though straight as an arrow while delivering the sports on TV, might be the funniest guy I've ever met. He was never a pro athlete, but he's a wonderful storyteller. And he cares deeply about local sports. He does a weekly report called "Senior of the Week," which features 83-year-old curlers and 92-year-old skiers—basically any active octogenarian is a candidate. My favourite of Billy's seniors are the mall walkers. Old people walking around malls to get exercise has apparently become very big in Ottawa. Billy and I develop a routine every time he returns from one of those shoots.

"What course did you do today?" I ask. He pauses, for drama, then deadpans, "Bayshore. Toughest track on the tour. That hairpin turn by Sears on Level 2? Deadly. We lost a couple of them there today. Heartbreaking."

News people often call sports the "toy department" of the newsroom. This is supposed to be a condescending insult, but I don't see it that way. I love toys. Who wouldn't want to hang out in the toy department all day? With Billy and Smitty around, it is always the best place to be.

In the summer of 1995, my buddy Darryl Stoliker and I drive to the East Coast for a few days' vacation. We go out in Halifax one night and crash at the apartment of some friends. The following morning is when the girl wakes me. The tone in her voice when she tells me to turn on the TV has me off the couch and scrambling for the remote in an instant. I turn to *Canada AM*, and the first image I see is a still photo of Smitty's face, filling up the entire screen. The words I hear the newscaster say are so unreal, so unfathomable, they don't register.

"Ottawa sportscaster Brian Smith was shot in the head last night as he walked out of CJOH-TV in Ottawa. He is in critical condition right now in hospital …" No. Not possible. This doesn't happen in Ottawa. This couldn't have happened to Smitty. Why would anyone want to hurt a guy who does the evening sports in one of the quietest, safest cities in North America? It takes me 10 minutes to grasp that it isn't some horrific mistake. I don't cry. I don't do anything. Just sit and stare.

I call my girlfriend (soon to be my wife), Cheryl, first, and she's a mess. She, like everyone else in Ottawa, had heard about the shooting the night before. But it's 1995, and I don't have a cell phone, so she couldn't reach me.

"It's awful here," is all I remember her saying. "Just please come home." Next I call CJOH and get our managing editor, Dave McGinn.

"It's not good," he says. "He's probably not going to make it. Listen, Billy is really having a hard time. We feel we should do a sportscast tonight … that's what Smitty would want. Can you get back and do it?"

A few hours later, I'm on a flight home, trying to comprehend the incomprehensible. The two-hour flight to Ottawa feels like 12. I want to know how he's doing, how everyone at the station is doing. And I want to know who did it, and why. I rack my brain to see if Smitty may have offended anyone in his nightly editorial comment that ends each sportscast. But to *shoot* him?

The taxi driver taking me from the airport to CJOH is glued to CFRA, Ottawa's talk radio station. We are five minutes away when the breaking-news music comes on.

"CJOH sportscaster Brian Smith has died in hospital …" I don't hear the rest.

The taxi pulls up, and our lobby is crawling with reporters. The same familiar faces I'm usually in scrums with at city council meetings are now throwing microphones in my face. They feel awful doing it. I can see it in their faces. I walk by without stopping.

The newsroom is a wake. People are sobbing, hugging, or just sitting silently at their cubicles, staring into nothing. Leanne

Cusack, one of the nicest people at the station, comes towards me looking to give and receive a consoling hug.

"No, not now," I say, bolting to the cubicle where Smitty usually sits to put together his show. I know if the mourning starts, there is no way I am going to be able to go on television.

It is 5:30. I am supposed to be on set in an hour doing Smitty's sportscast. Max Keeping calls me over. He is remarkably composed. He always is. A pillar. He asks if I'm okay, and then says we won't do a typical sportscast. We'll just chat—Max, his excellent co-anchor, Carol-Anne Meehan, and I—talk about Smitty and what he meant to us, then I'll cover the big sports news of the day briefly and throw to a long taped piece about Smitty's life. From that moment until the time I sit down on the set, I stay in work mode, trying to write the proper words into my computer. I'll never write a tougher lead than the one into Smitty's obituary piece.

We get through it okay, my voice breaking only at the sign-off at the end. When we go to commercial, I get up, walk straight to an empty stairwell at the far side of the building, and bawl my eyes out.

It turns out Smitty was killed by a schizophrenic man named Jeffrey Arenburg who believed the media was sending messages through his head. All he really wanted to do was get in front of a judge to ask him to stop it. And in his diseased mind, the best way to get in front of a judge was to drive to our TV station with a .22 calibre rifle and shoot the first person he recognized. Smitty was on his way to emcee a golf tournament dinner and was hustling out of the building as soon as his sportscast was over. Arenburg caught him right between the eyes from about 50 metres away. He was later found not criminally responsible for Smitty's death because of his illness and was sent to an institution in Penetanguishene. He was given an absolute discharge in 2006.

The days leading up to the funeral are brutal. People break down in the newsroom in the middle of conversations. Like with any tragedy, you just feel that nothing will ever be right again. The whole city feels like it has lost a friend. It is the first time I realize the bond viewers can forge with someone they watch every night on their television.

Thousands come to his wake and funeral. I wait in line to pay my respects to Alana, and not knowing what to say, I end up blurting out something dumb like, "If you ever need a golf partner, I'll be there." She and Smitty played golf almost every day. I don't even think she hears it. She is out of it—lost. Billy tells me a few days later that Alana called him in a panic from the cemetery, saying she couldn't find Smitty's grave. Billy soon figured out she had gone to the wrong cemetery. Lost.

The gathering after the funeral is awkward, as people keep coming up and asking if I am going to replace Smitty. It's hardly the appropriate thing to talk about on the day we bury him, so I end up leaving quickly. But I know it's coming. Sports doesn't take time off, even for tragedies, so they have to fill the position quickly. They ask me the day after the funeral. Billy will move to the 6 P.M. show, and they want me to take Billy's spot on the 11:30 P.M. Carolyn will stay in her weekend anchoring role, which is better for her family life. I talk to Billy first, to make sure he wants me as his partner. Then I accept.

Jesus. For most of my life, my dream is to be a sportscaster, and now it comes true, only because my friend is murdered? How is that right? How can I feel even the slightest sense of pride that I've achieved my goal? When the move is announced, people send me kind, warm notes of congratulations. But I'm mostly just sad and sick to my stomach. This is never going to feel right.

It's way worse for Billy. He never really wanted to do the 6 P.M. show. He was comfortable. Now he would be the guy doing Smitty's sportscast—replacing a man who had become far more beloved because of the tragic way he died. Smitty had gone from being a solid, popular sportscaster to a … legend. Billy did not want the burden of replacing him. But he did, and did it wonderfully. The last words of his editorial the night he takes over are "You don't replace a Brian Smith, you just borrow his chair."

I have little choice but to get over the awkward discomfort of getting into sports in the worst possible way. It takes almost a year for all of us at the station to feel somewhat normal again, but we do. Along the way, Billy and I become close friends. He is my mentor, my Mr. Miyagi from *The Karate Kid*, teaching me how to write sports for TV, how to be a storyteller. And he stresses, over and over, that the interview with the 88-year-old mall walker is just as important as the one you do with Wayne Gretzky when he comes to town. You should prepare the same way and treat them with equal respect. It is one of the most important lessons I've learned in the business.

Billy also understands that I'm a bit of a clown who likes to throw in smartass lines in my sportscasts. He encourages it, but also reminds me that I still have to be a journalist. His favourite hypothetical, repeated over and over to me, is "If Muhammad Ali dies in a plane crash, and you have to go on and deliver the news, people need to be able to take you seriously. They can't be looking at you, waiting for a punchline. You have to have credibility." In other words, make your wisecracks here and there, have fun, but walk the line carefully.

My time in the sports department with Billy and Carolyn is one of the best periods of my life. I get to cover the Rough Riders, the team I grew up watching, and the Ottawa Senators first playoff run, as Ron Tugnutt stands on his head for a month. But the circumstances of getting the job never stop bothering me. And so, after two years, I decide to leave CJOH. Billy and I go out for a beer, which turns into several. It becomes a seven-hour "I love you, man!" goodbye.

When I join TSN a year later, we talk on the phone often, as he critiques my performances on *SportsDesk* and our CFL panel. "Don't forget my Muhammad Ali warning," he repeats when I venture too far into shtick territory, which is fairly often.

One afternoon in the fall of 1999, a year into my career at TSN, I am driving home from a round of golf when my cell phone rings. It is a radio producer from the all-sports station in Ottawa.

"James, we were wondering if you could come on and talk about Billy."

"Billy who?" I say, trying to figure out what prominent athlete named Billy has been injured ... or arrested.

"Billy Patterson," he says. "You didn't hear?"

"Hear what?"

"He died this morning of a massive heart attack." I pull over to the side of the QEW, promise to call the producer back, and sob.

Billy was just 51. His wife, Pat, found him slumped over the bathtub that morning. They are pretty sure he died instantly. I think the pressure he put on himself to fill Smitty's shoes, and to do the perfect sportscast every night, took a toll. He leaves behind Pat, his lifelong companion, and two beautiful teenage daughters, Meghan and Sarah. Pat tells me at the funeral that Billy considered me the son he'd never had. Those words are, and will always be, the greatest honour of my career.

The day after he dies, the cover of the *Ottawa Sun* is a full-size photo of Billy, but on the side, there is a smaller headline for another totally unrelated story about a jail mix-up. The first two words of the headline are in large letters, right next to Billy's smiling face: "INMATE FREE." Yup, that's about right. Billy would have gotten a big kick out of that.

chapter 9

THE SPORTS NETWORK

One of the most common questions I'm asked, to this day, is "How did you get a job at TSN?"

I hope they mean, "How does one become a sportscaster for Canada's leading sports network?" and not, "How the heck did *you* get a job there?! With your odd Ben Stiller–ish features and questionable haircut?" Just to be sure, I'll try to answer both questions at once.

As soon as my ambitions finally started to expand beyond CJOH, TSN is where I wanted to go. Just as I'm sure some (many? most? all?) of you watch me now and think, "I could do that job as well as that clown," I would watch guys like Darren Dutchyshen and Mike Toth and think, "I could fit in with those guys on *SportsDesk*." But doing local sports in Ottawa in the mid-90s, I am equal parts cocky and lazy. I just figure they will hear about my riveting High School Athlete of the Week reports and come offer me the key to the network. So I never call, never send tapes, never make any attempt to contact anyone there, until the spring of 1997.

As much as I am having a blast with Billy and Carolyn doing sports at CJOH, I still don't feel right about getting the job because of Smitty's death. I do not want to spend the rest of my career as the guy who replaced Brian Smith. So I finally put together a demo tape of some of my best reports and anchoring moments. (FYI, neither the "Hats?" comment nor the gay porn moment make the final cut.)

I only send the tape to two places. TSN is one. The other is a new local station launching in the fall in Vancouver called VTV. My friend and colleague at CJOH Tim "Hacksaw" Latham—still the best video editor I've ever worked with—has applied there, and pushes me to do the same. I have fuzzy but fond memories of living in Victoria as a kid, and I've always wanted to move back to BC if I had the chance.

I figure I have a 50/50 shot at a job with VTV, and about a one in 50 with TSN, as no one ever seems to leave there and new faces rarely pop up. But a few weeks after I send the tape, the phone rings in my Ottawa condo.

"James, it's Keith Pelley from TSN." I recognize the name: the senior vice-president of production at TSN and second in command at the network (and the name I'd addressed my tape to).

"I watched your tape," Pelley says. "I like it. I really liked the jeans."

"Oh. Thanks Keith … the wha … what?"

"The jeans in that stand-up you did at the rink. Just don't see that much. It really worked."

My racing mind finally clicks in to what he's talking about. I had done a live report from the Ottawa Senators' rink on the building's opening night, giving fans a walking tour of the team's dressing room. I was wearing a jacket, dress shirt, and jeans. I'm relatively sure that combo only happened because my one pair of cheap dress pants (Big Steel Man—St. Laurent Centre) were at the dry cleaner, and I didn't think they'd be shooting me below the waist. Whatever. Apparently the jeans … worked.

"We'd like you to come down to Toronto for an audition."

A couple of weeks later I'm in a cab, on a rainy miserable Toronto day, pulling into TSN headquarters, thinking, "This is probably your one and only shot. Please don't screw it up."

It's a little surreal being in that newsroom you see every day in the background on *SportsDesk*. They sit me at a computer right next to long-time anchor Jim Van Horne and show me the lineup for the five-minute sportscast I'll be doing for my audition. I have to write a couple of on-camera intros and do a handful of highlight packages for various sports. I do my first run and feel it goes pretty well. But then Van Horne peeks around the corner of the set and says, "Punch it up a bit, give it more energy."

The comment terrifies me a little. Does it mean that the delivery I've perfected the last few years is roughly akin to that of a corpse? But I listen. After all, at that time, Van Horne might be the most respected, authoritative sports anchor in the country. And for him to take the time to care about my audition is very kind. So I do the same five-minute segment again, this time feeling like I'm yelling the entire time. "MOISÉS ALOU! DEEP TO CENTRE! OFF THE WALL! THAT'S AN RBI DOUBLE!"

But in my ear, the producer, Mark Milliere, says, "much better," and I'm done.

Then they take me to a different part of the newsroom, the "update position," and try to challenge my ad-libbing skills by saying, "Talk about Eric Lindros for a minute. Go."

Here's my initial thought transcription: *Lindros? Oh, ya, him. Shit. Big dude. Crazy parents. Wouldn't want to get hit by him. Saw him at a bar in Muskoka once. I was drinking a cooler. He laughed. That was pretty humiliating ...*

Fortunately, after gathering myself, my mouth is able to spew a few more polished thoughts on the Big E, and make it through my minute without any major stumbles.

I never see Keith Pelley that day. Mark Milliere just tells me someone will call me and sends me back into the cab and the rain to Ottawa. On TV shows like *American Idol*, auditions are always extremes. They are brilliant victories or embarrassing failures. They never show the people in the middle. But as I sit in that cab back to Pearson International, I really have zero idea whether I blew it or not. It went … okay, but no one was running up to hug me, saying, "We've finally found the perfect sports anchor! Our network is saved! Saved, I say, SAVED!!"

A few days later, I get another call, this one from Bob McLaughlin, the news director at VTV. He offers me a job as a senior news reporter.

"Why don't you hire me to do sports?" I ask.

"Because we aren't doing any. Our newscast is not going to have sports, unless something happens that warrants a story. Then our news reporters will cover it."

"You guys are idiots, then. Later." Oh wait. There shouldn't be quotes on that sentence. I don't actually say it. I just think it. How do you not cover sports in a city like Vancouver? Either way, I tell Bob I'll think about the news job and get back to him. He says he'll give me a week or so to make up my mind.

Pelley calls a few days later and tells me he's considering me for a weekend anchor position on *SportsDesk*. It's down to me and Lisa Bowes, who is already a reporter at TSN. He promises an answer soon. Then McLaughlin calls back, telling me he needs an answer within 24 hours. The offer is $60,000 a year, which is only slightly more than I'm making doing sports in Ottawa. But I loved living in BC as a kid, and I am excited about the chance to launch a new station in Vancouver.

Though I have zero bargaining position, I have no choice but to call Pelley and try to get an answer from TSN. I tell him TSN is where I want to go, but I have to give Vancouver an answer, and I don't want to lose both jobs. He says he'll call me back in an hour.

It's a stressful day. I know I'm finally leaving Ottawa, my home for the last 22 years, but my career could go in two completely different directions. Finally, the phone rings.

"Look James, we like you," Pelley says. "But Lisa has been with us for a while, so we're going to give her the job. I'd like to hire you someday. But it's not today."

I'm crestfallen, but I get it. I've watched Lisa. She is a good reporter and deserves her shot on the desk. I call Bob two minutes later and accept the job in Vancouver. My entire career, I wanted to be a sports anchor. And now, less than two years after finally getting there, I'm going back to news. My girlfriend, Cheryl, leaves her job with the government to come with me. Her willingness to drop her life for my questionable career move is just another sign she's a keeper. We load our Jack Russell terrier, Tanner, and everything we own in my beat-up SUV and head west.

I spend most of the three-day drive second-guessing the move. I figure Keith Pelley is just being nice. I blew the audition, and the TSN dream is probably dead. And now I've quit the Ottawa sports anchor job that was all I wanted growing up. Even the dog looks at me like I'm an idiot. I'm certain he's thinking, *You just ruined our lives, so I am going to pee all over our new apartment.*

chapter 10

WEST COAST KICKERS

My dog is clucking like a chicken as the fish flips and flops on the floor of the boat. Seriously. Tanner is a Jack Russell terrier who has always been afraid of water. Even when we run every morning on the beach in Vancouver, he won't go near the surf. But today, a bell has gone off. He has been watching me reel in the salmon for the last 10 minutes with one of those inquisitive-dog head-tilts, as if to say, "I know you are up to something, dude, but WTF is it?" But then the salmon hits the boat, and his world is instantly rocked. It all comes together in an instant. "*Whoa!* That thing is a *fish!* And it came out of THAT water! Water = fish! Fish = something I need in my mouth *right frickin' NOW!*"

From this moment forward, Tanner believes every single body of water contains fish. He spends the rest of his days sitting by swimming pools, bathtubs ... puddles, waiting for another salmon to come leaping out. Not even kidding. But on this day on the boat, he is tied up and can't get to the fish, so he starts making this strange half-bark, half-whine noise that sounds like a clucking chicken. And it's at this very moment, with the dog clucking and the salmon still flopping on my line, that my cell phone rings. My hands are occupied, so Cheryl grabs it.

"Don't answer it," I yell, completely fish focused. After all, we're out on gorgeous English Bay deep-sea fishing with her visiting parents, and I just caught my first fish, and my dog is suddenly funnier than Louis C.K. We've been in Vancouver only eight months, but we've fallen in love with the city. Moments like this make me think I could be happy here forever. No way I'm interrupting it with a phone call.

Cheryl answers anyway. She immediately gets an odd look on her face and hands me the phone. "You probably wanna take this."

I've always been drawn to silliness … stupidity … idiocy, you can choose your own word. I watch Letterman from the beginning, when it debuts as a low-rated morning show on NBC in 1980. I'm not sure Dave invented Stupid Comedy, but he perfected it. Throwing watermelons off buildings just to see the splat—that kind of highbrow entertainment resonated with me as a teenager. I know the ridiculously talented Jay Onrait also lists Dave as a primary early influence. I wonder if Letterman knows the impact he's had on Canadian sports broadcasters.

Growing up in Ottawa, my idiot friends and I make dumb Letterman-ish videos to amuse ourselves, but I never think of it as a career-useful skill. Not certain the exact moment when that changes, but it might have been in a Richmond, BC, church in 1998, when VTV lets me do a news report in a pink bunny costume.

TV news has always been very stiff, and I fell into that during my early years as a reporter in Ottawa. Even my fluff pieces, of which there are plenty (see Chapter 5), are played mainly straight. But my new station in Vancouver is eager to be different. My first week there, before we've even launched, I use my own home video camera to shoot a silly piece about my dog attending a Jack Russell trial (basically, a track meet for that crazy breed). I don't really expect it to air on television. I'm just killing time before the station goes to air.

Ivan Fecan, the head of CTV, is out in Vancouver, making sure the station launch goes well. A few days before we go to air, he asks to see some of the stories reporters already edited. I am sitting across the room, with headphones on, pretending not to be watching as he solemnly shakes his head, clearly frustrated by the typical news pieces he's seeing. Then my Jack Russell story comes on. I slouch down, trying to disappear in my chair. He doesn't say a word for 90 seconds or so, just stares at the screen with an intense frown until it finishes.

"This is it!" he bursts out to the executive producer and news director sitting with him, and to everyone else in earshot. "This kind of storytelling is exactly what this station should be about!"

Boom! Finally a network that will dedicate itself to true journalism: poorly shot home video comedy stories about dog races!

And just like that, I am handed a free ticket to Clowntown. Our assignment editor at VTV, Clive Jackson, a terrific old bloke who has a background in British tabloids, gives me a green light to do basically whatever I want, as long as it gives him an entertaining kicker—the last story of the newscast. Though once in a while, Clive would yell as I walked out the station door, "I need a toppa today Duthie! No funny stuff today. GO GET ME A TOPPA!" Topper (British accent) was Clive's word for a story to lead the newscast. I didn't give him many. Lots of kickers. Not many toppers.

Some days I grab a cameraman and just drive the streets of Vancouver, looking for something amusing to report on. We do hard-hitting stories on subjects like proper umbrella etiquette, a dog that fetches really big sticks out of English Bay, and a statue with an unusually large penis in the window of an art shop.

It's shocking *60 Minutes* doesn't try to hire me.

One day, we hear about a costume-themed wedding in nearby Richmond. I do the report dead straight, except for the pink bunny costume I wear throughout. It goes over so well, I briefly consider asking the station to allow me to do all my reports in the pink bunny suit. Full rabbit, no matter what story I'm covering—crime, politics, sports—it would have been AWESOME. Or career killing. There's a fine line.

My favourite piece we do at VTV comes out of the 1997 Asia-Pacific Economic Cooperation (APEC) summit, when a large group of world leaders comes to Vancouver. The city is buzzing with sightings of U.S. president Bill Clinton in Gastown and Prime Minister Jean Chrétien having sushi on Robson. There are also numerous leaders whose faces and names are not as familiar.

So I decide to have some fun with the celebrity-obsessed culture that has clearly infected Vancouver. VTV happens to have an affable young intern named Gord Yip, a husky young Asian man whose bald head makes him look more mature than his 20-odd years. We dress up Gord in a nice presidential-looking suit and have three other staffers put on trench coats, sunglasses, and earpieces, to look like secret service men. And we hit the streets.

One of my secret service agents is Steve Pratt, the former host of a kids show on YTV and now an entertainment producer at VTV. We hit it off from the moment we meet in Vancouver, as he shares my somewhat warped sense of what should be in a newscast. Pratt plays his presidential bodyguard role beyond brilliantly. I stifle giggles the entire time as he yells things into a non-existent microphone on the lapel of his trench coat, like, "This sidewalk needs to be cleared RIGHT NOW!"

The VTV bosses are nervous about the story. They don't like the idea of creating our own news and want to make sure we aren't lying to anyone about Gord's identity. But that is not the plan. We just want to see how people react to the mere notion that someone famous might be nearby. Perfectly legit social experiment.

And sure enough ... people freak. We stroll down Robson Street, the three "secret service" men leading the way, clearing a path while whispering in their pretend mics to no one. And Gord does nothing but look regal and nod to passersby. Within a block, people are swarming around him, taking photos and craning necks to get a good look. When they inevitably, excitedly, ask, "Who is it? Who is it?" I (the reporter following this Sultan of Somewhere around) answer simply, "It's Gord." To which the majority look

confused for a moment, then nod their heads in pretend understanding and say, "Oh, right, Gord. Cool! Can't believe I met him!"
The story is a hit when it airs that evening. And Gord the intern
basks in the glory for weeks.

The station quickly comes to its senses and abandons its
no-sports policy, hiring a terrific sportscaster from Edmonton
named Perry Solkowski (who is still there). I do a handful of
sportscasts filling in, but the station prefers I stick to shtick.
And oddly, I'm okay with that. It lets me be a lot more creative
than I can be reading hockey highlights. Plus, it lets me explore
my new city. Cheryl and I live in a small apartment in Yaletown,
with floor-to-ceiling windows giving a view of the mountains on
one side and False Creek on the other. We decide we could settle
down here in Vancouver.

Her parents come out to visit in March, and we rent a boat to
go fishing in English Bay. Which brings us back to the salmon, the
clucking Jack Russell, and the phone call.

Odds are, most of the important calls you get in your life will
come at home while you are on the couch in your underwear
eating pie. Well, mine anyway. It's simple math, really. That's my
most common location, attire, and meal choice. But the most
important phone call of my career comes right then and there, on
the boat in the bay with the fish and the dog and the girl and the
future in-laws, and me. Actually wearing pants.

"Hello, James, it's Keith Pelley from TSN. How are you?"

"Uhh … I'm great, Keith … odd timing, actually … I'm fishing
on English Bay and I actually have a fish flopping around the boat
right now making my dog go nuts."

Long pause.

"Man, you have a good life out there, don't you?"

"Yes, it's been really good. What's up?"

"Do you like football?" he asks.

What is this? The VP of TSN is interrupting my fishing day
to offer me tickets to a game?

"I love football," I reply, confused.

"Well, we want you to come to Toronto and be the host of the CFL on TSN. You'll host NBA, too, if you're up for it."

When Keith didn't hire me the summer before, I told him, "Please, don't call me in six months. If I am going to move across the country, I want to spend some time there." He promised. And he was true to his word. He didn't call me in six months. He waited eight.

And with apologies to Dorothy Boyd (Renée Zellweger) in *Jerry Maguire*, he has me at hello. TSN is my dream. To start there hosting football is surreal. All those years growing up in the stands of Frank Clair Stadium, watching the Rough Riders lose 49–4 (field goal and a rouge) will finally come in handy. I say yes without even waiting to hear the rest of the offer.

It's a two-year contract that will double the salary I am making as a news reporter in Vancouver. I ask Keith for 24 hours before he announces it, so I can resign at VTV, where they had been very good to me. The next morning, I'm in the office of our station manager, Jon Festinger, thanking him for the opportunity and expecting a simple handshake and "good luck" in return. Now, a couple of weeks before, riding the success of the bunny suit or some other piece of shtick, I had asked our news director for a $5,000 raise.

"We'd love to," he said. "But we have no money whatsoever in the budget, so any raise is impossible."

I was about to learn my first lesson in leverage.

"What if we match the salary TSN is offering?" Jon says, without the hint of a smile even though he is clearly practising some odd stand-up routine.

I actually giggle. "But that would be … double what I'm making. And last week, they told me there was no chance I could get $5,000."

"We could try to make it happen," he says.

I'm a little stunned, but it doesn't matter. I'm going to TSN, no matter what. I tell Jon this, but he asks me to sleep on it, to give him just one more night before I officially walk away. And he's a good man who has been a good boss, so I agree.

I call Pelley a few minutes later to ask him to delay the announcement of my hiring.

"Nothing is going to change," I tell him. "I am 100 percent coming to TSN, they just asked me to wait one more day."

"Well, let's bump up your salary another $10,000 each year," Pelley says without a hint of hesitation.

This is the part where I qualify for worst negotiator in the history of ever.

"You don't have to do that," I say. "I already told you yes. The salary we agreed on is fine."

"No, I want you to have a little extra. I want you to be completely sure in your mind that this is the right move for you."

And so I get my first raise, before I've even been officially hired. Minutes after I hang up the phone with Keith, there is another call for me in the newsroom.

"James, it's Scott Moore from Sportsnet in Toronto."

(Quick corporate refresher course: CTV started Sportsnet in 1998 to compete with TSN, which was independently owned. CTV also owned VTV, the station I was working for in Vancouver. A few years later, CTV would buy TSN, and then be forced by the Canadian Radio-television and Telecommunications Commission (CRTC) to sell Sportsnet. Sportsnet was purchased by Rogers. Bell bought CTV/TSN. Then they both bought Maple Leaf Sports and Entertainment (MLSE). Then you stopped reading this book because your head hurt.)

Moore, a former TSN producer, was hired by CTV to run Sportsnet. I was thinking of applying, but I'd been enjoying Vancouver too much to get around to it (the laziness again).

"Listen, I'll be honest, I don't really know you, but there are some people here at CTV who really don't want you to leave," Moore says. "Is there anything you'd be interested in doing at Sportsnet?"

Festinger clearly made a call to some executive, who called another, who called Moore, asking him to offer a national sports job to a local guy he's never seen ... who does news reports in bunny suits.

Moore is very understanding. I tell him I've committed to TSN, and nothing is going to change that. He wishes me luck, and the strangest job interview in the history of broadcasting is over in about three minutes. The next day, my resignation is official. And TSN sends out a press release saying they've hired an unknown news reporter from Vancouver to be the new face of their CFL and NBA coverage.

As I read it, I suddenly get extremely nervous and excited. And start clucking like a chicken. (Not really. Just trying to bookend the chapter properly.)

chapter 11

FRIDAY NIGHT LIGHTS

"Does anyone have any pants I can borrow?"

This is probably not the question you should be asking your first day on the job at a national television network. Especially when said network has a great deal invested in the show you are about to host. And yet, I must ask. Because I am pantless.

It is July after all. In local sports, no anchor with a trace of cool wears pants behind the desk in summer. I was shorts and sandals all the way in Ottawa. Even today, I can pretty much guarantee the guy giving you the local senior baseball scores at 11:30 P.M. on Channel 7 has cargo shorts on below that jacket and tie. Besides, it was wearing jeans on the air that caught the attention of my new boss Keith Pelley in the first place. If he liked me casually dressed on camera, he'd certainly be okay with shorts and flip-flops that are never going to be seen behind the fancy new TSN *Friday Night Football* panel desk. Plus, it's Canada Day. I'm pretty sure it's in the constitution that you have to wear shorts on Canada Day. (The fact that I didn't think it might be suitable to show a little professionalism on day one of my dream job still troubles me somewhat.)

No one says anything about my outfit during the pre-game meeting. Guess they figure I am going to change. It's only when we get on set a half hour before showtime that producer Pelley (TSN's senior vice-president has jumped back into the producer's chair for this one day, just to make sure his new host doesn't ruin the network) whispers in my earpiece, "Uhh ... where's the other half of your suit?"

"Don't have one, Keith. Thought I'd go with the shorts today, just to stay cool ... not sweat too much."

"Yeah ... well here's the thing, James. We have a reverse shot over your shoulder where you can see all the way to your feet."

Well, that's ... problematic. I sprint up to the small wardrobe room next to makeup where some of the commentators keep their suits and grab a pair of pants that roughly match my jacket. I'm not sure who they belong to—Michael Landsberg or Paul Romanuk, maybe. Definitely not Dutchy. His legs are thicker than my torso. I also borrow a pair of dress shoes. The only thing I can't find are socks. No biggie, I figure. The pants should be long enough that surely no one will notice.

I am not the only rookie that day. Just the only one who didn't bother to dress. Pelley has hired a brand-new panel, with former BC Lions general manager Eric Tillman and retired former Dallas Cowboy/Toronto Argo offensive lineman Chris Schultz as the analysts. Schultz is a giant of man, 6'7" with hands the size of those giant foam "We're #1" hands they sell at stadiums. Tillman is a soft-spoken, bright football executive with the thickest red hair I've ever seen. And it grows straight up, like an orange Chia Pet. I really want to pet it. But I wait a week or so to ask.

We're all nervous for our first game. There is tense silence in the studio as the minutes tick down to showtime. I can see Eric licking his lips constantly. When the floor director yells, "Thirty seconds to air!" Eric suddenly says, in a polite yet panicky manner, "Water! Could someone get me some water! Can't talk! Need water!" One of the camera operators scrambles to grab him a bottle, which he chugs like he just stumbled out of the Sahara. The desperate tone in Eric's voice cracks me up and relaxes me a little.

We are in good hands that day. Pelley is a very good producer who returned to TSN for a senior management position after doing NFL games with FOX. His calm, reassuring voice helps our debut go very well, with one tiny exception. When I get off the air, I check my phone and my voicemail is full. Of course it is! No doubt jammed with congratulatory messages from friends and fans all over the country. I punch in my password. Let's listen to the love flow, baby!

Voicemail Lady: You have 47 messages. First message.

Friend 1: Dude, WTF! nice cankles!

Voicemail Lady: Next message.

Friend 2: (Hysterical laughter) Now Canada ... knows ... what we all knew! You have ... the calves ... of a chicken!

Friend 3: What, they didn't include socks in your contract?! You need a better agent!

Oh. Crap. I quickly head to the control room to get a tape of the show. It looks fine, until they cut to that reverse shot behind me, where my bent leg has pushed my pants up about a foot, revealing a massive section of skinny bone-white calf leading to my sockless dress shoes. Ladies and gentlemen, your new football host! To this day, you will always find an extra pair of socks in my dressing room, just in case.

The football panel works well from day one. Tillman is smart and articulate and knows the league inside and out. And Chris Schultz is a star. He has a huge personality that matches his physique, and is a natural on TV. He occasionally makes up new multi-syllabic words mankind has never spoken before (he considers it a proud trademark now), but he is excellent at breaking down the game, and is so authoritative, he could speak in Pig Latin, and when he's done, you'd still go, "Man, that guy knows his shit!" In three years working with him on the panel, there is only one time where Schultzy may have slightly confused our viewers.

One of the few brain-testing challenges in TV is learning how to speak coherently to the audience while a producer is giving you instructions in your ear. Sometimes it's as simple as counting you down, so that you throw back to the game or to a commercial on time. You hear "10-9-8 …" and you have to finish your sentence exactly when he/she hits zero. But there are also times the producer's instructions are more complicated, especially if something goes wrong technically. There have been many moments where I've been on camera getting ready to throw to someone live when I hear this: "Keep talking, James, Farhan's microphone isn't working! Just keep going … they're trying to fix it … you might have to fill an extra 20 seconds here … or just go to the panel … wait … we got it … throw to Farhan *nowwww!*" It can be pure chaos inside your brain, but your job is to stay smooth, unfazed, and keep talking so no one at home knows anything is up.

For the first few weeks, Chris doesn't wear an earpiece. He wants nothing to do with having extra voices in his head. "There are already enough in there," he jokes. An analyst can get away with no earpiece most of the time, as the host can signal him to shut up if he is talking too long. But ideally, the producer likes to be able to communicate with everyone, so Schultzy finally decides he's ready to be hooked up.

The producer avoids talking to Chris as much as possible at first, but during halftime, Schultzy is on a long rant, so he has to get in the big guy's ear.

He says something along the lines of, "We're heavy! Get it back to James so he can throw back to the truck!" (Quick TV translations: "heavy" means we're over our allotted time, and "the truck" means the production truck on location at the game. So in other words, "Schultzy, shut up or we're going to miss the start of the second half!")

Well, this is what comes out of Schultzy's mouth to our national TV audience: "So the Stampeders have to establish a running game if they have any shot of getting back into this Schultzy we're heavy get it back to James so he can throw back to the truck."

He repeats every word exactly as it is spoken to him, at exactly the second it is spoken to him. I quickly throw it back to the game, and we all lose it, even Schultzy. To our likely confused viewers, it probably sounded like he was sleep-talking on air. "Stamps … running … Schultzy … heavy … truck!"

Of course, like everything else about television, Schultzy figures out the earpiece fast. And 15-plus years later, he's still one of the best football analysts on either side of the border.

We figure we won't have Tillman long. He knows the league and its players so well, another team will surely come calling. It ends up being the Toronto Argos, who hire him as their GM at season's end. But not before he shows up for a game after having dental surgery. We know we're in trouble in the pre-game meeting.

"So, Eric, what do you want to say off the top of the show about the Lions?"

"Guysth, I think I thould focusth on their thsecondary."

His frozen-mouth lisp instantly makes him funnier than Chris Rock, without telling a single joke. It's mildly better by showtime, but still so hilarious Chris and I have to bite our tongues to stop laughing through the entire broadcast.

CFL legend Matt Dunigan replaces Tillman on the panel the next season. Matt is a larger-than-life character and is a blast to work with from day one. If it weren't for the concussions, he could probably still play today. He's in ridiculous shape, with a body that looks more like a linebacker than a quarterback. One day, we're in the makeup room and Matt is trying on one of the new suits TSN supplies for us.

"Man, this is tight," he says. "Look tight to you, James?"

It looks really tight.

So just for kicks, Matt starts to flex. And instantly, the suit starts to tear at the seams. It is The Incredible Hulk, minus the green paint. One sleeve falls right off the jacket, then the other. And finally, the jacket rips in half down the middle. In about 30 seconds, it completely falls apart and lies in pieces on the floor.

"Think I need a size up," Dunigan deadpans.

There are a lot of long nights in the studio, especially when BC is beating Winnipeg 41–3 in the third quarter. So we find ways to amuse ourselves. Our panel set is in the same studio as the main Discovery Channel set. So directly opposite us, just behind our cameras, is a series of set props. There is a skeleton, a full set of knight's armour, and a small Polynesian-type idol with long hair that sticks straight up (distant ancestor of Eric Tillman?) but parts in the middle.

I always bring one of those big bags of mini-carrots to games to snack on. And before long, Matt and I are having intense competitions, throwing the carrots at the set pieces. (Overdue apology to the Discovery staff who were likely puzzled and angry about having to clean up carrot chunks every Monday after football weekends.) You get points for hitting the skeleton's head, points for nailing the knight. But the ultimate target is to split the hair of the idol. Matt usually wins our games, but one of my proudest athletic moments is splitting the hair of the idol before one of the greatest quarterbacks in CFL history. I well up a little thinking about it.

To this day, "Splitting the hair of the idol" is the phrase only Matt and I share to describe success.

TSN golf tournament, every year:

"Hey, Matty, how you hitting it today?"

"Splittin' the hair of the idol, James."

Out for dinner:

"Hey, Matt, how's your steak?"

"Splittin' the hair of the idol, brotha!"

Everyday conversation:

"So, Matt, how was your romantic weekend with your wife in Cabo?"

"Oh, we split the hair of that idol."

Yes, even innocent little games involving tossing vegetables at plastic dolls somehow end up sounding dirty.

chapter 12

VINCE AND THE GUY FROM *FRESH PRINCE*

I am darting in and out of traffic in downtown San Francisco, videotape in hand, desperation in head. We have 15 minutes to make deadline, and we are about a 14-minute drive away from the production house where we have to feed our tape back through space to Toronto. If we don't make it, our asses are on the line.

To say it is raining cats and dogs on this February afternoon is a cruel understatement. More like goats and llamas. My chest and nipples are clearly visible through my soaked dress shirt. I look so hot, I really should be in a Whitesnake video. (Apologies if you are eating while reading this.)

My producer Martin Paul is feverishly trying to hail a cab. I have given up on that and have now resorted to jumping in front of moving cars to stop them, then trying to bribe the half-terrified drivers to take us there.

"I will give you $100 to get me to this address!" yells the drenched (yet oddly well-dressed) psycho, as he bangs on countless drivers' side windows. Most nervously hit the lock button and speed away. We're screwed.

It's the Friday of NBA All-Star Weekend 2000. Hosting *NBA on TSN* is the other half of my first job at TSN, as it begins just as the CFL season is ending, and vice versa. (Aside: The bosses decide I should shun the suit and ties for our NBA coverage to go with a younger, hipper look. Somehow this ends up being mock turtle-necks and plaid jackets. After all, nothing gives you NBA street cred like a mock. I should have really accessorized with a pipe.)

On this miserable Northern California afternoon, we have just finished an interview with Toronto Raptor teammates and cousins Vince Carter and Tracy McGrady. They have spoken candidly about their desire to stay in Toronto and win multiple championships together (and ... cue hysterical retrospective laughter!!!).

I like Vince (February 2000 Vince, anyway). Away from the court and cameras, he is still a polite, soft-spoken kid. As we wait for the crew to set up lights, he asks me about Alcatraz, and whether it's worth his time to take the boat trip out there. He tells me *The Rock* is one of his favourite movies. I tell him *Escape from Alcatraz*, the Clint Eastwood classic, is better. He has never heard of it. I feel like a grandpa.

McGrady shows up a couple of minutes later. I'd only have one other real conversation with T-Mac. It came after I did play-by-play for a Raptors game in Chicago. I was waiting for my cab, and he was waiting for his limo.

"I have a question about TSN," he says.

"Fire away."

"What is that curling shit?"

"Ah, it's a pretty popular sport in Canada."

"Seriously? People watch that? Guys with brooms standing around pointing at those big pucks with the handles?"

"Rocks. They call them rocks. And yes, lots of people apparently like it."

"Damn," he says, shaking his head. Then the limo pulls up with a girl in a fur coat in the back, and off T-Mac goes, into the Chicago night. Pucks with handles. Will never forget that.

T-Mac and Vince are great together in the interview. They are still young and unspoiled, and in many ways, they are the buzz of All-Star Weekend. Especially Vince. His mere entry in the slam-dunk contest has revitalized the event. It had been cancelled two years before. Many believed there were no more tricks to be done. Many were about to be a whole heap of wrong.

Miracle! Marty has found a cab, likely preventing me from being arrested for harassment of innocent commuters. We get there a couple of minutes late, but are able to extend our satellite window a few minutes to get the interview sent back through space to Toronto. This costs the company money, but I don't feel guilty. I feel like a drowned rodent.

We've dried out by Saturday night, and I'm sitting in the arena in Oakland, down near the court before the skills competition begins. I spot Alfonso Ribeiro, Carlton Banks from *The Fresh Prince of Bel-Air*, sitting a few seats over. In the 15 minutes or so I'm there, a dozen people yell, "Hey, Carlton! Do the dance, Carlton! Do the dance!" For the few of you who have never watched *The Fresh Prince* (I feel only sadness for you), Carlton is the ultra-nerdy, preppy, rich cousin of Will Smith, Philadelphia's streetwise kid. And his dance is ... well just google it. You won't be disappointed.

Ribeiro is dressed very LA chic and has a model by his side, but he can't escape Carlton. Soon, a group of well-lubricated fans start chanting it: "Do the dance! Do the dance!" Carlton does not do the dance. Carlton looks like he wishes he'd never done the dance. And I quickly realize this is Alfonso Ribeiro's life. Unless he someday lands a career-resuscitating role as a recovering meth addict in a gritty Ben Affleck film, Alfonso is Carlton for eternity. Every. Single. Day. Everywhere. He. Goes.

"C'mon, Carlton! Just do the damn dance!"

It's the curse of the One Defining Role actor. I would interview Cuba Gooding Jr. a few years later, and I ask him how many times a day people want him to say, "Show me the money!"

"Hundreds, my man," he answers, defeated. "You don't even wanna know." Of course, I then have to ask him to say it for the sake of the interview. If he hates me, I don't blame him.

I abandon Carlton's nightmare to climb up to our set, inside a first-level luxury suite. All-Star Saturday Night is broadcast on TNT (Turner Network Television) in the United States, and TSN picks up the feed. But because of the hype over Vince, TSN NBA analyst Brian Heaney and I are there to open the show and do brief segments in and out of commercial breaks. Heaney played briefly in the NBA and became a coaching legend at St. Mary's in Halifax. He's a conservative, fundamentals-first coach. He doesn't seem much into dunk contests. He's also very cool and measured. In the two years I have worked with him, I have never seen him really excited. That's about to change.

The building is buzzing as Carter's turn approaches. He has tried his best to crush the hype, saying in his TNT interview just before the contest that the whole thing has been "blown out of proportion." He then walks out on the court and proceeds to blow proportion out of proportion.

As he prepares for his first dunk, the players all stand, many carrying ludicrously large 2000-era video cameras. Carter starts near the baseline, leaps, goes between his legs, and windmill jams. The building explodes. Heaney looks at me, mouth gaping open. Shaquille O'Neal falls backwards like he's been shot. That dunk would become commonplace within the next decade, but in 2000, it has never been seen before. And it's otherworldly. In my earpiece, I'm hearing the TNT commentators calling it "maybe the best dunk ever."

His second dunk is equally absurd, a ferocious 180-degree windmill from a starting point behind the basket. This time, the crowd reaction isn't quite as loud, as I believe they are a little stunned at what they are seeing. Watch the dunk contests before 2000. No one had ever dunked like Vince.

For dunk number three, Tracy McGrady takes a position under the basket, which only adds to the anticipation. He has the ball and is somehow going to set up his cousin. The building goes quiet as Carter starts his run towards the key, but the pass is a little off, and he abandons the attempt. But he's given enough away. I can hear TNT analyst Kenny Smith in my earpiece, saying, "He's going to take it between his legs and dunk it!" After showing T-Mac exactly the height he wants the ball, Carter goes back to his launch position and takes off.

Smith is right. McGrady bounces the ball off the floor and Carter grabs it, already in mid-air. He goes between his legs and destroys the rim. And Oakland blows up. Every person in the building reacts like they have just won the $380 million Powerball. Fans in front of me are leaping off their chairs into their neighbours' arms, falling into the aisles like a flash mob doing choreographed pretend heart attacks. Then I notice Brian Heaney, the calmest, most conservative commentator at our network. He has fallen off his chair and is lying on the floor of the suite, rolling around in uncontrollable laughter. Hours later over a beer, he can't explain what happened. He was so blown away by the sheer lunacy of Carter's acrobatics, he simply lost it.

I have been lucky enough to attend many of the biggest sporting events on the planet. I have still never witnessed an atmosphere like that night in Oakland. Think about it. There was no home team to root for. No buzzer beater or Hail Mary in an actual game that mattered to anyone. Just a silly made-for-TV skills contest. And yet, that crowd went as nuts as a crowd can possibly go.

Carter nails one more mind-blower in the final, where he finishes by hanging from the rim at his elbow joint. He then wraps up the title with an anti-climactic two-handed version of the famous Jordan leap-from-the-foul-line jam (except Vince was a good foot inside the line). It doesn't matter. The legend has already been cemented by the first three dunks.

I sprint to the locker room and get to the front of the pack rushing to Carter's stall. Vince knows me now after the long sit-down interview the day before, and turns to me for the first question. At which point, I get the semi-brilliant/semi-idiotic (there's always a fine line) idea to turn to the rest of the media and say, "We're TSN from Canada. We were promised a live one-on-one, so stay back for three questions please." This was:

a. Not true. There was no such promise, and if anyone actually looked, there were no cables sticking out of our camera. There was no chance this was live.
b. An opening for some big angry audio guy from Philly to shove a boom mic down my throat.

But shockingly, they all seem to buy it. We get our one-on-one and race to the truck to feed it back. Carter's magic show is now the lead on *SportsDesk*, pushing hockey highlights from the top of the show on a Saturday night for the first time in anyone's memory. Carter instantly becomes one of the most popular athletes in Canada that night, a label he would throw away in train wreck fashion a couple of years later. He would go on to have a decent, but surprisingly quiet, career.

But man, that night in Oakland. I have still never seen anything like it. He brought the house down. He turned an ultra-calm, hard-to-impress analyst into a little boy having a giggle fit on the carpet. And though I have no proof of this, I think he just might have made Carlton do the dance.

chapter 13

"THE DESK"

This, in a single sentence, is why I love television: Doing a ridiculous bit about your infatuation with a hot Russian tennis star on a sports highlight show can lead to meeting … THE HOT RUSSIAN TENNIS STAR!

One night, hosting *SportsDesk* (just before it became *SportsCentre*), I am doing an intro to men's tennis highlights. I ask the director to put up a still of Anna Kournikova instead. My Kournikova obsession is a running gag on the show. In the middle of a sentence about Roger Federer, I stop, as if catching the Kournikova image in my periphery.

"What are you doing here?" I ask, now speaking directly to a graphic that I can't even see, because it is superimposed by a computer over my shoulder. "This story isn't even about you. You are barely even playing anymore. Get out of my head! GET OUT OF MY HEAD!!!"

The director, on cue, dissolves the graphic off the screen, leaving me staring into nothing, at which point, I reach out into the empty space where the graphic had been, grasping at air, while saying faintly, desperately, "Please don't go."

When you anchor a show like *SportsCentre*, you tend to forget people are watching. Amusing the crew is your only real goal. If you get a stifled giggle from a camera operator, you've won. But apparently, people are actually watching. Including, on this night anyway, someone from Tennis Canada, who took note of my Kournikova issues, and didn't forget. A couple of years later, I get a call from my boss:

Boss: Hey, James, sorry to bug you. Wondering if you could help us out with an event …

Me: No shot. Summer. Me no work.

Boss: Oh … well, it could be fun. It's a tennis thing …

Me: Don't do tennis. Only contact sports. And swimsuit competitions.

Boss: Are you sure … they want you to be the umpire for a celebrity match with McEnroe and Courier and Carling Bassett and …

Me: Legends tennis? Seriously, kill me now. I'd rather watch reruns of *Full House*.

Boss: Oh … and Anna Kournikova will be there too.

Me: I'm in. Love tennis! Whatever you need, Boss! You know me … company guy all the way!

Apparently, they had asked for me because someone had seen that silly intro on *SportsDesk* and remembered my, um, enthusiasm. And so a couple of weeks later, I am in the big lifeguard chair at the Rexall Centre in Toronto, umpiring the match. And by "umpiring," I mean relentlessly hitting on Kournikova for two hours (with my lovely wife, Cheryl, in the crowd, completely unfazed because she is used to being married to an idiot). The evening basically goes like this:

Kournikova hits a forehand well long.

Me: In!

Courier: Are you kidding me?! I know this is a fun match, but that was out by three feet.

Me: Never doubt Miss Kournikova's ability to paint the line! Unsportsmanlike conduct penalty. Three extra points to Miss Kournikova. Game, Kournikova!

Courier: Unsportsmanlike conduct isn't even a tennis rule.

Me: Abuse of pretend umpire! Set to Miss Kournikova's team! Anna, do you need a refreshment break ... or thigh massage?

It grows more and more desperate as the night wears on, peaking (bottoming out ... whatever) as I sing her boyfriend Enrique Englesias's hit "Hero" to her, while Bassett is attempting to serve. As the match ends, Anna is clearly smitten with me. And by "smitten," I mean she politely shakes my hand while carefully avoiding any eye contact. So all in all, a horrific night for tennis umpiring, a pretty solid night for me. That is the gift of hosting "The Desk," our nickname for TSN's flagship show.

But not all my moments on "The Desk" lead to such magic. The worst thing about any national TV anchor's job is that when you have a bad day, you can't just hide in your cubicle until 5 P.M. and hope tomorrow goes better. When we have bad days, several hundred thousand witness it. I've had too many screw-ups to list, but the one I always remember from my early days was doing a curling highlight package on the 6 P.M. weekend *SportsDesk.* One of the curlers in the pack is Connie Laliberte, pronounced LALI-Berty—simple enough. But curling is not my greatest area of strength, and I've never said her name out loud before. So I carefully cross it out the seven or eight times it appears on the script and scribble my own phoneticized version: "La-Liberty." Which is completely wrong. Phonetics, like curling, not a forte. But that's how I say it the first time it comes up in the highlights. La-Liberty. As soon as the butchering occurs, producer Greg Sands gets in my ear to correct me. "It's LALI-Berty," Sandsy says calmly. No problem! Except the second time I have to say it, the high school French immersion portion of my brain decides to put a hard Gatineau twang on the end: "La-Lee-bear-tai."

"It's LALI-Berty," Sandsy says sternly into my ear. Now I'm rattled. As I continue with the highlights, every time her name comes up, the letters seem written in some alien language. And I destroy her name every ... possible ... way.

Me: Lali-ber-tai with the in-turn draw.

Sandsy: LALI-Berty!!!

Me: La-lie-ber-tie scores two in the seventh ...

Sandsy: SAY IT RIGHT!!!

Me: And then lying two in the ninth, La-li-bert? (I actually did it in the form of a question)

Sandsy: (Silence. I figure he's quit on the spot.)

Me (still live on air): And in extra ends ... (pause) ... Connie ... takes it 7–5.

Sandsy: Thank God.

While I was hosting CFL and NBA in my early years at TSN, I would anchor *SportsDesk* on the weekends. Back then, the main show was the 11 P.M. weeknight *SportsDesk*, anchored at the time by Rod Smith and Darren Dutchyshen. (Rodsky & Dutch—one of the best commercials our promo guys have ever made—YouTube it.) But in the fall of 2000, Dutch is given the chance to host a new show called *That's Hockey 2*. The bosses ask if I'd like to give up my football and basketball roles and take his spot full time. It's not an easy call—more of a lateral move than a promotion—but I'm generally a restless soul, and Rod Smith is one of my favourite people on the planet, so I take it.

We have endless fun. Rod is not only a great broadcaster, he's also the perfect Ed McMahon, laughing at all of my lines, even the lame ones (so basically, all of them). Once or twice, he even guffaws when I'm not trying to be funny. You see, when one anchor is talking, the other is often going over his next script, so he's barely paying attention. Rod becomes so used to me being an idiot, his mind starts to believe that every time I pause, I've delivered a punchline. So we have a couple of moments like this:

Me: And with that, Owen Nolan has now scored in five straight games.

Rod: (Chuckling) Five straight. Heh, heh.

I quickly realize I could be content doing this show with Rod for the rest of my career. Instead, we are done in six months.

Jim Van Horne, a TSN institution hosting the 6 P.M. *SportsDesk* and the man who helped me that day of my audition, leaves for a job in radio. Around the same time, *That's Hockey 2* gets scrapped. The shuffle button is hit again. Rod takes Jim's job on the early show, and Dutch and I are partnered on the 11 P.M. *SportsDesk*. We spend an eventful year and a half together, while TSN is purchased by CTV, moves to a new building, and *SportsDesk* becomes *SportsCentre*.

Dutchy and I are an odd mix at first. He, the loud, brash, beefy Saskatchewan farm boy. Me, the quirky, not so beefy, product of the Ottawa suburbs. Dutch is one of the most passionate people I've ever met. It's his single-greatest strength as a sportscaster. There is no one who loves doing the highlights every night more than him. I struggle at first. His personality is so strong, I have trouble getting a word in. But after a couple of months, it starts to click. Dutch has this tendency to say things you aren't supposed to say on television, especially in 2001. And they make me laugh, harder than a supposedly professional broadcaster is supposed to laugh while doing a supposedly professional broadcast. My all-time favourite line of his comes on a home run by a player named Edgar Rentería:

"3–2 in the seventh, Edgar Rentería [Rent-or-REE-a] at the dish, deep to left, Rentería ... Gonorrhea!" I'm done. No chance at recovery. Just go to commercial.

The summer months are the toughest hosting *SportsCentre* because there is so little going on. Baseball highlights fill up much of the show. Out of pure boredom, I invent something called Home Run Call Theme Night. Each show, I pick a random theme, and every time there is a home run in a highlight pack, I blurt out a word related to that theme. For instance, one early theme is types of cheese. So:

"Giants–Cardinals, bottom one, Barry Bonds deep to right ... Gouda!"

"Whitesox–A's, 3–3 in the sixth, when Frank Thomas connects with a man on ... Havarti!"

It is pointless, but it amuses me and makes the slow summer shows more tolerable. One night, in a tribute to Dutchy, the home run call theme is towns in Saskatchewan. I pick a few with funny names off a map and save my favourite for last: "Cubs down to their last out when Sammy Sosa takes John Smoltz to straight-away centre ... Big Beaver!" Without missing a beat, Dutchy replies, "Been there." I can't even finish the highlight pack.

There is only one show I can recall where Dutch and I didn't spend most of the night laughing. It was the *SportsCentre* that aired September 11, 2001.

I am sitting on the couch feeding my baby daughter Darian that morning, while my two-year-old son, Jared, is, for some reason only he knows, playing hockey with one of those giant exercise balls that is twice his size. My cell rings, and it's my buddy, Dave Shaw.

"Turn on the TV right now," he says.

"What channel?"

"Any channel."

The second plane has just hit the towers. For most of the day, I am unable to compute, overwhelmed by the enormity of the tragedy. But as the afternoon rolls on, I realize we are supposed to do a sports show that night. Never has our job felt so small and irrelevant. Dutch and I talk on the phone, and neither one of us wants to go on the air. It feels senseless, offensive almost, to do our show on this night. But our bosses decide the show will go on.

And in retrospect, they were right. There are no highlights. The games have all been cancelled. But there are interviews from athletes about the tragedy and news about when games will be rescheduled. People need some level of normal at times like that. And I suppose for those who watch us every night, we give them a bit of that. I spend the next couple of days trying to figure out where sports fits into something like this. And end up writing this column for our website:

THE FINAL TOLL—September 15, 2001

We, in sports, seem determined to attach a number to everything, and the nightmare of September 11 is no different. The "Sports World," this imaginary bubble we supposedly live in, lost LA Kings scouts Ace Bailey and Mark Bavis.

Two. A neat, tidy death toll, perfect for the tickers at the bottom of the screen. But wrong. We also lost:

Soccer moms, and Little League dads, and big sisters who became corporate bigwigs, but could still whip you at 21 when they came home for Thanksgiving. We lost star shortstops from the corporate softball league, and secretaries who didn't play, but always brought the oranges, and cheered like you were Derek Jeter. We lost 11-year-old boys who could have been the next Jordan or Gretzky, and four-year-old girls who could have been the next Mia Hamm or Serena Williams, not to mention whom they could have become in the *real* world.

We lost fans. We lost Mets fans and Yankees fans, and fans that couldn't stand either, which was a damn brave stance in New York. We lost Jets fans who'd always go to the game with the same three buddies, each shirtless with a big green painted letter stretching from navel to neck. And no matter how cold, they'd remain skin to the wind, screaming: "J-E-T-S, Jets!" Even when it was 21–3 Colts. We lost bosses you couldn't stand, until they invited you to the box at the Rangers game and you both wore your Messier shirts, and forever bonded. We lost girlfriends who left you alone on Sunday afternoons in the fall, or better yet, sat right next to you and cursed like a convict when Kerry Collins threw a pick. We lost guys from the mailroom who'd spend a couple of days' wages to sit in the nosebleeds with their girl at a Knicks game, and stockbrokers in Boss suits who'd spend a couple grand to impress a model with courtsides. But they'd cheer just as wildly. New York has great fans. We also lost Red Sox fans, Bruins fans, Patriots fans, Capitals fans, Redskins fans, Wizards fans, and probably at least a fan or two for every team out there. Even the Bengals.

We lost fathers who'd take you to mini-putt and blow a six-inch gimme on 18 every time to lose by one, so he'd have to take you for ice cream yet again. We lost mothers who somehow found time to run households with a bunch of kids, corporate divisions with hundreds of employees, and marathons in under four hours. We lost Grandpas who took you out for your first round on a real course, and pretended they didn't see when you teed it up on the fairway.

We lost coaches who'd work 60-hour weeks, and then spend their Saturdays trying to teach six-year-olds to stay in position, and not all chase the same ball. We lost entire lines from the Firefighters Shinny League.

And you know what the saddest part of all is? Sport was just a tiny part of who these people were.

We lost *all* of them.

chapter 14

P × P

I am standing, to make sure I get a perfect view of the play. I want to nail this call. And even though I'm a Niners fan, I realize I have to do it neutrally. The excitement in the voice has to be the same for a Cowboys knockdown or pick as it is for a San Francisco touchdown. The huddle breaks. I'm ready.

"Montana over centre. He takes the snap and rolls right! Here comes the pressure, throws off his back foot … for Clark! He's got it! Touchdown Niners! Touchdown Niners! San Francisco is going to the Super Bowl for the first time!"

It's perfect.

I adjust my underwear, allow myself a quick yelp of glee for the Niners win, grab my can of Wink (I loved Wink, the most underrated lemon-lime pop in the history of soda), and sit back down on the couch in my parents' basement, content with my call of another historic sports moment. I'm 15. I probably should get out more.

Getting any sportscasting job is a dream for teenage me. Being like Smitty or Billy, doing the local sports on CJOH, would be unreal. But my true fantasy, born way back in public school, is to do football play-by-play.

From about age 10, I turn down the volume on our basement TV and do my own commentary on Sunday afternoons. Not for the whole game. Pat Summerall is too good to miss for three full hours. I call a series here and there, maybe a quarter. Then I turn the volume back up to listen, while eating cherry pie filling right out of the can. The big cans, too. It's a minor miracle I don't weigh 270 pounds by university.

One Sunday in December 1980, NBC decides to air a New York Jets–Miami Dolphins game with no commentators. I treat this as my own network audition and carry the whole broadcast by myself. By age 14, I fully believe I am ready to replace Howard Cosell on *Monday Night Football*. Though the pale yellow blazer frightens me somewhat. I prefer doing games in my New York Islander PJs with the jam stains. I figure ABC will agree to this request once they hear how good I am.

Present-day confession: When aspiring young play-by-play wannabes (who can't get a hold of actual play-by-play guys like Chris Cuthbert or Gord Miller) ask me for advice, I always recommend doing every game they can to get experience—high school football, minor hockey on the community cable station, and every sport they'll let you do for the campus TV or radio station in college or university. *"Time now for the third place épée match between Mohawk and Seneca at the Ontario Regional College Fencing Championships. Should be a dandy."*

Me? I did none of that. Not a single event. Those days with the volume turned down in our wood-panelled basement at 10 Valewood Crescent, Gloucester, Ontario, end up being the only play-by-play assignments I ever do, pre-TSN. Even when the network hires me, they never even ask about my experience in the booth. Would have been a tricky conversation:

"So, James, we know you can anchor, but how much play-by-play have you done?"

"Lots. I've done several hundred NFL and CFL games."

"Really? Wow. Impressive. What network was that?"
"Ahhh … that was for … errr … PBTV."
"Pardon?"
"Parents' Basement Television. Smaller network run out of Blackburn Hamlet."

I might be the only broadcaster in history whose very first play-by-play gig is a regular season NBA game for a national network.

It is 1999, and I'm in my second year at TSN. The play-by-play dream had been shoved aside for a decade now as I went from news reporter, to local sport anchor, back to news reporter in Vancouver, and finally anchor/host at TSN. Then one week, both our regular basketball play-by-play guys, Paul Romanuk and Rod Black, are busy at other events, so our head of production, Rick Chisholm, decides to give the kid from the basement with the jammies a shot. I'll call the Raptors and Hawks from Atlanta. I still remember looking at the game-day media program and having trouble registering it:

TSN: P x P James Duthie

Basketball, I still believe, is the easiest of the major sports to do play-by-play for—not easy to be great at, but probably your best shot at not embarrassing yourself calling a professional sporting event for the first time. There are only 10 guys on the court. You are sitting a few feet away from them. And none of them have helmets on. I figure I can get through without mixing up Muggsy Bogues and Charles Oakley.

It goes pretty well, though I say "Scores!" repeatedly for baskets. Can't take the hockey out of the boy. And at one point, I decide to be clever and announce Dikembe Mutombo's full African name during play.

"Hey, folks, did you know Dikembe's full name is Dikembe Mutombo Mpolondo Mukamba Jean-Jacques Wamutombo?" I believe I miss two baskets and a foul getting that out.

I had spent several days trying to come up with some brilliant catchphrase to say if Vince Carter pulled off one of his already trademark dunks. My personal favourite is "It places the lotion in the basket!" Though I'm not sure quoting Buffalo Bill from *Silence of the Lambs* would work with a hoops audience. Turns out Carter catches me off guard in the middle of rattling off some inane story I had prepared to fill air. So as he completes one of the best dunks of his young career, all I get out is "Vince Carter ... airborne!" Pretty weak. But it does get played on ESPN that night, so ... small victories.

A few weeks later, I do play-by-play for the Canadian University Basketball Championships in Halifax. During the first commercial break, our analyst, Brian Heaney, grabs me by the arm and says, "Stop talking so much! You keep cutting me off!" This terrifies me to the point where I barely speak for the rest of the first half. Later, one of my bosses says, "I like how you backed off and let the pictures tell the story." Yeah, that is my ... technique. Has nothing to do with the fact I thought my colour guy was going to shove my headset up my nostril.

Halifax is my first championship game, and once again, I spend considerable time trying to figure out how I'm going to call the last few seconds. I saw an interview with Al Michaels once where he said his "Do you believe in miracles? Yes!" call was completely off the cuff. Though he is one of the best ever, I don't buy it. I think the vast majority of the time, even the most experienced play-by-play guys will have a line ready, just so they don't blow the moment that could be replayed for eternity. I'm guessing Michaels came up with his "miracles" line sometime very late in the game when it became clear the Americans had a shot.

This game is between the Saint Mary's Huskies and the Alberta Golden Bears. I have something mega-cheesy like "The Bears are golden!" ready for an Alberta win. (In retrospect, I'm extremely glad they didn't win.) But I struggle coming up with something for Saint Mary's. People have told me to just keep it simple, like "And the Huskies are national champions!" Screw that.

In my mind, TSN will soon realize the only play-by-play I should be doing is back in my parents' basement, and thus this might be my only chance ever to call a championship, so I'm going to come up with something at least semi-original.

During the game, I notice there are some fans barking like dogs when the Huskies get a basket, and I get an idea. The game stays very close until the last few seconds when Saint Mary's goes up by four to seal it. With about three seconds left, I blurt out my championship opus:

"Every dog has its day. Huskies, this one ... is yours!"

Okay, it's not exactly "Do you believe in miracles!" But at least I get it out without stumbling and bumbling. At a bar a decade later, a former Saint Mary's student walks up to me, recites the line, then gives me a hug. This makes me happy.

I do a handful more basketball games, including a Raptors–Wizards tilt in 2002 in Toronto when Michael Jordan misses a buzzer beater. "Jordan ... for the win ... No!!! Not this time, Michael Jordan!" Again, hardly poetic, but I am proud of the moment. Calling a Jordan game, even old guy Wizards Jordan, is unforgettable. I also do one equestrian jumping event in the summer, where my expert commentary amounts to saying "Ohhh!" every time a horse knocks a rail off.

After a while doing the fill-in commentating on hoops and horses, I finally get a crack at my real dream. TSN asks me to do a handful of CFL play-by-play gigs. Football play-by-play, it turns out, is much more challenging than basketball. And football play-by-play in a booth high above the field is much more challenging than sitting on your couch with a can of cherry pie filling in hand.

I survive my first game, a forgettable blowout win by the Eskimos in Edmonton. My second game has the lowly Ottawa Renegades in BC to play the Lions. I fly out a couple of days early to watch practices and make sure my depth charts and notes are 100 percent accurate. For some inexplicable reason, my one game of experience has me confident enough that I decide to go out the night before

the game with some of the guys from the crew. As happens occasionally on the road, one beer leads to another, and soon it is 3 A.M.,
and my director, Andy, and I are at some questionable establishment
with people who work on Microsoft founder Paul Allen's yacht,
which is parked at the marina by the Westin Bayshore. I come very
close to getting on that boat, just for the story. Of course, with my
luck, it would have set sail at dawn, and I would have had to call
my boss and tell him I couldn't call the game because I was "at sea."

Thankfully, I choose to stay on land and keep my job. But the
night has taken a toll. As we prepare to tape an on-camera chat for
the pre-game show, our terrific producer, Jon Hynes, asks the
cameraman if he has white-balanced properly.

"You need to fix that, Duthie looks green," he says. Leif
Pettersen, our colour analyst, who I've told about the night before,
chuckles and says, "Jon, I don't think the camera is the problem."

Leif is a TSN legend. A former CFL star with model looks—
maybe the most confident man I've ever met. He is also very good
with me that night—coolly filling in all the gaps when I need to
pause to throw up in my mouth. But Leif is also in a hurry. He has
booked the red-eye home so he can watch his daughter's equestrian event the next day. To catch the flight, he knows he'll have to
leave the second the game ends. But the Lions are destroying the
Renegades, and sometimes CFL blowouts tend to run long. So
with about two and a half minutes left on the clock, Leif calmly
taps me on the shoulder and gives me the "I'm outta here," signal.
He takes off his headset and strolls out of the booth.

At first, I believe this is a prank to teach the rookie play-by-play
guy who stayed out too late a lesson. It isn't. My colour guy is gonzo.

I gather myself to call a play—some garbage time eight-yard
completion—and then Jon Hynes does what producers do after
most plays, saying, "Okay, Leif, here comes your replay."

I hit my talk-back button (also called a cough button), which
cuts your microphone to the audience and allows you to speak to
the producer, and say, "Ah, he's gone, Jon."

"What do you mean? To the bathroom?"

"No, I mean he's gone. To the airport."

Silence. And so the green (literally) rookie does the last two and a half minutes of the game by himself. I might have been horrified if it were close, but it's 48–15 or something, and the absurdity of the last 24 hours now hits me like a linebacker's helmet to the sternum, and I start laughing. If the tape of that game exists, the last two minutes are full of mostly dead air, only because I have pressed my cough button so the viewers can't hear my guffaws.

Those kinds of stories take on legendary status in our business. Over the years, that 2:43 morphs into 5 minutes, then 10, then the whole fourth quarter. In 2007, I run into Leif at an airport in Columbus, Ohio, and he just laughs and shakes his head.

"I was out the other night and some guys wanted to hear about the time I left the game at halftime! The way I see it, I gave you your big break. You owe me!"

A year later, Leif passed away after a massive heart attack. He was one of TSN's great characters. And by the way, he made that flight and his daughter's equestrian event, which is all that really matters.

My next Ottawa Renegades game has a different, but equally bizarre, ending. As I wrote at the start of this book, I grew up at Lansdowne Park in Ottawa. My parents had season tickets forever, and I went to every game, from age 8 to 30, sitting between Mom and Dad and listening to Ernie Calcutt call the game on my Walkman. Going back there to do a game for TSN remains one of the greatest moments of my career. And it might have been my greatest single call. Had anyone seen it.

The game is a good one ... back and forth between the Renegades and the Saskatchewan Roughriders. The Renegades are up late, with quarterback Nealon Greene and the Roughriders needing a touchdown to win. They drive the ball down inside the 10 and have one play left to try to win it. In the second before the snap, I'm trying to calm myself. *Don't talk too much. Let the pictures tell the story. Less is more.*

The play goes like this: Greene scrambles around, throws to the end zone, and the ball is knocked away. Renegades win. Crowd goes crazy. My call is brief, simple, and in my mind … perfect.

"Greene … back to pass … throws … game over!"

As I let the crowd carry the celebration, I nearly dislocate my shoulder patting myself on the back. I can see the fantasy headline in the fantasy newspaper that would never ever exist anywhere except my fantasy world: "LOCAL HERO RETURNS WITH BRILLIANT CALL OF RENEGADES WIN!"

Then Jon Hynes gets in my ear, with a tone far too serious for someone who should clearly be congratulating me on my brilliance.

Jon: Dude, tell everybody what happened on the play.

I hit the cough button.

Me: Why? They saw it. It was perfect.

Jon: They didn't see it.

Me: Whaa?

Jon: We lost video. No one saw the play. They just heard you.
And … you didn't really say what happened.

Me: [quiet sobs]

Seems that also happened to be the first night we tested high definition. We had a second production truck at the game just to make sure all the HD cameras and cables worked, as we were going to debut it within a few weeks. With about a minute left in the game, the HD crew says, "That's a wrap" and starts to put away their equipment. But instead of pulling out the plug on the HD video feed, a technician pulled out the main feed. And viewers across the country were left with me, saying ... errr ... pretty much nothing, over a black screen.

My brilliant TV call thus becomes the worst *radio* call in history. It's probably fitting that not long after, my brief play-by-play career comes to an end, as other opportunities come up. So the dream of calling a Super Bowl fades to black. But I could still cover one. And I was going to beg and grovel until I did.

chapter 15

THE SUPER BOWL (220 MINUTES WITH ANDY ROONEY)

Andy Rooney is not happy with his juice box.

This does not exactly qualify as news in the man-bites-dog sense. After all, Rooney has made a career out of being everyone's Uncle Grumpy. But I always figured that was just his made-for-TV shtick. Until I sit down next to him at the 2002 Super Bowl.

Rooney is a TV legend, after doing a segment called "Two Minutes with Andy Rooney" on the great CBS news show *60 Minutes* for, oh, about … 70 years. He would close the show every week by whining amusingly about something that bothered him. Could be some major world political issue, but more often than not, it is some trivial slice-of-life thing along the lines of *"Why can't I get my blueberry muffin to come out of the wrapper in one piece? Half my muffin always get stuck on the wrapper. We can send a man to the moon, but we can't get a no-stick muffin wrapper? That drives me nuts."*

Is there a better job than complaining about muffin wrappers for two minutes a week? I'd always been a fan of whiny Andy. And now, suddenly, here he is. High in the nosebleeds of the Louisiana Superdome, an hour before Super Bowl XXXVI, everyone's favourite octogenarian curmudgeon, in the seat next to mine.

I say hello, and Andy nods, but he's already going through the bag of goodies the NFL leaves under every media member's seat. This includes a packed lunch, a seat cushion, and a cheap portable radio to listen to the game. The following is a rough transcription of his lunch-box opening play-by-play (it helps if you do it aloud in Andy's voice):

"What the hell? A juice box?!?" He looks over at me as if it was my idea. "What am I, seven? Is this a field trip? I hate these things! You can't get the straw out of the plastic, and then it won't fit in right, and it's too full and squirts all over your sweater. And what's this supposed to be? A turkey sandwich? With a packet of mustard? Where's the mayo? Who puts mustard on a turkey sandwich when they could have mayo? Is there a mayo shortage in Louisiana? And yet they also give us ketchup? Well, that can't be for the sandwich, so what the hell is it for … this stupid little chewy bar? That's just what I need at the biggest sporting event on the planet, a ketchup-covered apple Nutri-Grain bar. And what's this thing … oh … the radio. It's plastic! Wow, they really went all out for these, didn't they? Is Fisher-Price the technology supplier for this Super Bowl?"

And so it goes for the next ten minutes or so. Andy quiets down once the game starts. Seems he gets his cheap plastic radio to work to his satisfaction. When U2 comes on at halftime, he just puts his head between his legs and covers his ears. Andy apparently wants no part of Bono and The Edge.

Spending (roughly) 220 minutes with Andy Rooney was not what I had envisioned when I received one of the assignments that I got in the business for. Not only am I covering a Super Bowl, but a Super Bowl in New Orleans. Which is the equivalent of saying, "Not only did we get a nanny, but a bikini-clad supermodel nanny!" (Do not repeat this metaphor to my wife.)

New Orleans is made for Super Bowls. It should really be there every other year, minimum. Bourbon Street is an adult carnival. At one bar, Dennis Rodman walks in and buys shooters for every person in the place—had to be five hundred. (His reported financial issues years later make a great deal of sense.) Another night, we lose Chris Schultz, which isn't that odd, because Schultzy has a habit of disappearing for hours on end. We have long since given up looking for him when, standing on the ground level of a three-floor bar, I suddenly get a draft-beer Gatorade shower. I look up, and there on the top floor with an empty jug is Schultzy, grinning. I'd be mad at most people, but Schultzy is like a puppy (albeit a giant menacing one) who pees on your rug. It's hard not to love him, no matter what he does. Plus, if I ever did get mad at him, he would snap me like a twig. So my options are limited.

The week has been great; the game is even better. It is the first Super Bowl since 9/11, and as U2 performs "Where the Streets Have No Name," they scroll the names of every 9/11 victim across the roof of the Superdome. It is spine tingling.

The Rams are double-digit favourites, but the Patriots hang around all night, and as the game heads to the fourth quarter, there is upset in the air. The lousy part about covering a Super Bowl, for the TV crews anyway, is that you miss most of the fourth quarter. With about 10 minutes left in the game, they corral you to take you downstairs to field level. This process takes so long that by the time you get down in the bowels of the building, the game is winding down. They cattle us all on a concrete walkway about 50 yards from one of the end zone entrances. So roughly two hundred of us watch the end of the game on an 18-inch monitor hung from the ceiling.

And what an end. Tom Brady, a second-year previously unknown QB who replaced the injured Drew Bledsoe mid-season, leads the Patriots on a stirring last-minute drive into field-goal range. Adam Vinatieri hits a 49-yarder, and the Pats stun the heavily favoured Rams. As the ball splits the uprights, a cameraman from a Boston station standing next to me says, matter-of-factly, "Well my next week is f*%#ed."

We race onto the field moments later and get into position to do live reports for *SportsCentre*. We aren't expecting to get many players. With all the U.S. networks there, our Canadian cable network isn't exactly top priority. But since the Patriots have won, they are giddy and are talking to everyone. So we get a string of guys popping by, including Vinatieri, with the Vince Lombardi

Trophy tucked under his arm. For a kid whose favourite show growing up was *NFL Films Presents*, it's unforgettable.

But the big prize is Brady, who of course we have zero shot at getting. We are in a commercial break when I see him, heading back towards the locker room after doing ESPN. I scream, "Tom!" and try to wave him our way. And to my shock, he nods and takes a few steps in our direction. *Holy crap.* I'm about to get the Super Bowl MVP, live. That thought barely registers before a mob of PR people, league officials, and other salivating media types turns Brady back towards the tunnel. He looks back at me briefly, shrugs with a "Sorry, dude, but my world just got too crazy for Canadian cable" grin, and disappears into a future of superstardom, supermodels, and many more Super Bowls. See ya, Tom. Enjoy the ride.

When I take the *NHL on TSN* job seven months later, I figure my Super Bowl days are done. But then comes the warm wonderful gift of Lockout 2005. And here I am in late January, on a connector from Charlotte to Jacksonville for Super Bowl XXXIX.

Here is my seating arrangement on the flight. Directly in front of me: Emmitt Smith. Directly behind me: golfer Jim Furyk. Directly across from me: Donovan McNabb's mother. I keep thinking, this would make a really good episode of *Off the Record*. Somewhere Landsberg is seething. Emmitt and I have a long chat, and he confides in me that he is about to retire (he would announce it that week). Okay, technically, all he says to me is, "Quit kicking the back of my chair!" But to me, that means his back is bad, so he must be ready to hang 'em up. So I'm still taking credit for the scoop. "TSN has learned," baby. It's all about "TSN has learned."

It takes me all of three minutes after our arrival to remember I am at the most overhyped media monstrosity in the universe. Two camera crews are waiting at the airport, desperate for the exclusive interview with ... McNabb's mom.

It is the strangest Super Bowl location ever. It's not that Jacksonville is ugly. It's just that ... THERE'S NOTHING HERE!

(All-caps = cry for help.) I believe the city's official motto is "Welcome to Jacksonville, only two hours from Orlando!" It's like awarding the Grey Cup to Belleville. The people are nice, though. Seems like they imported every senior from around the state just to smile at you.

Airport: Hi! Welcome to Jacksonville!

Airport baggage claim: Hi! Welcome to Jacksonville! You need help with them bags?

Airport bathroom entrance: Hi! Welcome to Jacksonville! Enjoy your pee!

The seniors are everywhere. It's the first Super Bowl ever where the toughest dinner reservation to get is 4 P.M.

We're not actually staying in Jacksonville. We're in a motel 45 minutes outside of the city. It's a three-star, which, under the local rating system, means no one has been murdered in your room in the last week. Funny thing, see. When they awarded the game to Jacksonville, they apparently forgot to ask if they had any places for people to stay. In New Orleans, there were 20,000 hotel rooms within a six-block radius of Bourbon Street. In Jacksonville, there are 1,800 rooms, period. So you can rent a booth at the Waffle House for $400 U.S. a night. Waffles not included.

On Media Day, I witness a large male reporter ask Tom Brady, "What makes you so sexy?" Brady gives him that cute, blushing, "Aw, Shucks" smiley answer he gives every complimentary question, though I'm guessing he would have popped him if there was no one around. I also watch a guy in a superhero outfit leaping on players' backs. And I think to myself, *What happened to you, Terry Bradshaw?* But my new personal favourite media icon is a "reporter" from Mexico who conducts all his interviews with a hand puppet wearing a tiny football helmet screaming questions in Spanish. I tell our ace reporter Farhan Lalji that he needs to steal this technique and bring it back home for things like, I dunno, Canucks practices. He doesn't laugh.

On the Thursday night before the game, Schultz and I tape a bit with Chris Berman on the massive ESPN set. Thursday, I learn, is the night when Chris tapes all of his segments for Friday and Saturday. We are trying to get done in a hurry so he can get back to work. I slip into Chris's host seat, and he moves into one of the analyst chairs next to Schultzy. Berman loves Canada, so is happy to do the piece, and it goes well. I quickly scoop up my papers and makeup powder, and we head off, back to our hotel in the boonies. Just as we are getting back, my producer Dennis's phone rings. "No, I don't think so," I hear him say hesitantly. "But I'll ask." He hangs up.

"You didn't by chance take any of Chris Berman's notes or makeup, did you?"

"Of course not," I respond without looking, chiding Dennis with my eyes for even asking. Then I look. And in my little bag is ... every one of Chris Berman's handwritten scripts, plus a plastic sandwich bag containing all of his makeup.

"Err, okay, maybe I might have."

And that was the night I shut down ESPN for two hours, as Chris Berman (apparently) tore apart the set, looking for his notes, which had all been "right there in front of me!" About six months later, I run into Berman on the practice range covering the U.S. Open Golf championship. I don't even get the hello out.

"Hey, Chris, James Duthie from T ... "

"The guy who stole all my notes and makeup! Great to see you again. Please don't go near my stuff."

Occasionally, someone asks me the difference between covering the NFL and CFL, both of which I love. Here's the story I tell them. One day in Jacksonville, we get delayed crossing a street to the convention centre. Police block off the road. We figure we must be caught in some midday parade. Instead, it's about a five-car motorcade.

"The President?" I ask one of Jacksonville's finest, who is directing traffic.

"No, sir, it's Mr. Tagliabue [the NFL commissioner]."

Later in the week, Farhan and I hit a couple of parties in town. As we're driving out of the downtown around one in the morning, we see affable CFL commissioner Tom Wright on the side of the road. Our windows are down and one of us yells, "Tom?" as we pass by. (We are speeding through a light in busy traffic onto an on-ramp so we can't really stop.) As we zoom by, we hear the CFL commissioner yell, "Guys, I need a *riiiiiiiiide!*" (The stretching out of the last word is his sad desperate voice fading into the distance.) Too late, we're gone. And that, ladies and gentlemen, sums up the difference between the CFL and NFL— the transportation options of their commissioners.

Two days before the game, I'm at a security entrance outside the stadium watching Michael Irvin lose it. Seems the future Pro Football Hall-of-Famer has forgotten his media credential, and even though every one of the guys in the yellow vests working at the checkpoint knows exactly who Michael Irvin is, they aren't letting him in. Irvin is only there to do an interview with an ABC affiliate. That station is lined up, with the rest of the media (including us), on a large catwalk outside the stadium. We are the only other ones at security, so I stand there watching Irvin get more and more frustrated. Then he yells out the following (I type it in my BlackBerry right away because it is instantly my favourite quote of all time):

"C'mon, boys! I ain't gonna hurt your stadium! I don't wanna cause no harm to anyone! I'll leave my bag here! I got nothin' on me that could destroy your stadium! I PROMISE I WILL NOT BLOW UP YOUR STADIUM!"

When I stop giggling, I tell security Irvin is going to do an interview with us (white lie) and we'll escort him in and out if that helps. They relent, and let him in. I hated Irvin as a Cowboy, but he seems like a decent guy. He thanks us and heads off to do his interview. We are still taping our stuff when he strolls by later, and says, "Hey, the guys who got me in! You want me on the panel today?" So he sits down and does a segment with us. And I can vouch for him. At no point did he attempt to blow up their stadium.

We get to the game Sunday, and guess who is in the seat next to me?

"Jacksonville? Why the hell are we in Jacksonville for a Super Bowl? Where are we going next year, Des Moines, Iowa?"

"Hi, Andy. Good to see you again."

(Apparently, they have the same seating arrangement for every Super Bowl, as Andy Rooney has been next to the TSN seats the last two years I missed as well.) I strike up a long conversation with him this time, since we're now Super Bowl buds. I explain to him who the Black Eyed Peas are as they perform in the pre-game show.

"Well, I do like the girl," he says, as Fergie gyrates on the big screen. Andy and I are tight now.

The game is just okay. The Patriots win again, holding off Donovan McNabb and the Eagles. I realize as the confetti is falling that this might be my last Super Bowl, unless there's another hockey lockout. And that will never happen! I mean, no one could ever be that stupid, right? (I could really use an Andy Rooney rant on that one.)

Andy would do his last *60 Minutes* segment on October 2, 2011. He would pass away a month later. I was sad. I still think of him every Super Bowl. And every time I pack a juice box in my kids' lunches. Those straws are a pain in the ass.

chapter 16

AZALEAS AND URINALS

Long before we called them bucket lists, I had one.

I am 12 when I write my first draft (which at 12, you believe is your final draft). And right at the top: going to The Masters. No wait. It's second. Number one is dating a cheerleader with a paw painted on her face. I have a thing for the Clemson University football team. And 12 is that Middle Earth age for boys when they are just coming out of loving cute cuddly animals ... and just getting into loving hot cuddly cheerleaders. So a cheerleader from your favourite football team with an orange paw painted on her cheek is pretty much heaven. And so is Augusta.

My love for golf comes young, nurtured at an ultra-exclusive chichi country club my pal Mark Ward and I go to every day in the summer. It's called Innes Road Mini-Golf and Driving Range ($1.75 for a round, $4.00 for a large bucket. Great milkshakes). We play full 72-hole mini-golf tournaments, have fries for lunch, then try to hit the guy in the ball-collecting tractor all afternoon on the range. I am smitten with golf years before I ever set foot on a real course.

At 10, I am watching every second of any tournament American network TV gives me on the weekends. John Deere Classic, B.C. Open, Hartford Open—they are all majors in my barely developed sports brain. I worship Calvin Peete, one of the first black players on the PGA Tour. Peete and Tony Esposito are my favourite athletes. I'm thinking I might be the only kid in the history of the planet with that idol combo.

Any PGA event will do for me. But The Masters is spell-binding. By 12, the second week in April is challenging Christmas as my favourite time of year. And from the moment I arrive at TSN some two decades later, I ask (plead … same diff) to cover The Masters. And in 2002, six months before I move to the *NHL on TSN* full time, they relent, and send me.

I had always imagined driving down a long, winding country road surrounded by Georgia pines to get to Augusta National. Seems I was a little off. The course, it turns out, is not far off the interstate, tucked behind a typical North American highway exit road, full of chain restaurants and strip malls. We drive in early the first morning, butterflies the size of flamingos in my belly, and just a few blocks from Magnolia Lane, we pass a Hooters. In fact, there is a Hooters girl standing by the road, spinning a Hula Hoop and yelling at passing cars, "C'mon in for the Hooters Masters break-fast special!" Weird. Jim Nantz has never mentioned this in his flowery openings.

Ah, Nantz. That's probably one of the reasons I bit so hard on The Masters as a kid—the way the commentators talk about it like hallowed ground. Nantz (who is generally an excellent broad-caster) will come on and say things like, "A gentle breeze whispers its way through the Georgia pines, stirring up the ghosts of Augusta's past. The azaleas sway to and fro in unison, as if bowing to the spirit of Bobby Jones …"

So there's a half-club wind, Jim? Is that what I'm to take from all that? As we're driving past the Hooters girl, I imagine Nantz making the same commute that morning, waxing poetic all the way.

"A small drop of sweat meanders its way towards her ripe, supple bosom, like a fallen leaf in Ray's Creek wanders through Amen Corner. Oh, Hooters girl. Yours is the sweet morning dew of … Augusta. Amen

indeed, baby … Amen indeed. I'll see you at eight. Have a gin and tonic ready for me."

Once you get off the strip and onto the grounds, Augusta National is exactly like it looks on TV. Actually, it's better. It is one of the few places I've been to in the world that is more beautiful than I'd imagined. And I had imagined it really, really beautiful. The first thing that strikes you when walking the course is the severity of the slopes. Not just on the greens, everywhere. The eighth is straight uphill. You don't need a caddie, you need a Sherpa. Ditto 18. The first time I walk up it, carrying a cameraman's tripod, I practically need CPR at the end. Television, no matter how good the HD, does not do Augusta's topography justice.

It is heaven. Unless it rains. And for Masters week 2002, it rains a ton. Thursday and Friday are a mess. They aren't able to complete the first two rounds before darkness falls Friday night.

On the Saturday morning, I follow Arnold Palmer up 18, where he finishes his final competitive round at Augusta. It's an incredible moment. People are crying in the gallery. I am determined to get a one-on-one with the legend, but the tournament PR people say, "No shot." He is only doing interviews with CBS and the Golf Channel. So I stake out the parking lot. I casually ask one of the young attendants which car belongs to Mr. Palmer. He offers it up in a second. And my cameraman and I plant ourselves next to it, and wait. Sure enough, after about a half hour, here comes Arnold. No entourage, no security, no PR flacks … just Arnie and his car keys. As politely as possible, I ask if he might answer a couple of questions for Canadian TV. He proceeds to give us a teary-eyed three-minute interview. Then the most popular golfer ever gets in his car, waves, and drives away. I'm pumped. Dean Willers, my pal and cameraman, says, "You just did Arnold Palmer's last interview at The Masters." (Aside: A year later, Arnold changes his mind and comes back to play one more Masters. I'm a little disappointed. He ruined my tiny piece of history. It's a little selfish of Arnie to do that to me. But I forgive him.)

Still basking in the glow of my Palmer parking lot exclusive, and with a couple of hours to kill before the start of Round 3, I decide to explore the many cabins at Augusta National. The press pass gives you great access. You can go almost anywhere. I stroll into one cabin and stumble upon Tiger Woods's mother and his (then) girlfriend Elin Nordegren sitting on a couch chatting. There is no one else in the building. So I sit down on the adjacent chair and make myself comfortable. The Woods women ignore me and go on chatting. After maybe 20 minutes, in walks Tiger.

He is much different from the stone-faced robo-golfer I see on my TV and in his news conferences that I've attended. He is more like a giddy high school nerd smitten with his girlfriend. They hug and kiss, and he asks Elin to run back to the house and grab him some socks he left on the bed. (I remember this because it strikes me as bizarre that there isn't some Nike guy with a truck with three thousand pairs of socks at Tiger's disposal.)

Even though Woods and his ladies seem completely oblivious to the fact I'm there, I'm still starting to feel awkward, so I get up and follow a sign upstairs to the men's room. It's a relatively small washroom with three urinals and a stall. As always, I choose the middle urinal. This is an important lesson for you young men on the brink of adulthood: ALWAYS CHOOSE THE MIDDLE URINAL. I never trust guys who take the corner urinals when they have a choice. They always angle themselves to the corner like they have something to hide. It shows a lack of confidence. Be strong. Choose the middle urinal. If there is one useful takeaway from this book, that is it. As I stand confidently at the middle urinal getting rid of last hour's Gatorade, the door opens behind me. I glance over my shoulder, and sure enough, it's Tiger Woods. Now, I've been around plenty of famous athletes by this point and rarely get rattled. But this is Tiger Woods, 2002 World Domination Version. He is the most famous athlete on the planet. And he's shoulder-to-shoulder with me at the urinal to my left. (He surely would have chosen the middle urinal if it were available.)

So for a moment, I'm a little flummoxed. You see, there is an unwritten (until now) guide to urinal etiquette for men. In a small washroom like this, when there are only two of you, you need to at least acknowledge the other guy with a nod or a "What up." But at the same time, you don't want your glance to linger, for fear he thinks you are … you know … bird watching.

"Wow, Tiger is pulling out the driver! And I've got my … putter."

So after a moment of hesitation, I come up with "Hey." Pretty solid. Succinct. I'm proud of it. Tiger responds with a "Hey" of his own. This is going well.

With Tiger just four strokes off the lead and a couple of hours from starting his third round, I decide to follow up with a simple "Good luck."

He is still opening his belt and unzipping at this point, so he chuckles, glances down, and comes back with the following: "I should be all right. I do this several times a day."

Ba-da-bing!

Yup. On the morning of moving day in the biggest tournament in the world, the grumpy superstar known for cursing at his errant drives and giving death stares to any cameraman who clicks near his downswing cracks up a stranger with a pee joke. This still impresses me as much as any of his major wins.

Tiger would shoot 66 that day and follow it up with a 71 on Sunday to beat Retief Goosen by three and win his second straight green jacket. It was the height of his glory. A few years later, things went a little … umm … south with Elin, and his game. And some … (this is awkward) … very different Tiger urine stories emerged in the tabloids.

We'd meet again, Tiger and I. But not before my career took another hard pull-hook left.

chapter 17

THE ACCIDENTAL HOST

I am walking towards the green at 18, needing a two-putt to break 80.

Let's clarify this scenario. I don't want anyone who plays golf with me calling BS before they even get into the chapter. The public track we are playing in Muskoka, north of Toronto, is short and easy. I don't believe there is a single tree. I don't break 80 often. But on this day, I have a shot.

My buddies and I are finishing off a guys' golf weekend. The sun is going down on a beautiful early October Sunday. It's been a crazy, wonderful three years. Cheryl and I have moved from Vancouver to Toronto, gotten married, had two kids (Jared and Darian), and we're weeks from conceiving a third (a second daughter named Gracie, though I don't know that yet ... I'm not that good). I've moved from hosting CFL and NBA to hosting *SportsCentre* full time. And 2002 has been one of my favourite years, getting to cross a Masters and a Super Bowl off that childhood bucket list. (I even think Cheryl painted the paw on her face and put the cheerleader outfit on one time for me. You know how Saturday nights in the suburbs work.) Anyway, life is spectacular. And I figure it's time to just settle in for a few years. I've had enough change in my life.

And then, the phone rings. Man, isn't that always when the phone rings?

When TSN got the NHL rights back many months earlier, I didn't really bat an eye. I was having a blast doing *SportsCentre* with Dutchy, and getting the odd football and basketball play-by-play gig. I don't even throw my name in the hat for any of the *NHL on TSN* jobs. I love hockey, but I look around and figure we have enough hockey guys. Gord Miller is our main hockey host, and he's very good at it. So it never even crosses my mind to consider applying. By August, everyone in the building is buzzing about this incredible studio being built on the other side of the CTV compound for the *NHL on TSN*, complete with a rink with synthetic ice. I don't even bother to go check it out. I'll wait to see it on TV.

Turns out Gord isn't the host after all. He gets the main play-by-play job instead. Our boss, Keith Pelley, has a vision to create an MTV-style (MTV in 2002—whole different network) studio show with a host who walks and talks and throws to a bunch of different segments—analysts debating, players doing demos on the rink, and live bands performing during the intermissions. One day, word filters through the newsroom that he has hired an unknown broadcaster from Vancouver named Linda Freeman to be the host.

Unknown to most, but not to me. Linda and I worked together at VTV. She started doing the weather and ended up hosting a funky morning show. And she was very good. Smart, quick on her feet, and incredibly nice off air—one of the best people I meet during my time in BC.

It is a historic hire for TSN. No woman had ever hosted a national hockey broadcast in Canada. Some of the guys are groaning and rolling their eyes when they hear a former weather-girl is our new hockey host, but I am happy for her. I have no idea if Linda knows anything about hockey, but it sounds like this will be a very different kind of hockey show.

In early September, there's a huge *NHL on TSN* launch party at The Docks in Toronto. They even hire extras to scream like groupies when the on-air personalities enter the party on the red carpet. These girls are screaming at Dutchy and me like we're a boy band, so I say to one of them, "Thanks for the love ... by the way, what's my name?" She shrugs sheepishly. Hilarious.

I see Linda briefly at the launch party and wish her well, then frankly forget about the *NHL on TSN*. Until that boys' golfing weekend.

The first call actually comes on Friday evening, after we are already multiple beverages in, sitting on the deck of a cottage we've rented. It is Keith Pelley, in his office or his car, somewhere on speakerphone.

"Hey, James, quick question for you ... when you worked with Linda in Vancouver, what did you think of her as a broadcaster?" Odd question.

"I liked her. Good broadcaster, great person."

There are a few seconds of strange silence.

"Okay, appreciate it. Have a great weekend."

He hangs up, leaving me with no idea what to make of the call. I figure maybe they've had a few kinks in rehearsals, but I don't waste much time on it. I see my Ottawa buds only once every couple of years, so the call is forgotten in about 30 seconds.

But then the phone rings again on Sunday, walking up the eighteenth fairway, two putts from 79. I would have let it go if I hadn't seen it was Rick Chisholm's number. Rick is TSN's senior VP, and Keith's right-hand man.

"Hey, James, do you think I could stop by your house tonight?"

Rick has been my direct boss since the day I was hired in 1998. He's a wonderful guy. We've played some golf together and had a few lunches. But he has never, ever, asked to come to my house.

"Uhh, well I'm golfing up north, Ricky, but I'll probably be home around eight. What's up?"

"I'll see you at eight. We'll talk then."

I three-putt for 80.

I spend the two-hour drive home using my buddies as a sounding board, trying to figure out why TSN's second in command wants to see me on a Sunday night. I don't think I'm fired. Haven't made an offensive joke in ... well, a couple of shows, anyway. I start to figure it must have something to do with the Friday phone call. And by the time I hit Barrie on Highway 400, a half hour from home, I am starting to put two and two together.

Rick gets to my place just minutes after me. My house, with a toddler, a baby, and a dog, is madness, so we go for a walk. We small-talk for about five minutes, until I decide to cut to the chase.

"Ricky, I think I know what's up ... but ... what's up?"

"We want you to host the *NHL on TSN*."

"You mean, like ... now? The season that starts in 48 hours?"

"Yes."

"What happened to Linda?"

"She's still going to be on the show, but we've decided, and she agrees, that hosting is too much for her right now. We need someone who knows hockey a little better. And we feel you are the best host we have."

Kind words, but my first reaction is to say no. (Yes, I know any Canadian hockey fan reading this is thinking, *You are nuts.*) But this just isn't part of my career plan. Plus the proud part of me is thinking, *If you really wanted me to host the* NHL on TSN, *why didn't you ask me six months ago?* So I waffle.

"I need to think about it, Ricky."

"You don't have time. We need the new host in studio tomorrow morning for rehearsals."

So we walk in silence for a couple of minutes, and I do the quickest pro–con chart in history. Cons: 1) no more football play-by-play, 2) no more *SportsCentre*, and 3) I haven't prepped at all for this job and could be walking into a disaster. Pros: 1) I am a Canadian kid who grew up loving hockey, and I have just been asked to host NHL games on a national network. The list doesn't need to go any further.

"Okay, Ricky. I'm in."

We agree to deal with the contract details later. (Agents would say I am nuts for this and blew the ultimate leverage—but I trust Rick and TSN, and they would take care of me a few months later.) The next morning, I pull into our building as the new host of the *NHL on TSN*. A host who has never set foot in the studio and has no idea what the show is about (besides ... hockey). The season starts tomorrow.

As I pull into the CTV parking lot, I stop for a woman hurriedly crossing towards her car. She glances back. It's Linda Freeman, the woman I'm replacing. It's a weird moment. Reminds me of the scene in *Pulp Fiction* when Butch (Bruce Willis) stops at the light and Marsellus (Ving Rhames), the gangster he just ripped off, happens to be crossing. Thankfully, our scene doesn't end in a dungeon with the Gimp.

Linda comes over and jumps in the passenger side. She doesn't slap or slug me, so that's a good start. In fact, she couldn't be nicer. She says she's relieved—the hosting gig turned out to be too much for someone who hadn't done any sports broadcasting, and she wasn't comfortable. I still feel awkward—taking this job from someone I know and like—but it helps to know she isn't bitter. (Linda ends up doing a handful of features before leaving TSN a couple of months into the season.)

I walk into the building and straight into a production meeting for opening night. The group of producers looks tired ... beaten. They have been going non-stop for weeks trying to get the various show segments ready. Now they have a new host the day before it goes to air. I have a ton of questions but choose to just sit quietly and learn as much as I can.

"Okay, let's go over the opening night lineup," says one of the producers. "We're going to start the show with the puppets."

Sounds goo ... Wait. What?

chapter 18

PUPPETS, STRIPPERS, AND MONKEYS

In the chronological history of the *NHL on TSN*, the studio prop order goes like this:

1. Puppets
2. Stripper
3. Monkey

When they make movies based on true stories, they often blend several characters into one, just to simplify things. Thus, our film would likely have a stripper who uses a monkey puppet. I would watch that.

The puppets are born out of a vision to do something completely different with TSN's new hockey show. In the spring of 2002, just before the network officially takes back national cable broadcast rights, TSN president Keith Pelley holds several brainstorming sessions with people inside and outside of TSN to come up with fresh ideas. Somehow out of that comes a pair of puppets named Nick and Doug, a cross between Statler and Waldorf from *The Muppet Show* (who themselves were a takeoff of Harold Ballard and King Clancy in their private box watching Toronto Maple Leafs games), and Wayne and Garth from *Wayne's World*. The plan is for Nick and Doug to pop up here and there during the show to make witty observations about the game and the league.

If we'd had *The Daily Show*'s writers and complete editorial freedom, the puppets might have worked. Instead, they are doomed from day one. And there are few things sadder than a doomed puppet. They need to be edgy to be funny. But when you are a national rights holder for a league, edgy doesn't fly. Nick and Doug's writers end up doing safe (translation: lame) bits that draw groans from the studio crew. (When the crew groans audibly, you are in trouble. I've prompted groans myself. I know groans. And the puppets had the groan meter going through the roof.) Here is a word-for-word transcription of a random puppet bit:

Doug: Well, this is the time of year some teams put their rental players on the market.

Nick: Rental players?

Doug: You know, the players teams pick up just for the playoff season.

Nick: Oh. Do the Sabres have any rental players?

Doug: Yup, Alexei Zhitnik.

Nick: Zhitnik!? He's only scored one goal in the past 18 games! I'd say that's more of a rent-a-wreck!

Doug: I'm just sayin' he's available.

You can read it over if you want, but no, you didn't miss anything. That was it. Puppet comedy. They are fired after one season, their puppet corpses left backstage for years after, hanging lifeless over some lighting stand, with creepy puppet grins still on their faces. One of our producers finally rescued one, and it still sits on his desk. A stuffed ode to the wacky first year of the *NHL on TSN*.

And man, it is wacky. I am more circus ringmaster than host. Besides the puppets, there are live bands, comedians, and a variety of analysts skating on our synthetic ice rink or sitting at different desks around the studio. Opening night, 48 hours after that fateful visit from my boss, Rick, I am on air, semi-sprinting from spot to spot introducing all of the elements of the show. Bob McKenzie and Dave Hodge are at one desk, former players Ric Nattress and Dave Reid are on the rink firing pucks, and Ron Wilson sits alone at another desk, making sarcastic cracks at me as I try to bounce around our giant studio without face planting.

Some of it works well. Some of it fails miserably. One segment, called Talk Amongst Yourselves, has Bob and Dave already in the middle of a conversation when we go to them. So basically, I tee up a topic, then say something lame like, "Bob McKenzie and Dave Hodge are discussing that very subject right now! Let's listen in!" And we cut to them in the middle of a sentence. Bob and Dave are great. But the premise that they just happen to be discussing something and we're all going to eavesdrop for a couple of minutes is beyond hokey. Talk Amongst Yourselves dies quickly and thankfully.

I didn't know Dave and Bob very well back then. But I can quickly tell they are miserable with the show. They are two of the most respected hockey people in Canada, and this new *NHL on TSN* circus is clearly not their idea of how to broadcast our game. Meanwhile, I'm mostly oblivious, still that little boy stuck in dreamland, walking my dog's leash while the dog waits at home. Growing up as the son of a police officer and a teacher, I was basically raised to do what people in authority positions tell me. So I do. And frankly, I'm just not strong-willed or perceptive enough yet to say, "This is stupid. We shouldn't be doing this."

I would get better at that as the years go on, but in the fall of 2003, I am basically Pavlov's puppy. But Bob and Dave are not. They voice their complaints to the bosses (loudly), and a couple of months into the season, some changes are made to try to get the show running smoothly. Though smoothly is not to be confused with less wacky. We do a pre-game show segment in January announcing TSN's All-Star selections. One of our producers at the time had been out the previous weekend and met a young lady who was trying to get into television. He told us she was a dancer—the kind who circles a pole made of brass. When we meet her, we have no reason not to believe him. (I won't use her name because she may be somebody's mom now.)

He suggests we have her unveil our All-Star choices in Vanna White fashion. Let me correct that: in Vanna White posing for *Penthouse* fashion. It still boggles my mind that this idea got approved. But I'll take the fall, because I didn't walk off the set like I should have. Instead, I am the one on camera with her, as she lies across the studio desk in tight jeans and a tighter tube top, saying things like "Our last forward is that pesky devil John Madden," in the most seductive way John Madden's name has ever been spoken. In retrospect, I'm surprised we didn't have a pole on set. Social media does not exist in 2003. This, methinks, saves several jobs that night. We never see her again.

Even the guest segments we do are on the nutty side that first season. The panel has still not been born yet, so we have different characters on the show every week. One night, Al Iafrate drives on the set on his motorcycle, live as I'm opening the show. We have a radar gun behind our net on the rink to see if he can come close to his legendary 105 miles per hour slapshot at the 1993 All-Star Game in Montreal. Problem is, there isn't enough space, so he has to shoot from a small riser, where he has no room to wind up or step into the shot. Al has also chosen flip-flops as his footwear for the day. Odd for a national TV appearance, but, hey, we don't judge. So off this tiny riser, in flip-flops, with zero warm-up, the long-since retired defenceman fires. 98 mile per hour. Ridiculous.

Doug Gilmour laces up his skates on our fake ice one night to recreate his famous double OT playoff series–winning goal on Curtis Joseph and the St. Louis Blues. Just to make it as unrealistic as possible, I am playing the role of Joseph, wearing a suit and no skates. At the end of the segment, I decide to throw this smartass line in: "When we come back, Doug will recreate his famous milk commercial with the cow legs." Doug is standing just behind me, smiling sweetly as he cracks me in the back of the calf with his stick, just below camera range. It almost buckles me, though on the tape, you only notice a wince as the shot cuts immediately to commercial. I have a two-inch purple welt for a week. Doug calls it a love tap. I quietly thank the gods of every religion that I never took a real Gilmour whack.

For another segment, former Washington Capital Mike Marson joins us in full martial arts gear. Since retiring, he has earned a fifth-degree black belt in Japanese Shotokan. One of the things Mike does as part of his routine is to HIT HIMSELF AS HARD AS HE CAN IN THE HEAD WITH A SLEDGEHAMMER! (Sorry. Not usually an all-caps guy, but I felt this required it.) Mike does this to prove … umm … I still have no clue. Something about the power of the mind to control pain, I believe. If this were present day, with our knowledge of head injuries, someone would have thrown us in jail for allowing Mike to do this. But in 2003, we are all saying, "Hey, a hockey player is going to pound his forehead with a sledgehammer on our show! This is awesome! Woot!" (Actually I don't even think "woot" is around in 2003. We probably say, "Yippee!" We aren't very cool.)

So during a live national hockey broadcast, Mike grabs his sledgehammer and pounds himself in the front of the head multiple times. As I move in to interview him right after, he already has a massive egg growing in the middle of his forehead and looks like he's about to pass out. In retrospect, maybe the stripper isn't our biggest mistake that first year.

With the failure of the puppets and the stripper, and the lunacy of the sledgehammer incident, we decide to play it safe for a while. So we hire a monkey to predict the outcome of the playoffs. (!)

The monkey is the (unintentional) idea of Eric Neuschwander, one of our producers and one of the funnier guys at the network.

At the time, Eric happens to be into one of those nature shows called *Monkey Business*, about chimpanzees at a sanctuary. So during a pre-playoff meeting where all sorts of bad ideas are being thrown around about how to spice up our playoff coverage, Eric tries to get a cheap laugh by saying, "Why don't we just get a monkey to predict who will win the Stanley Cup!"

He doesn't get the laugh. Instead, he gets thoughtful pauses from high-ranking executives, followed by nods of approval, followed by "Love it! That's entertainment!" Followed by, "Great work, Eric, now go find us a monkey!" And that, in a nutshell, is how television works.

After calling every zoo in southern Ontario, Eric finds a macaque at the Bowmanville Zoo, east of Toronto, that is smart enough to learn tricks. He decides spinning a Crown and Anchor wheel would be easy enough to learn, so he rents one at a party store and takes it to the zoo. Turns out her name is Maggie and she has a weakness for Skittles. Her trainer prompts her for a few minutes, and suddenly Maggie is spinning like she's being watching Pat Sajak for decades.

Soon, she is in our studio, sitting on my shoulder and urinating on my suit, picking the winners of all eight first-round series in the 2003 Stanley Cup Playoffs. It might have been a one-and-done segment, like the stripper. Except that Maggie spins her wheel and picks the seventh-seeded Anaheim Mighty Ducks to upset the Detroit Red Wings in the first round. Obviously, that will never happen. Until it does. And now the monkey is a prophet and is invited back for Round 2. She picks the Ducks again, this time to upset Dallas. Which, of course, they do. And now the monkey is making news across North America.

She quickly becomes my nemesis. I spend several hours a day answering emails about the monkey. People on the street start yelling things at me like "Hey, Monkey-Boy!" "Where's your monkey, Duthie?!" and the always hilarious "Hey, Duthie, did you spank your monkey today?"

My three-year-old son starts telling his nursery school class that his dad works at a zoo. (Actually, that's fairly accurate.) Beautiful women stop me, only to ask if the monkey is as cute in person as it is on TV.

You want to know what the monkey is like, ladies? She stinks. The dry cleaner can't get the monkey smell out of my suits. She flings her poop all over the studio. Even Tie Domi didn't do that. (You know I love you, Tie. Do not punch me in the face over this. I promise I'll change it to Roenick for the paperback.) And at the rate Maggie's popularity is growing, she will be hosting the show next year, and I will be doing the Tweed Seniors Shuffleboard Tournament on community cable. Insecure, fragile, jealous TV ego-heads like me can't handle this kind of threat. I'm reduced to the position of monkey publicist, taking calls from reporters as far away as Europe and being deluged with questions like:

"Why is the monkey so much smarter than your analysts?"

"Does the monkey handicap the NBA, too?"

"Is the monkey single?"

Real cute.

TSN.ca asks me to write a ludicrous column (which is pretty much the only kind I can write) where I interview the monkey. It's a terrible idea. So of course, I do it. Excerpt:

JD: Tell me about your background.

MM: Well, I lived in the jungle until I was captured by a man with a big yellow hat. [Laughs] My Curious George material is pure gold.

JD: How do you explain your stunning success in predicting those Anaheim upsets?

MM: Hockey is in my blood. I was up for the lead in that *MVP* movie about the hockey-playing monkey. It was bull$*#@ I didn't get it. That chimp slept with somebody.

JD: That's disgusting.

MM: It's a dirty business, pal.

JD: But really, why the Ducks? Had you been charting J.S.
Giguere's consistent statistical improvement over the last
three years? Did you, like Paul Kariya, buy into the defence-
first mentality? Or is it the fact their PIM per game is a
paltry 7.8?

MM: Actually, there's a duck who sneaks me cigarettes at the zoo.
I owed the species.

JD: What's next for you?

MM: You name it. Endorsements. Psychic hotlines. Movies. I'm
talking with Sigourney Weaver about remaking *Gorillas in
the Mist*.

JD: But … you're … not a gorilla.

MM: I've spoken to De Niro about how he put on the weight for
the end of *Raging Bull*. Gorilla is not that tough. I can do
gorilla.

Maggie also correctly predicts Anaheim beating Minnesota
in the Western final. But she finally gets it wrong when she takes
them in the Stanley Cup final, as the Ducks lose to New Jersey in
seven games. Ha, suck it monkey! (I never actually say that. On air,
anyway.)

While the puppets and stripper were short-lived, Maggie is
such a hit she becomes a staple on our show in the playoffs for the
next five years. One night, the producers bring in a lemur to spice
things up. They call it Jacques Le-mur. This is highbrow comedy to
us. The lemur sits on my head while Maggie spins her wheel.
Here's the thing with lemurs. They have claws, and they always
like to sit upright. So Jacques digs its claws into my skull, while I
put on a fake TV smile and encourage the monkey to do her

spinning. I can feel a slow trickle of blood down the back of my neck. Or maybe it's cerebrospinal fluid and I'm about to die. Either way, this did not come up in journalism school.

I survive the lemur attack (I call it that now to try to impress my kids) and my half decade with Maggie. And we survive that crazy early time of the *NHL on TSN*. Yes, some of it was awful. But, man, we had a lot of fun. Along the way, the TSN brain trust makes a couple of key leadership changes. First, following the advice of Bob McKenzie (and by advice, I mean Bob likely said, "You better hire this bleeping guy or I quit!"), they hire Steve Dryden, the former editor of *The Hockey News*, to oversee the content of the show. Steve is a true journalist and probably the hardest-working man I've ever met. He would quickly become the conscience of the *NHL on TSN*. Then they bring over Mark Milliere, an extremely bright TV guy who runs *SportsCentre*, to oversee the entire *NHL on TSN* production. Those two key changes would guide us towards a more traditional (though still sometimes wacky) hockey show, where content and personalities replace puppets and primates. But not before one more major hiccup: the season that never was.

chapter 19

HELL AND HEAVEN (ONE LOCKOUT AND THREE GOLF MAJORS)

Glenn Healy and Brian Burke are yelling at each other, one into each of my ears. For now, I am The Guy in the Middle, instead of The Guy on the Left. Poor positioning decision. And now I have a migraine.

It is the fall of 2004, and we are all miserable. I'm supposed to be hosting hockey games. Instead, I host mind games. Heals and Burkie are very bright guys who make valid arguments for both sides of the NHL/NHLPA dispute threatening the season. But we're all sick of the talk already. We start doing regular lockout panel chats in September. So ... roughly five a week ... two a day since January ... sometimes three ... carry the one ... crap, better get my phone calculator ... equals ... somewhere around 150 lockout discussions. Or about 147 more than Gary Bettman and Bob Goodenow have had over the same period.

And for what? I feel the same way I did after I saw *Lost in Translation*: "So that's it? What the hell did that mean?"

Speaking of translation (the lockout has also weakened my segue strength), out of boredom and frustration, I write an easy reference guide to help fans fully comprehend the lockout-lingo they have been hearing on *SportsCentre* every night:

Significant Philosophical Differences—*Gary hates Bob. Bob hates Gary.*

Cost Certainty—*A guarantee that the price you pay for Leafs tickets will continue to rise under a salary cap.*

Impasse and Implementation—*When you argue with your wife over the logic of buying $2,000 imported drapes, and then come home from work the next day to find she's already had them installed. Sorry. I have some scars.*

Revenue Sharing—*When a sizable portion of your paycheque goes to the guy who installs the imported drapes. Deep scars.*

Hard Cap—*What Bettman and Goodenow better wear in any public place where there may be hockey fans carrying projectiles.*

We show classic hockey games to fill the holes in our schedule. Which sounds like a great idea in theory, until you realize how bad most old games are. I am initially excited when we decide to show the entire 1976 Canada Cup, which holds a dear place in the heart of 10-year-old me. Then the games start, and I realize compared to today's game, the 1976 Canada Cup looks like the Red Deer Seniors' Beer League.

CBC cancels *Hockey Day in Canada* because of the lockout. TSN decides we'll do it instead. And so mid-February, I am hosting the show with Healy from the World Pond Hockey Championship in Plaster Rock, New Brunswick. It is minus 40. The only production staff we have are in the truck running the show, so I am alone outside on the lake with our cameraman. Every half hour or so, producer Dave Stiff says, "Okay, we need to fill five minutes and we're on in 90 seconds!" And I skate madly across the 30 or so rinks they've built on the lake to find someone to interview. At one desperate point late in the day, I grab the intercom microphone from the organizer and plead, "Could the team from the Cayman Islands please come here immediately because we are on in 30 seconds and I really have no one else left."

Some of the many talented guys (and gals) on the right I've worked with. A vintage 2000 *SportsDesk* poster featuring my then partner Rod Smith, Jim Van Horne, and Gino Reda; with my friend and sportscasting mentor Brian Smith, whose murder in 1995 devastated Ottawa and changed my career; with my 2010 Vancouver Olympics co-host, *CTV National News* anchor Lisa LaFlamme; The Panel—Aaron Ward, Darren Dreger, and Bob McKenzie—at the Cup final in Boston in 2013.

When my own dreams of being a pro athlete ended early due to lack of talent, I never imagined I would spend my life interviewing legends. Here, with the Hockey Hall of Fame Class of 2014: Peter Forsberg, Rob Blake, Mike Modano, and Dominik Hašek.

Somehow my career path went from covering local news in Ottawa for CJOH-TV to rapping in ridiculous videos wearing a Nintendo Power Glove for no apparent reason ("Out for a Rip," 2014).

Football fun. My trainer Chris Schultz berating me during my failed "tryout" with the Argos in 1999; interviewing New England Patriots kicker Adam Vinatieri after he kicked the game-winning field goal in Super Bowl XXXVI (2002); with Calgary Stampeders quarterback Bo Levi Mitchell after he won MVP in the 2014 Grey Cup.

Things they never taught me in journalism school: how to deal with a lemur digging its claws into your skull on live TV (2006), how to take selfies with llamas (and Cabbie) on live TV (*TradeCentre*, 2015), how to sing the gospel chorus of a song about a delay-of-game penalty ("Puck over Glass," 2013).

The most elaborate and ridiculous *NHL on TSN* Films production: *The Panel Hangover*. Lost on the beach with Darren Dreger and producer Richard Hodgson (Zach Galifianakis); pre-filming stare down with Aaron Ward; filming the key phone-call scene with L.A. Kings star Anze Kopitar and our crew in Los Angeles. Photos by Alex Quinonez.

The best thing about covering hockey is that even the biggest stars are genuinely nice guys. Interviewing Sidney Crosby at the 2007 NHL Awards; Wayne Gretzky before the gold medal game in Vancouver in 2010; former Vancouver goalies Roberto Luongo and Cory Schneider, with Schneider's stand-in dummy. Luongo runs him over in the final scene in one of our many Luongo films.

The best things about my life: getting to meet incredible, inspirational people like Jonathan Pitre, "the butterfly child" (on our set in 2014), and getting to share it with my family (with my wife, Cheryl, at the 2013 Canadian Screen Awards, and with Jared, Darian, and Gracie on the CTV Olympics set in London in 2012).

The night before, Heals and I are having a late dinner in the motel restaurant when word breaks of a possible settlement. Rumour has it Mario Lemieux and Wayne Gretzky are flying to New York on Sunday, and the lockout will be over. Heals makes one phone call (to Goodenow) and in a minute knows the story is not true. But TSN desperately wants us to drive the 45 minutes back to the lake (where our production truck is parked) to do a live-hit into *SportsCentre*. Heals sips his wine calmly and says, "The story is wrong, we're not going." Over the next half hour, four different executives call, each one more senior than the last, begging Heals to go, because everyone is reporting the lockout is about to end. Heals doesn't budge, finishing his glass before finally agreeing to do a phone interview from his room (a sitcom in itself as drunken pond hockey players from the floor hear him on TV, then run to his room yelling, hoping to get their slurred voices heard on TSN). Heals is right. The story falls apart the next day. Mario and Wayne do not ride in to save the day, and the season is mercifully cancelled days later.

It still makes me sick that we lost an entire year of hockey. But at that moment, I have other things to ponder. Like, "What the heck am I going to do now?" It's a few weeks after that I get the call that cheers me up for the first time in months.

"Hey, do you want to cover golf this summer?" Damn straight.

It's now mid-June and I am at Pinehurst No. 2 in North Carolina for the U.S. Open. I'm under attack. Our TSN set is right beside the range, about 190 yards from where the players hit. Canadian PGA pro Ian Leggatt decides to practise low hooks by aiming at Bob Weeks and me while we are on the air. (This is apparently what golfers do to amuse themselves. Try to kill innocent broadcasters. Now I understand why Johnny Miller's booth has bulletproof glass.)

There are three steel bars that hold up the set, all directly behind our heads. Every couple of minutes ... *ping!* And we both hit the deck. I learn two things about Ian Leggatt that day. One: Don't let the fact he's one of the nice guys on tour fool you. He's a sick freak. Two: He is deadly accurate with a pull five iron.

The best part of this U.S. Open is watching an unknown named Jason Gore almost become the next John Daly. Cinderella in size 38 slacks. Heading into Pinehurst, Gore is a no-name Nationwide Tour player in the midst of a week from hell. He 1) had his car broken into while staying at some cheap motel on the way to Carolina, 2) has a new baby with two ear infections keeping him up all night, 3) has less than 30 grand in earnings for the year, and 4) has a spot in the final pairing on Sunday with Retief Goosen.

Gore is more fun than the Hooters Company Picnic. After a Tiger-like celebration of a birdie on Saturday to get into the last group, he whispers to his caddie, "Did I just point that ball into the hole? I'm such a cheese ball."

In the middle of his news conference, he stops and asks, "Am I saying 'Uh' too much? Oh man, I know you guys are going to rip me."

When we finish an interview with him after the Saturday round, he walks away and says to his wife, "Honey, I just did Canadian TV!" As if it is the coolest thing that had ever happened to him. And Sunday, I am standing near him on the seventh tee, after he birdies to get within one of the lead. With a lovestruck gallery screaming like they're teenage girls and he's a boy band, Gore turns to his caddie, giggling, and says, "Holy shit, this is fun!"

Not for much longer. He would blow up on the back and shoot 84. Which, in a way, makes him even more likable. A decade later, he has one PGA Tour win to his name, but he has never come close to the magic of those first three and a half rounds at Pinehurst.

A month later, we take the red-eye from Toronto to London, a connector to Edinburgh, Scotland, and head straight towards St. Andrews for the British Open.

"The peat. Ah, the peat."

I will repeat this line from the *Seinfeld* Nazi episode endlessly as cameraman Dean Willers, producer Jamie Reidel, and I drive through the Scottish countryside. I find it endlessly amusing. Not sure the crew agrees as they try to shove me out of the moving vehicle after the twenty-seventh time I say it.

This is no ordinary Open. It is the last one for Jack Nicklaus, the greatest golfer who ever lived. I'm a suck for sentimentality. Heck, I rented *My Dog Skip* for the kids, and bawled for an hour after. So Jack's last stroll up 18 has me a little moist-eyed and pretending to have allergies. I'm standing about 50 yards short of the green, right in the middle of the mosh-pit-thick gallery that has lined the entire eighteenth hole. It's remarkable how much the Scots worship Jack. He is God here. The week of The Open, they release a new five-pound note with his face on it. You know you are big when they put you on money. Imagine how cool it would be to pay for a burger with a picture of yourself? *"Hey, you got change for a Me?"*

I stare at Nicklaus strolling up 18 towards us for a minute, then turn to watch the faces of the gallery as he walks by. There are probably 50 people, mostly middle-aged men, within a 15-metre radius of me, and almost every one of them is screaming Jack's name and bawling at the same time.

When he drains his birdie putt on 18, they react as if he's won The Open, not missed the cut. Minutes later in the press tent, where cheering and asking for autographs are usually the greatest taboos, they give Jack a standing ovation, and almost every reporter asks him to sign their program or media pass. I'm not into autographs, but I have a British Open golf ball in my pocket that I bought for my son, Jared, now five. I figure if there were ever a signature that would mean something, it would be from the Golden Bear, moments after he finishes his last Open championship.

They announce that Jack is not doing one-on-one interviews, but I have mastered the hijack one-on-one, where you wait outside and interview the subject as he leaves. Jack comes out, and I ask if I can walk with him and ask a couple of final questions before he departs St. Andrews for the final time.

"Sure, son," he says. And so I do a quick three-question interview with him. When it's over, I clumsily pull the ball from my pocket and say, "Mr. Nicklaus, would you mind signing this?"

Jack smiles. "Sorry, the one thing I don't sign is golf balls." He pats me on the shoulder, and is gone. The only time in my career I ask for an autograph, and I blow it. (I later find Jack Nicklaus–signed golf balls available online. They better be fakes.)

With Nicklaus gone Friday, the spotlight turns back to Tiger, who is lapping the world again. TSN has covered most of Woods's major victories, but the one thing we've never gotten is a one-on-one interview with him afterwards. Jamie, Dean, and I are determined to end that streak this weekend.

I spend a good chunk of Saturday searching for Tiger's agent, Mark Steinberg. I find him on the very last hole and slide up next to him as he strolls up 18, in the gallery next to his main meal ticket. Tiger had recently shot a special in Toronto that had aired on TSN, so I use that as my in.

"Hey, Mark, James Duthie from TSN in Canada. Great to see you. Really enjoyed the show Tiger did for us in Toronto. It was a big hit." (I have no idea if it was a hit.)

"Oh, TSN, right. We enjoyed that," he says.

"Listen, it would be great if we could get a brief one-on-one with Tiger if—when—he wins tomorrow."

"It's next to impossible with the amount of time he has," Steinberg replies. "But look for me, and I'll see what I can do."

I also ask one of the media coordinators, a tall British man with a perma-scowl, who says, "Zero chance. Just get him at the podium with everyone else."

I do some minor Sherlock Holmes work and find the portable where the winner will do his two interviews. One is with ABC/ESPN, the North American broadcaster. The other is with the BBC.

Tiger wins by five. Dean and I plant ourselves just outside the one-on-one portable. The grumpy media guy sees us at one point and says, "You're wasting your time. It's not happening."

But as Tiger and his entourage approach and enter the building, I see Steinberg and say, "Mark, James from TSN ... that one-on-one we talked about?" He hesitates for a second, then nods. "Get in here." The media grouch tries to block our way. Steinberg intervenes. "They're okay. Tiger will do them, too."

And so we get our first post–major victory interview with Tiger. As Dean is setting up the camera, I ponder bringing up the urinal encounter from Augusta, but worry it might sound creepy. "Hey, remember when we peed together and you made a funny?" So instead, I just congratulate him on the win.

"Thanks, homeslice," Tiger replies with a smile.

Homeslice? I don't think I've heard anyone say that since Dwayne Wayne on *A Different World*. Woods is much warmer in person than you would imagine. (Of course, it helps that he just won a major.) But he might consider working on his street lingo.

The NHL lockout ends while we're in Scotland. We get the news in a pub. The Scots go nuts! They drink and party all night. On a Tuesday! And they keep it up all week! I never knew they loved hockey so much. Sorry, what? You mean they alwa ... Oh. Right.

Shortly after I get off the plane from Scotland, I'm off to New York for the first piece of business of the new ice age: The NHL Draft Lottery, otherwise known as The Crosby Show. Every team will have a chance at getting the first overall pick and the greatest prospect in a generation. The night before the lottery, I get a shoeshine in Times Square. I ask my shiner if he has heard of Sidney Crosby.

"Is that Bill's kid?"

Oh boy. Well, that's an easy mistake. Thinking Sidney *Crosby* is Bill *Cosby*'s kid! (Since that night, while everyone else calls Crosby Sid the Kid, I call him Theo Huxtable.) It seems The Next One is not quite as big a deal in New York as he is in Canada in the summer of 2005. But to the group of NHL owners and general managers who have gathered here, he is *everything*.

We share a couple of drinks with a small group of GMs in a New York steakhouse on the eve of the lottery. The topic of conversation is the dollar value of one of the balls in the machine. John Ferguson Jr., the general manager of the Toronto Maple Leafs, is asked if he could buy all 48 balls at $1 million a piece, would he? Without hesitation, he says, "I'd make that deal." What about $2 million each? JFJ ponders it for about a second, then says, "Probably." Chuckles follow, but in retrospect, 96 million for Crosby would have been a steal for the Leafs, if it weren't just beer-talk fantasy.

The next day, I am standing before 30 GMs and owners, as we count down the draft order in reverse towards number one: the ticket to Sid. It is a surreal scene. A room full of tough, hard-assed hockey guys shaking in their loafers. Many of them tell me later they can't ever remember being that nervous. When his team makes it to the final five, Carolina owner Peter Karmanos looks like he is about to go into cardiac arrest. I almost call for paddles.

We all know how it ends. Pittsburgh's Ken Sawyer and Anaheim's Brian Burke are standing onstage, waiting for the moment that will change their franchise's future. During the commercial before the announcement, I jokingly ask them to hold hands like the final two do on *American Idol*, but Burke tells me to "Go f&%#" … err, I mean, he politely declines. As Gary Bettman announces the Penguins have won, Ken Sawyer almost falls over. And hockey fans all over the world all have the same thought: *Who the hell is Ken Sawyer?*

With Crosby a Penguin, and hockey's return on the horizon, my summer takes one last golf detour. I complete my own personal grand slam, covering the PGA Championship at Baltusrol Golf Club in New Jersey. Baltusrol is named after a farmer named Baltus Rol who was murdered here. It just edged out the other name they considered: Scene of Horrific Murder Country Club (which personally I like better).

A second murder is almost committed during Round 1 of the PGA Championship. Victim: Me. Killer: David Duval.

Duval had been the best player in golf, winning a ton of tournaments including the British Open. But then there were injuries and off-course issues, and he just ... lost it. And I mean *really* lost, like those dudes on the island with the monster and the polar bears, and the hatch (keeping all my TV and film metaphors 2005-era appropriate in this chapter). Watching Duval now is what it must have been like watching fat Elvis in Vegas. You remember what he once was and almost have to look away. Though in Duval's case, that would not be smart, because he could duck-hook a Nike One in your ear (foreshadowing).

Duval was in Mike Weir's group at the British Open, and he is again at the PGA. Since we usually follow Weir around, I've seen *waaay* too much David Duval this summer. Dave in fescue. Dave in trees. Dave in ponds. But the moment of truth, the apex of ugliness, comes on 13 in Round 1 of the PGA.

Duval hooks his drive 75 yards left of the fairway, past a small snack shack and into a little garden. I happen to be snacking, and I watch the ball bounce by my head and roll to a stop a few feet away. There is almost no one else around, so I decide to stay and watch the carnage. First Double D tries to get a free drop because his supposed line to the green (which he has no shot at) is obstructed by the snack shack.

"Nope. It's a permanent building," says the official.

"Who made that decision?" Duval snaps back.

I can't hear the name the official gives, but I hear Duval's retort.

"Well, he's an asshole."

It gets worse. Duval has a bunch of movable objects between his ball and the fairway. The most prominent is an ice-cream cart. It takes him several minutes to find the ice-cream girl, who is on a smoke break. And when he finally does, she says, "I ain't movin' it." (She eventually does.)

Then there are the two garbage cans. Since no one else is around to help (I am the lone witness to this train wreck, catatonic while watching it), Duval has to move them himself. The sight of a British Open champion hauling garbage is part painful, part priceless. I am tempted to roll up my hot dog wrapper and say, "Hey, Dave ... could you take care of this for me?"

Then comes the final kick in the pants. The woman running the snack shack has been busy rewrapping three-day-old banana muffins or something, and hasn't been paying attention to Duval's nightmare, but is aware he's been there a while. Duval is staring into space seething, waiting for his caddie to bring over a club so he can chip back onto the fairway. The woman glances up at who she thinks is just another thirsty member of the gallery and says, "Sir, no matter how long you stand there, I cannot serve alcohol until after eleven." I almost choke on my last bite of hot dog.

I leave the group after that hole (Duval somehow makes bogey), then go to meet them at 18 later to interview Weir after his round. I am walking with Michael Grange from *The Globe and Mail* amidst the trees next to 18, telling him the story of Duval at 13. We are a good 30 yards over a creek and up a hill from the fairway when we hear the clear crack of golf ball on branch. I duck. A second later, a ball falls right at my feet. I look down and the black swish is as clear as day.

Duval.

That will be my one lasting memory of Baltusrol, my final golf tournament before returning full time to hockey. Not the heat, which was a ludicrous 42 Celsius without the humidex. I believe hefty Tim Herron sweated a new water hazard. Not the bizarre Monday finish and Phil Mickelson's winning chip. Nope. I'll be telling the story about the once-great golfer in the wraparound shades who almost gave me dimples ... on my scalp. Not sure why, but I have cheered for Duval from that day forward.

Life is strange. 2004/05 began as the worst year of my career, my annus horribilis. It ends as one of the most memorable. It also ushers in a new, spectacular era of hockey. And the glory days for the boys on the panel.

chapter 20

THE GUYS ON THE RIGHT

When 5'5" (in heels) goalie Darren Pang played in junior and the minors, he would sleep in the luggage rack on the bus. He once climbed into the overhead bin on a plane, just to get a giggle out of teammates. So when he spots a regular-sized aquarium sitting outside our studio one night before the show (the Discovery Channel show *Daily Planet* is right next to us), he can't resist. He somehow squeezes his tiny frame in and waits for one of us to come out.

Problem is, we don't. We're in the middle of some heavy conversation inside the studio ("No way! *Jackass* two was way better than *Jackass* one!") So our tiny bald contortionist stays squished in his little box for a half hour. I finally walk out and see him, face pressed against the glass with his goofy grin. Any length to get a laugh. It's a basic Panel principle.

The most rewarding part of being the guy on the left all these years is hanging out with the guys on the right. In 13 years hosting The Panel (I will capitalize it from here forward as it feels like a person to me), I've gotten to sit next to endlessly entertaining players, smart-as-a-whip coaches (see Chapter 21) and the top insiders in hockey. It has been the best seat in the house.

Getting superstar players on The Panel is an eternal challenge. In the NFL and NBA, the biggest names seem to go straight from retirement to ESPN or TNT. But in hockey, most slide into executive suits or disappear quietly with the many millions they've made. Ours is a sport where having a big personality and speaking out has always been discouraged. What we love about our hockey players is what hurts their ability to be good on TV: they're too nice. It takes kahunas to sit on The Panel and criticize guys you have played with or against. It also takes effort to stay current and watch games every night. Most just aren't willing to do it. It makes me appreciate the roster of regulars we've had over the years. None had Hall-of-Fame careers, but all of them are characters.

We've had countless active players make brief cameos on The Panel when their teams don't make the playoffs or get knocked out early. Ex-players-turned-broadcasters Panger, Glenn Healy, Mike Johnson, Michael Peca, and Matthew Barnaby all had long stints as regulars or semi-regulars. They are terrific storytellers, and better company. The Guys on the Right could be a book instead of a chapter (sequel?). But for the purpose of keeping this particular chapter under 70,000 words, I'll stick to telling you about the guys on our current roster.

Almost everywhere I go, I get asked, "What is [insert TSN analyst's name here] really like?" I figure the best way to answer that is to tell you a story or two about each one.

Wardo

Aaron Ward is as generous a friend as they come. He has picked up more tabs than the rest of The Panel combined. But he is also a mild psychopath—the most dangerous prankster I've ever met. There is not a crew dinner on the road that is complete without Wardo "shoeing" one of us—pouring a scoop of hollandaise or barbecue sauce on top of your (inevitably brand-new suede) shoes. How a 6'2", 240-pound man can crawl under a table unnoticed, when all of us are expecting it, baffles me. He is basically Batman.

During his days in the minors in Adirondack, a rookie named Yan Golubovsky throws Wardo's clothes in the shower. A typical human's response would be to do the same to get even. But Wardo is not typical. So instead, he gets a cinder block, fishing line, and a bobber. With 20 minutes left in practice one day, he asks a teammate to fire a puck off his ankle. He fakes an injury so he can leave the ice early. Golubovsky has a brand-new sports car he is very proud of. Wardo steals the car keys from his pocket. He ties the fishing line to the cinder block, ties the bobber to the line, ties the keys to the bobber, walks across the street, and throws the cinder block in the Hudson River. He then returns to the dressing room and waits, the cat who ate the canary, until Golubovsky realizes his keys are gone. I truly believe watching that young Russian jump into the frigid Hudson to retrieve his keys brought Wardo as much joy as any of the three Stanley Cups he went on to win.

Aaron Ward has worked his ass off watching tape and calling coaches and players to become one of the top studio analysts anywhere. He also gives me access to his ridiculously large collection of expensive ties, so I have to suck up to him.

The O-Dog

Jeff O'Neill was a hockey prodigy, a ridiculous offensive talent who went fifth overall in the 1994 NHL draft. He scored 30 goals three times, 41 in his best year in Carolina. He could also blow money with the best of them.

During his heyday with the Canes, O-Dog attends the Jim Valvano Celebrity Golf Classic, in honour of the late great NC State basketball coach. Jeff has a new girl with him he is trying to impress, so he starts bidding on all sorts of silent auction items. He wages a bidding war on an autographed Peyton Manning helmet against Meatloaf, the singer. When it starts getting out of hand, O-Dog looks right at his *Bat Out of Hell* adversary and says, "How high you gonna go, Meat?" (O-Dog says a lot of amusing things on The Panel, but this will eternally be my favourite sentence he has ever spoken.) Later that evening, he pays 40 grand for a tour of TNT's NBA set and a chance to meet Charles Barkley and the guys. Forty grand, just so the girl thinks he's a big shooter. He never even goes on the tour.

In the social section of the Raleigh paper a few days later, there is no mention of the 47K O'Neill spent for the charity. But they do make note that he was seen at 2 A.M. in a bar later that night "bumming a cigarette," and that a little girl he met on the golf course during the event remarked, "Your breath smells like beer."

No wonder O-Dog wasn't really fond of the media. But now, he's part of it. Seconds into his first-ever TV segment on The Panel (for an internet play-of-the-year contest), I know he is going to be a star. He just has it. O-Dog is one of the funniest, most opinionated hockey analysts to come along in ages. Plus he has a neck tattoo. When I retire, I vow to get a neck tattoo with The Panel's faces on it, in O-Dog's honour. I will be one badass senior citizen.

Ray

Ray Ferraro once scored 108 goals in one season with the Brandon Wheat Kings. I know this because he reminds me every time I see him. The hockey gods reward Ray for this amazing feat by having him spend most of his NHL career playing for really lousy teams.

While Ray is with the Atlanta Thrashers, head coach Curt Fraser comes into the room after the first period and warns his players not to take any more tripping penalties. So of course, Ray takes one early in the second. He can see his coach seething from the bench. The same bench Ray would be glued to for the rest of the night. But with a minute left, and the Thrashers down one, the goalie is pulled and calls Ray's name as he comes to the bench. Ray leaps over the boards, skates in, finds a rebound, and scores the tying goal. On the plane later, he is watching a movie when Fraser walks back and rips off his headphones. "Did you swear at me?" Fraser yells, veins popping. "I saw it on the little camera in the penalty box!" Fraser had been watching the game on the plane and saw clear video evidence of Ray cursing at him from across the ice. Ray tries to deny it, but neither that nor the tying goal helps. He is deep in the doghouse for a month, playing on the fourth line.

Weeks later, after another bad Thrashers period, Fraser bursts into the room fuming, breaks a stick against the wall, and chucks the rest of it across the room. It hits a beam on the roof, ricochets back, and strikes Ray in the head. Fraser feels so bad, he immediately puts Ferraro back in the good books. Better linemates and more ice time follow. Ferraro's good pal Andrew Brunette still calls it the turning point of Ray's career. He would go on to score just shy of 900 points in the NHL.

Ray doesn't get on The Panel often because he is usually between the benches, seeing the game like an alien with 50 sets of eyes. He is the best game analyst in hockey, bar none. His current segment, What's Bugging Ray? is one of my all-time favourites, because the grumpier Ray gets, the smarter and funnier he gets. He is a brilliant, legendary carver. Unless you are the guy getting carved. Which sadly is me, at most dinners on the road.

Noodles

There are countless hilarious reasons in my imagination for a guy to get the nickname Noodles. Sadly, it came rather simply for goalie Jamie McLennan. He couldn't stand the greasy diners his team would stop at in junior, so he would cook Kraft Dinner on the team bus in a crock-pot. Hence: Noodles.

Noodles begins his first professional hockey season in the New York Islanders farm system. After starting with Richmond in the East Coast Hockey League, he is promoted to the American

Hockey League's Capital District Islanders. He joins the team for a pair of games in Newfoundland against the St. John's Maple Leafs. Noodles is keen to impress the AHL Islanders goalie coach, Billy Smith, the backstop of the New York Islanders dynasty, and one of the nastiest goalies the game has ever seen.

He starts the first game and shuts out the Leafs in the first period. As he skates out to start the second, he sees a giant-headed feathered bird standing in his crease taunting him. That would be Buddy, the AHL Leafs mascot—who is supposed to be a puffin—Newfoundland's official provincial bird. The hometown crowd goes nuts as their puffin pretends to put a hex on the rookie goalie. Noodles gets to the net and tries to ignore Buddy, gently nudging him out of the way. But the puffin pushes back. Noodles isn't sure what to do. He has never been goaded into a fight by a man in a ridiculous bird costume before. Finally, just before the puck drop, Buddy leaves to resume his mascot antics in the stands.

Noodles and his Islanders go on to win the game, and he is named the first star, surely impressing his legendary goalie coach. He is pumped when Smith is waiting at his stall, asking to speak with him outside the room. Here come the compliments! Or not.

"Don't you ever let a mascot stand in your crease!" Billy barks. "That is your space and you control it!"

"But, Billy, I had a great game," Noodles protests.

"I don't care how many pucks you stop. Don't you ever let a f&%#ing mascot stand in your crease. If he's there next game, you f&%#ing run him over. Do you understand?"

Noodles mumbles yes, but is quietly terrified. He tries to avoid all eye contact with coach Butch Goring at practice the next day, hoping he won't get the start in the second game. But at the end of the skate, Butch taps him on the pads and says, "You're starting tomorrow night, kid."

The rookie goalie spends the next 24 hours obsessing about a giant puffin. He is so rattled, he gives up three goals in the first period. As he skates on for the second, he looks to the other end of the ice, and sure enough, Buddy the bird is waiting in his crease, taunting him. So Noodles makes one of those split-second decisions hockey players have to make hundreds of times a game. He decides he is going to crush the puffin.

He starts skating full speed the entire length of the ice, and without breaking stride, buries Buddy the bird into the corner. The puffin, thankfully, is not dead. It (he?) is able to get up and skulk off the ice. Noodles gets booed relentlessly by the St. John's crowd, and gives up several more goals in a blowout loss. Once again, Billy Smith is waiting at his stall. But this time, he is grinning.

"That's how you do it, kid! That's how you become a man in this league. That's how you get respect!"

Noodles earns my respect years later in similar fashion, by running Roberto Luongo over with a Zamboni. It is the start of a brilliant comedic acting career in our series of Luongo films (see Chapter 25). He has also developed into an excellent goaltending analyst on our show, and a radio star (with O-Dog and Bryan Hayes on *Leafs Lunch* on TSN 1050, the most entertaining hockey radio program anywhere).

My next piece of literature is going to be called *The Day Noodles Ran over Buddy the Puffin*. It will be a children's pop-up book.

Marty

Growing up, goalie Martin Biron is an admitted bully to his younger brother Mathieu, three years his junior. Mathieu is good at everything, so Marty beats him up, cheats—whatever it takes to make Mathieu go home crying. But younger brothers grow, and soon Mathieu is 6'5" and breaking into the NHL the same year as Marty.

On November 24, 2003, the two face each other. Mathieu's Florida Panthers are home to Marty's Buffalo Sabres. Down 1–0 in the first, the Sabres turn the puck over in the offensive zone and Stephen Weiss takes off up the ice with the young defenceman Biron skating hard to join the rush. Weiss slides a perfect pass to the front of the net and Marty sees only a glimpse of the long stick that redirects the puck inside the post on his glove side. As he turns to watch puck hit twine, Marty hears a very distinctive "Yeah!" He knows it instantly. After all, he'd been hearing it for years in the basement, on the street, and at the outdoor rinks growing up. He turns to see Number 34 for the Panthers leaping up and down. Mathieu had scored on big bro.

That same night, brothers Tiki and Ronde Barber are facing each other on *Monday Night Football*. During the game, Al Michaels announces that for the first time since Phil and Tony Esposito did it 23 years before, a brother has scored on a brother in the NHL. Michaels then shows the highlight. The Biron brothers make history and get on *Monday Night Football* on the same night. It remains the last brother-on-brother goal in the NHL.

Someone grabs the puck after the goal and hands it to Mathieu. He would put it on a plaque and present it to Marty at their summer charity golf tournament. Little bro gets the last laugh.

Marty tells that story with so much pride. It's almost as if his career highlight was seeing the joy on his brother's face. Which is pretty much all you need to know about Marty. He was one of the first active players we ever had on The Panel. He was a natural, so we welcomed him back as soon as he retired. Plus, he has blue wolf eyes that hypnotize viewers so they can't look away. It's helpful for ratings.

Jonesy

In 1988, Keith Jones is a junior C player who figures he has zero shot at playing pro. On the day of the '88 draft, he doesn't even know it's on. He goes to Flamboro Downs racetrack with his girlfriend. When he gets back home, his dad is waiting on the porch. He says to Keith, "You've been drafted!" Keith responds. "What?!? Are we going to war?"

Jonesy goes on to play a decade in the NHL, racking up 117 goals, 765 penalty minutes, and roughly 798,562 stories.

Once, while playing with the Flyers, he loses his left-handed stick in the Bruins zone. Instead of going to get it, Jonesy rips the right-handed stick out of Bruins forward Anson Carter's hands. He gets the puck, dangles a couple of guys, and tries a wraparound with the curve going the wrong way. While all this is going on, Carter picks up Jonesy's stick and plays the rest of the shift with it. Ray Bourque is screaming at the ref the entire time about the thievery, but to no avail. When the whistle blows, Jonesy skates to centre ice and drops Carter's stick, like a stage performer taking a bow. Bourque just stands there, shaking his head at the lunacy he has just witnessed.

We soon get to witness that same lunacy on The Panel. I am driving one day in Toronto, listening to Jonesy tell story after hilarious story on the radio with Mike Hogan. I call Steve Dryden and say, "We have to get this guy on our show." He would become a staple for the next decade. Jonesy loves making brash predictions, mostly just to get a laugh out of us. During our *NHL on TSN* fantasy draft in 2008, he picks Marian Hossa first overall, bypassing the likes of Sidney Crosby and Alexander Ovechkin. He predicts Hossa will score 70 goals with Detroit (he had 66 *points* the year before). We remind Jonesy of this, oh, every time he's in.

Sadly, that isn't much anymore. He works a ton at NBC, so his appearances are rare. I still believe the only reason he ever visits The Panel is so he can have Swiss Chalet. He orders the dirty bird every single time he is in. It's a crock he hasn't landed an endorsement.

Bobby Mac

I saved my two closest Panel pals for last.

Bobby McKenzie is a legend, plain and simple. I may host The Panel, but he wears the C. Many of the players who come in for cameo appearances tell me afterwards that the most nerve-racking part was not being on live TV, but sitting next to Bob. It has probably hurt our ability to have lively debates at times, because most guys hear Bob's opinion on a topic and go, *Crap, I can't disagree with that. Bob is never wrong.*

He can also be a hard-ass, which I love. If Bob feels The Panel is being worked too hard, he becomes our union steward.

Producer: Hey guys, that segment you just taped was really long. You have to do it again.

Bob: No.

Producer: Okay. Segment is good!

Hall-of-Famer Phil Esposito found out the hard way not to mess with Bobby Mac. Bob is working with *The Hockey News* when he writes a piece saying the NHL should not have given the Tampa expansion franchise to the Esposito group, but to Peter Karmanos and Compuware (who would later buy the Hartford Whalers). After Bob moves on to the *Toronto Star,* he is talking to a player in the Lightning dressing room at Maple Leaf Gardens when Esposito comes in.

"Hey you, get the f&%# out of here!" he yells at Bob. Bob is startled, as he has always had a good relationship with Esposito. He tries to calm him down, but Espo won't relent.

"You heard me, get the F&%# out of here!"

"No, Phil. I have a right to be here. I'm not leaving."

Esposito then strikes Bob in the neck with the heel of his hand, sending him reeling backwards. Bob is shocked and leaves the dressing room to regroup. He sees Esposito in the hall minutes later and tries again to talk to him, to figure out what just happened. Espo tells him to get lost again. So Bob fights back.

"Quit being unreasonable, Phil. I could charge you with assault."

"Go ahead. You're nothing. I'm Phil Esposito."

The nothing part pushes Bob over the edge.

"Okay, Phil. Remember this moment. Because you f&%#ed with the wrong guy."

Bob walks down the hall, picks up a phone, and calls 911. "My name is Bob McKenzie, I work for the *Toronto Star*. And I've just been assaulted by Phil Esposito." Esposito apparently gets wind of this and is headed to Buffalo by the time the police arrive.

Maybe Esposito figures it will just go away with time. But here's the rub with Bob. He doesn't go away. If you're his friend, you have him forever. If you cross him, by … say … smacking him in the neck and calling him "nothing," he will never forget.

Esposito tells police he will surrender the next time he comes to Toronto. Overtures are made from Espo's lawyers, asking for some resolution. Bob refuses. Finally, the day before the court case, the Lightning are back in Toronto and the two sides agree to meet at a lawyer's office in the afternoon. Esposito tells Bob he's really sorry and feels sick about what happened. He begs Bob to drop the charge. Bob listens quietly and then responds:

"Here's the thing, Phil. I wanted to forget and move on. But in front of a whole bunch of people, you said I was nothing. And I couldn't do anything to you. Well, here we are, and who's asking the 'nothing' to help him out? I'll drop it, Phil, if you apologize in a letter."

"Okay, Bob, I can do that," Esposito responds.

"Actually, Phil, I took the trouble of writing the letter for you. Here it is." Bob pulls out a page-and-a-half letter, detailing the entire incident, and Esposito's apology, exactly the way Bob wants it. After first resisting, Esposito finally relents and signs the letter. He also agrees to appear with Bob in front of the media at the game, and apologize publicly, which he does.

Bob still has that letter. Oh, and by the way, he likes Phil Esposito and gets along fine with him now. They've done radio shows together several times. Espo is a good guy who had a bad night. And picked the wrong guy to have it with.

I've had a couple thousand nights on The Panel with Bob. I don't remember many bad ones. There is no one I'd rather have as my bookend on the right.

Dregs

Bobby Mac is with me on The Panel from day one. Darren Dreger comes over a few years later, after hosting at Sportsnet.

I didn't know Dregs very well while we were at rival networks. But we bond one night after losing to the CBC's Scott Russell at the Gemini Awards. I have been to enough of these shows to figure out that seating means everything. If they have you seated near the front and the aisle, there is a good chance you are winning. If you are near the back or the middle, you're screwed. On this night, Dregs and I are both nominated in the same category as Scott. When we get to the theatre, Scott is front and centre. I am back in about row W. Then I look around and find Dregs, who is in the balcony section, roughly row ZZ! If his name were announced, he would have to rappel down to the stage. He shakes his head, leaves, and goes to the bar outside the theatre, well before the award is announced. I meet him there, and we have a couple of beers and chuckles over our seating snub.

The only time my Awards Seating Theory (AST) fails is in 2011, when *Off the Record* host Michael Landsberg and I are nominated with Russell, Ron MacLean, and Scott Oake in the Best Sports Host category. The venue is inside the CBC building (home station advantage for the other guys). There is a small section of seats at the front, then standing room for the crowd, then another section of seats at the very back. Ron and the two Scotts are right up front, while Michael and I are seated together in one of the last rows at the back. On the bright side, this allows me to have multiple beverages and enjoy the evening without worrying about having to make a speech. Then they get to our category. "And the winner is ... James Duthie!" Uh-oh. It takes me about three minutes to get to the stage, which turns out to be valuable time to think of something semi-coherent to say.

Dregs joins TSN after being recruited heavily by Bobby Mac, who takes out his main insider competition and eases his workload in one brilliant stroke. Dregs comes across as serious and straight on television, but off it, he is an evil comedic genius. If you leave your phone alone for a minute, he will be sending emails from your account to our boss, saying things like, "Cannot work with Aaron Ward anymore. He has to go. Call me ASAP." No one stirs up more trouble than Dregs. And no one is a more loyal friend to everyone on The Panel.

He is also a pure news hound. In 2009, he writes a story saying NHL Players' Association leader Paul Kelly's future is being questioned. He then convinces our bosses he has to go to Chicago to cover the union's meetings. At that time, very little ever came out of union meetings. Comparing them to watching paint dry is an insult to drying paint. But Dregs has a gut feeling something is up. He is the only reporter at The Drake Hotel that night, when the meeting takes a crazy turn, as player reps start to rebel against Kelly. Twitter is still in its infancy as a breaking news wire in 2009. That night, standing in the lobby of The Drake, Dregs live tweets every twist, including Kelly's firing at 3:30 A.M.

He gets nominated for a Gemini for his reporting that night. No balcony seat this time, making the walk to the stage short when his name is announced as the winner.

Dregs and Bob are the best insiders in hockey. When we add Pierre Lebrun to Insider Trading in 2010, it creates a formidable trio. Pierre works the phone like a telemarketer. Plus, he always buys The Panel a really expensive dinner at the Cup final. This is the number-one trait we look for in a new panelist.

Collectively, it's quite a cast of characters coming in and out of our studio each game night. But if I may steal from Pat Healy (Matt Dillon) in *There's Something About Mary*, "those goofy bastards are the best thing I've got going."

chapter 21

THE QUIZ SUCKS

"You can tell James Duthie to shove that Quiz."
    —John Tortorella, at his news conference on his first day
        coaching the New York Rangers

The three stages of an NHL coaching life cycle are as follows:

1. Hired
2. Fired
3. Panel

Often, the cycle repeats itself several times. By my count, we've had a full roster's worth of ex-NHL coaches on The Panel: Paul Maurice, Marc Crawford, Bob Clarke, Ron Wilson, Mike Babcock, Peter Laviolette, Tom Renney, John Anderson, Craig MacTavish, Andy Murray, Bobby Francis, John Tortorella, Mike Keenan, Claude Noel, Joel Quenneville and Claude Julien (together for just one *TradeCentre* appearance), Kevin Constantine, Mike Milbury, and Pierre McGuire. Not to mention executives between gigs like Brian Burke, Jay Feaster, John Ferguson, and Craig Button (now a TSN regular and one of the most knowledgeable junior hockey experts anywhere). Of the coaches, only McGuire and Milbury were content being full-time broadcasters. The rest were between jobs, and The Panel was a decent place for them to watch a lot of hockey and maybe keep their name fresh in the minds of the general managers, especially the next one who decides that "a change of direction is needed."

The coaches I work with on The Panel are not the same guys you see behind the bench. They are, for the most part, happy, relaxed, generally terrific guys. In other words, not at all like the guys you see ripping the reporter in the post-game scrum, trying to climb over the partition to get at the opposing coach, or grabbing certain body parts (that have to be pixelled out on *SportsCentre*) to make feelings clear to an official. General rule for television (and life): when we have to pixel out your junk, you've had a bad day (sorry, Joel).

The former coach-panelist I am asked about the most, by a landslide, is John Tortorella. Torts the coach can be nuts. This is irrefutable. Once in Tampa, he thought Dan Boyle was taking too long to come back from an injury. So Torts went around the dressing room and took down every shot of Boyle from the Lightning's Stanley Cup season. When Boyle arrived and saw this, he lost it, and the two almost came to blows. Torts loves Dan Boyle. He just had one of those moments.

Torts joins The Panel after being fired by the Tampa Bay Lightning at the end of the previous season. My boss, Mark Milliere, arranges a "get to know you" dinner for the three of us in downtown Toronto before the season starts. I feel like the guy who shows up is an imposter. Away from the pressure of coaching and post-game news conferences, Torts is the exact opposite of what you'd imagine. He is a choirboy: quiet, polite, doesn't drink or smoke, and usually goes to bed around 9 P.M. (which is going to make West Coast doubleheaders interesting). The angry cursing madman I know from TV is nowhere to be seen. I quickly realize it's only when he starts speaking passionately about hockey that Torts goes full Bruce Banner Hulk.

His first appearance on TSN is our annual season-preview show. We have a pool on how long it will take him to swear on air.

Some take two weeks, some several months. I predict 40 minutes into this first show. I am wrong.

It takes him 14 minutes.

It happens the second time he speaks. A random *shit* in the middle of a sentence. When we go to commercial, I say, "Torts, you have to be careful. We can't swear on this show. And by the way, I won the pool."

"I didn't swear," he says, clearly perplexed.

"Uh, yeah, you said *shit*, Coach."

"C'mon? Really? Are you sure?" We have to show him the tape to prove it. This moment instantly explains every Torts post-game tirade. When he speaks from the heart, whatever comes out … comes out. He can't control or, apparently, remember it.

Torts is mostly on his best behaviour after that. He lashes out once in a while, mostly at the questions on The Quiz ("Canada's favourite game show"—copyright). "The Quiz sucks" becomes his catchphrase and his *NHL on TSN* epitaph. My favourite Torts moment doesn't happen on television. It comes a month or so into his brief tenure on The Panel, while we are eating pizza during a long doubleheader of Wednesday night hockey. He looks at Bob and Dregs and me quite seriously and says, "You know what, guys? I love everything about these nights. I love hanging out with you, eating pizza, and watching hockey. It's the best. I just wish I didn't have to go on TV."

I laugh so hard, I cough up two mushrooms and a pepperoni. So he's saying, *Can I keep doing this, but just skip the part you are paying me to do?*

He is gone a few weeks later, hired by the New York Rangers, where he picks up where he left off in Tampa—angry post-game tirades mixed with the squirting-fan-with-water-bottle incident behind the bench. But the other Torts I got to know is still there. At the 2012 All-Star Weekend in Ottawa, I meet a family from Chicago with a little boy named Vinnie Bonamici who is battling cancer. The Make-A-Wish Foundation has given them tickets to the game. It's only an hour to the start of the skills competition, but I take a flyer and text Torts, asking if I could bring Vinnie down to meet Patrick Kane, his idol, after it's over.

A half hour before showtime, my phone rings. "Bring him down now. I'll be waiting for you," Torts says. Sure enough, he's standing there as we walk out of the elevator. He proceeds to take Vinnie into both dressing rooms to meet all the players and then brings him on the bench with him. He basically dedicates his entire night to the boy.

I still text Torts once in a while to ask him about a player or league-related issue. His responses always end exactly the same way: "Hope your family is well. The Quiz sucks." I miss him. I've always told people no one has ever hated being on TV quite like Torts. And yet in the spring of 2015, out of the blue, my phone rings.

"I'd like to do TV again," Torts says. And there is no laughter or "Gotcha!" that follows. He means it. If I had a mouth full of wine, I would have spit it in sitcom-shock fashion. Torts starts making appearances on ESPN a few weeks later. They don't do The Quiz. He's happy.

Torts is far from the only coaching character we've had on The Panel. Kevin Constantine seemed like a straitlaced X's and O's guy until he tells me one night he can walk on his hands. So during a late-night triple-overtime playoff intermission, when we tend to get giddy, we make him. And for 30 seconds, he Cirque de Soleils back and forth across the set on live television. Then he throws Cheezies at the camera with me when we run out of things to say before quadruple overtime.

Mike Babcock is intense during his stint early in the *NHL on TSN* days. The Panel often yells, "Mark it!" when we want a certain play saved for possible use during an intermission. Babcock yells, "Mark it!" every 15 seconds. So we basically have to save the entire period for him. No one before or since has watched the games as closely as Babcock did.

Bob Clarke is as tough a panelist as he was a player. He shows up one night with one of his fingers gone above the knuckle, fresh wounds and bloody bandages still visible.

"What the hell happened, Bob?" we ask in unison.

"Ah, I had some ligament damage and couldn't control the finger. They said they could splint it to the other one, but I just told them to cut it off. The splint was going to get in the way of my golf game."

Hockey players: toughness eternal.

Clarkie only comes in a handful of times a season, but he's one of our favourites. He's not TV savvy like Pierre McGuire or Paul Maurice, but he always has strong opinions and great stories. Though he does single-handedly destroy the myth of The Quiz one night.

There is much more pre-planning in television than anyone lets on. For The Quiz, our producers have to prepare video for the answers. They also have to font (display) the contestant's answers on the screen as soon as they are made. So we tell the panelists the questions beforehand and get their responses. I know most of you have likely figured this out. But there are viewers who want to think it's no different from *Jeopardy* and the answers are all off the cuff. One night, late in December 2008, Clarkie gets a little confused.

Question three of The Quiz is: "What was the feel-good story of the year?" The multiple-choice options are

a. Chicago's rebirth
b. the shootout [still popular back then]
c. Joel Ward
d. the Winter Classic

Clarkie goes first and answers: "The year of the euro!"

And the nation collectively says, "WTF?" That was supposed to be his answer to the next question: "How will 2008 be remembered?" I could just move on, but I can't let Clarkie look senile. So I stop and explain to the viewers that we showed the guys the questions beforehand and he has just gotten a little ahead of himself. The illusion of The Quiz is shattered in an instant. It's like seeing behind the curtain in *The Wizard of Oz*. Our fault, really. You shouldn't prep Bob Clarke. He's way better winging it.

I'm not even sure we pay Clarkie. I think he's a little bored with semi-retired life, playing golf in Florida with his four-finger grip. He is the one guy who comes in just because it's fun. Most of the others have ulterior motives. We get that. The Panel is basically a coaching placement agency. And we have about a 97 percent success rate.

It can be awkward when they're about to leave us. Darren or Bob will be on The Panel and report that the coach sitting next to him is the leading contender for a job.

In 2009, while Peter Laviolette is on The Panel, Dregs learns from another source that Lavy is the leading contender to become the next head coach of the Philadelphia Flyers. We're sitting in Steve Dryden's office having our pre-game meeting when Dregs lets Lavy know he has this information and is going to report it that night.

"You can't do that," Lavy says.

An extremely heated half-hour discussion follows. Lavy argues that if Dregs reports it, it will look like Lavy fed him the information, which he didn't. And that could damage the trust between the Flyers and their potential new coach. But Dregs has to do his job. So he reports it. Lavy's fears prove unfounded. He still gets the job. But it made for one awkward night in the studio.

There is no bitterness. Lavy understands the game. And he is fully aware he may need The Panel again someday. Early in the 2014/15 season, I text him looking for some insight on Filip Forsberg, the spectacular young Swedish forward the Predators stole from Washington (Forsberg for Martin Erat—one of the most lopsided deals in years). Lavy gives me a couple of quotes about what a good young player Forsberg is, but is careful not to build his young star up too much, leading to this text exchange.

Lavy: "Now leave him alone and talk about Ekblad. Hope you're well, Jimmy."

Me: "I miss the way you tell me to get lost, Pete."

Lavy: "I ended it with 'hope you're well.' Need to be polite … ya know … just in case."

chapter 22

BLOOPERS, RIOTS, AND
KNIFE ATTACKS

It is moments after Game 7 of the 2011 Stanley Cup final, and deep in the bowels of the rink in Vancouver, The Panel is a mess (two-thirds of it, anyway). I am trying not to throw up, and my suit has a tear on the sleeve where Aaron Ward sliced me with a knife a few nights before. (The fact that I have forgotten this and put it on again today reflects the state I am in.) Ray Ferraro is standing next to me, looking like Edward Norton after he beats himself up in *Fight Club*. His face is stitched up and swollen, the wounds still fresh. We need to finish our post-game work for *SportsCentre* and get back to the hotel. Badly. Bob is the only one in good shape, but he is checking his phone, and looks concerned.

"There are cars on fire outside, boys," he says. "We'll be going home through a riot."

The most memorable moments of Panel life happen when things go horribly wrong. We have done tens of thousands of segments over the years ("units" Bob calls them, as in, "Three more units left tonight, boys!"). Because of the quality guys we have, both on The Panel and in the control room, the vast majority of our units are solid and smooth. But the best comedy happens during the few that aren't.

At the 2009 Stanley Cup final in Detroit, Dregs brings an octopus on the set. He has octopi info he plans to use at the end of his "Insider" segment. So he pulls it out of the bag on live TV and starts twirling it around his head, the way the real Red Wings octopus guy does. Unfortunately, our little tentacled friend left this world quite a while ago and is starting to fall apart. So as Dregs twirls, little chunks of octopus go flying all over the set. It ends up on suits, in eyes, in hair. I believe Dregs does his next segment with a small chunk dangling from his ear. We permanently ban all cephalopods from the show on the spot.

Dregs is not the first panelist to twirl his arm wildly above his head on our show, with bad results. Bob Errey, an analyst with the Pittsburgh Penguins, joins us in studio for a game. For a typical intermission, each guy on The Panel will pick out one or two things to talk about from the game. We'll get video edited that we roll while the panelist makes his point. But once in a while, things get chaotic in the control room and the video doesn't get rolled on time. Bobby Mac and I have a signal we use off camera to remind the director and producer it's time for the video. We put one arm and finger in the air and twirl it, like a cowboy about to toss a lasso. (It's pretty much the universal TV symbol for "Roll it!" except Bobby and I tend to do it rather violently.) So while Errey is alone on camera doing solid analysis about a key moment of the game, the video is nowhere to be seen. Errey has been in the business a while so he is handling it well, but we can tell he's struggling to find more to say without seeing his clip. So Bob and I start doing our thing, spinning our arms madly above our heads, hoping our guys in the control room see us and roll it. Problem is, Errey has never been on The Panel before and has no idea what we are doing. Though he is speaking to the camera, he catches us out of the corner of his eye, and in that split second, decides we must be somehow describing what he is talking about. So as Errey talks about some effective Penguins penalty kill, he starts twirling his arm wildly above his head, too.

There is no chance anyone at home will understand, and there is no way for us to explain it to them. This realization cracks Bobby Mac and me up for the rest of the night, and for many nights since. Errey's video eventually does come. When we go to commercial, between guffaws, we try to explain what we were trying to do with our arm signals.

"Oh, man," he says, a little embarrassed, but immediately finding the comedy in it. "You guys were doing it so passionately, I figured it meant something and I better play along," he says with a laugh. Our "Roll it!" gesture will now forever be known as "The Errey."

Errey need not worry. We've all embarrassed ourselves much worse than that during our time on The Panel. Usually, it's a slip of the tongue that leads to something ridiculous coming out of our mouths. The playoffs are a breeding ground for bloopers. You are on TV every night for two months in a row, often until the wee hours of the morning. (West Coast triple overtime can be particularly troublesome.) One Saturday afternoon after a very late night, I am doing some highlights of a Rangers–Capitals game. We are given scripts for these, letting us know who scored and when, but we usually do our own ad-libs. One particular highlight from this game has a Washington player carrying the puck around the net with one hand on his stick while his other arm fights off a Ranger defender. He makes a great pass out front and the Capitals score. I had seen the play from the night before, so I ignore the script and do my own description. This is what comes out, loud and proud: "Look at him! Beating a man off with one arm!"

My greatest mistake is not the unfortunate hockey-porn wording. It is pausing after I say it and glancing to my left at Bob and Darren Pang. They are also exhausted and loopy, and they react like this is the single-funniest thing they have ever heard in their lives. And when they start laughing, I start laughing. I still have a minute's worth of highlights left, but I'm done. The rest is muffled giggles, followed by laughs, followed by tears.

Yes, we know losing it over silly sexual double entendres isn't particularly mature or professional. But when you have been locked in a studio for a month, sleep-deprived and glassy-eyed, these things happen.

Gino Reda is hosting the World Juniors in 2003 from Halifax when he has to voice-over what we call a "hero shot," a short replay right after, or just before, a commercial break. In this case, the shot is a low-angle look at Canadian player Brendan Bell scoring and then skating right towards the camera and smashing his arms against the boards after a goal. Gino, also exhausted from a long day, chooses the following unfortunate phrase to describe what he is seeing: "There is Brendan Bell… coming in your face … all … night … long."

Well, that would be … unpleasant.

Not all Panel bloopers are mistakes. During the 2011 playoffs, Paul Bissonnette (BizNasty) joins us for a couple of days. Paul is a fourth-line scrapper who has become one of the more popular players in the league because of his hilarious musings on Twitter. He is a nice, young, good-looking single guy who lives for two things:

1. Hockey.
2. Meeting hot girls.

And I may have these in the wrong order. We are covering the Vancouver–Nashville series, with the Canucks up three games to one, and at home for Game 5, but trailing. During an intermission, I ask BizNasty, "If you were on the Canucks, what would you be thinking about the prospect of going back to Nashville?"

Biz answers, dead serious, "I'd be excited about it. Nashville is amazing. The bars are great and the women there are unreal!"

"No, no, I meant the idea of the series going six games."

"Oh, right. They wouldn't want that. Probably want to finish it tonight. But Nashville is great." Don't ever change, Biz.

The Stanley Cup final that year is eventful for The Panel. Final stats: one knife attack, one broken nose, and one riot.

Vancouver wins the first two games over Boston, and with two days off before Game 3, our entire crew heads out to dinner at Davio's restaurant in Boston. Canucks owner Francesco Aquilini and GM Mike Gillis drop by for a while. Aquilini is in a great mood—two wins from glory—and buys several bottles of wine and an $1,800 bottle of tequila for our crew. (How is that even possible? Rare exotic worm?)

Aaron Ward shares a story about one of the last times he was at this restaurant. It was the Bruins season-ending party, after being eliminated by Carolina in 2009. The drinks were flowing and the players were roasting each other. According to Wardo, Tim Thomas became agitated that he was being ignored in the roast and went a little squirrelly, angrily ranting about the team and breaking the blade of a large steak knife with his hands. The owner of Davio's kept the knife as a souvenir and he brings it out now to show us. I'm foggy on what led to the next event—I might have made a crack about Scott Walker's sucker punch on Wardo in that Carolina series—okay, maybe 17 cracks. And the next thing you know, Wardo is chasing me down the street outside the restaurant with a similar knife. It's not easy to out-sprint an armed attacker when you are full of steak, and in stitches. Unless of course your attacker is in the same state. I don't actually believe I'm going to die. But Wardo does like to push things to the edge, so I figure there's a chance I may lose a hand or something. Instead, he slices the sleeve of my suit jacket like some ninja sushi chef. It is one of the suits Armani gave me for the Olympics the year before. So I think I'd have rather lost the hand. I make a mental note not to bring up the Scott Walker thing again when Wardo has access to wine and weaponry.

Boston comes back and takes the series the distance. The night before Game 7 in Vancouver, I make a rare and horrendous decision to go to an Indian place with a friend for food and a drink. (I rarely go out the night before games—especially Game 7 of a Cup final.) Whether it's bad tandoori or the mango mojitos (they were three for one—I have no other reasonable explanation for this decision), I am a complete mess the next day. I feel like I am going to toss my naan at any moment.

Our pre-game set is located in a community centre directly across False Creek from the rink. The Panel desk sits on a balcony outside. The exterior walls of the building are all floor-to-ceiling glass. I am sitting on set with Bob, resting my head on the desk, trying not to pass out. Ray is the last to arrive, and with just a couple of minutes left to showtime, he hustles towards the door and ... walks right into it, smashing his nose wide open, in a B horror movie blood-gush. Dregs is the only one of us to actually witness this. He does what all concerned friends would do: sends Ray to the hospital, then immediately makes a brilliant comic recreation of the incident with his phone, which he sends to all of us.

I likely would have milked that injury, staying in hospital for days, trying to get #prayforJames trending. But Ray is a hockey player, so of course, he is back at the rink by game time, with multiple stitches on his badly swollen nose.

We are quite the pair. I watch the game with my head buried between my knees at every whistle, attempting to nap during inter-missions. (CBC is broadcasting it. We are just doing *SportsCentre* afterwards.) The Bruins win 4–0, and moments after the Stanley Cup is handed out, we are on the air live. My hands are shaking so much, I can barely hold the mic. Ray looks like he just got out of the cage with George St. Pierre. Bob, as usual, is the glue holding it all together, though there is a distinct possibility he will get both puked and bled on at any moment.

And in the midst of this *SNL* skit, the riot breaks out. We stay on the air covering it for a while, before grabbing a media bus back to our hotel. It is a surreal ride, with car fires and SWAT teams everywhere. This cannot be Canada. Especially after a hockey game.

We grab some food at the hotel, and I feel recovered enough to risk going out to retrieve a credit card I'd left at the bar the night before (damn mojitos). As I'm walking towards the hotel's front door, I run into a couple of our crew members who say, "You shouldn't go out there. It isn't safe."

"I'll be fine," I reply. "Worst has to be over by now." As I am about to exit the door, a man being chased by the police dives right through it, sending glass shattering across the lobby. He is quickly jumped by about six SWAT guys.

"Alrighty then. I think I might stay in."

I watch the rest of the riot from my room. It's a horrible night for one of my favourite cities in the world.

The only tiny positive is that it gives Ray a better fake story for his nose injury. I tell him he should just tell people he cut it fighting off a gang of looters, while protecting a shopkeeper and his children. There's a reason Ferraro rhymes with hero (sort of).

The screw-ups in studio, the nights out on the road, Clarkie's missing finger, Ray's broken nose. These are the stories we'll remember forever. But they are the aberrations. The Panel has done more than a thousand games, hundreds of other hockey-related shows and specials, and countless *SportsCentre* segments. We've probably had close to one hundred different cast members along the way. And we've always taken great pride in providing smart, informed, entertaining hockey talk. That part we take very seriously.

But you tend not to remember the great discussions you've had on concussions, or goalie interference, or who deserved the Hart in 2011. So instead, we laugh about the tales I've just told you, which we'll probably confuse and embellish as we grow old and senile: *And then right after Wardo cut Duthie's finger off, Ray dove through the glass to get away from the SWAT team and fell 17 floors into False Creek! Bob dove in and saved him. Again!*

chapter 23

THE *TRADECENTRE* TELETHON

The phone rings at 3:45 A.M. Sorry pings, not rings. (It is March 9, 2004, and I have an old-school BlackBerry.) You know those sudden jolting wake-ups that interrupt the sweetest, deepest of dreams? One second, you're rubbing sunscreen on Eva Mendes's back while she lies in the sand ... of the bunker beside 18 at Augusta ... where you just won your third green jacket ... wearing a mask and flippers for the entire final round (I have no idea) ... and *PING! PING!*

Suddenly Eva's gone, and you jump up in your bed and have no idea where you are or why it sounds like there are five fire trucks in your bed.

This is one of those wake-ups. I'd only been asleep for 90 minutes or so. It is the early morning of NHL Trade Deadline. We'd hung around late at work when Bob McKenzie got wind of a big Colorado–Phoenix trade involving Derek Morris, Chris Gratton, and others. I am still home and in bed by 12:30, but have trouble getting to sleep, already doing the math on how soon I have to get back up (6:00 A.M.) for the longest day of every year.

I finally grasp that it is my phone and not Ladders 65–68 driving into my ear. *PING PING! PING PING!*

"Wha ... uhh ... helloooo?"

"James, it's Mark."

Mark? Mark who? Mark Ward or Mark Tadiello, my two best friends from high school? Mark Messier? Mark's Work Wearhouse saying my polar fleece socks are in? Mark Wahlberg? (I'm still groggy.)

"Wha ... what time is it?"

"It's 3:45. Sorry to wake you. But we need you in right now." (Oh. Mark Milliere. My boss.) "It's been a crazy night. Todd Bertuzzi badly injured Steve Moore. We're going on early."

"How early?"

"As soon as you get here."

I shower and make the half-hour drive to TSN. Our producer and director are there, but no one else. The studio is dark. They are determined to go live as soon as possible, and so at 5:27, I am sitting at my desk, with one cameraman pointing a single light at me. (The lighting guy also hasn't arrived.) *TradeCentre* is known for breaking records for number of commentators. But this show will apparently begin with one.

We end up holding off for another half hour. Glenn Healy shows up and the two of us begin the show alone. The moment anyone shows up, they join us. By 7:30, it's a full house, and one of the longest *TradeCentre*s ever is in full swing.

At least we had something to talk about that day, as awful as it was. There have been other *TradeCentre*s where it's so slow, you can see the tumbleweeds roll across the set. The mornings are always the worst. Even in busy years, trades don't start until around noon, sometimes later. Until then, we are a telethon of speculation. Except no one calls in to donate. In 2013, we do four and a half hours of Network Time Killers (as Letterman used to call them) until the first trade, a blockbuster seeing Chicago send minor-leaguer Rob Flick to Boston for minor leaguer Maxime Sauve. *And the balance of power in the NHL has shifted dramatically!*

Flick later joins us for a phone interview, where I have to resist opening with, "Rob, tell me something about yourself, because I don't know a freakin' thing."

All the big news had happened early that year: the last-minute lockout settlement to save a half-season, Brian Burke being fired by the Toronto Maple Leafs, the Iginla trade (more on that later). During the show, someone from a number I don't recognize sends me an endless stream of texts, ripping our coverage.

10:33 A.M.: "This show is brutal."

11:10 A.M.: "ZZZZZZZZZZ"

11:45 A.M.: "Somebody kill me now."

12:37 P.M.: "What a gutless interview. Ask some hard questions."

1:52 P.M.: "Couldn't they get Gino to host?"

I figure it is one of my buddies, and I'm amused for a while. But after the thirteenth text or so, I've had enough.

2:35 P.M.: "Okay, uncle. I don't have your contact in my phone. Who is this?"

2:36 P.M.: "It's Burkie! Miss me?"

Actually, I do. One of our annual rituals on *TradeCentre* is interviewing Brian Burke, with his shirt open and tie off, draped around his neck like he's been working for six straight days trying to save the planet from a meteor about to hit it. He inevitably shoots down all my questions with one-word answers and a menacing stare. It's endless fun. I'm sadistic like that.

At around 5 P.M. that same day, one of the slowest ever, after nine hours on the air, our always calm producer Geoff Macht says in my earpiece, "Need you to fill a couple more minutes here." I turn to the panel and have … zero. And so I say, for the first time ever (though I have thought it often), "So, do you think … Is there a trade that … Has any team … [pause]. Who am I kidding?

I literally have nothing left to ask you guys." Which doesn't bode well for the hour we still have to fill.

Then there are years when the deals never stop. In 2008, we have Wade Belak (RIP) on the phone early in the day after he is traded from Toronto to Florida. A minute into the interview, another trade breaks. I ask Belak to stay on the line, saying, "We'll get right back to you." But then, it's trade after trade after trade for the rest of the day. About seven hours later, I get a text from the always darkly funny Marc Crawford: "Is Wade Belak still on hold?"

One Trade Deadline just before I started hosting, we get Ron Tugnutt on the phone and ask him how he learned he'd been dealt. "I was in the bathroom and heard it on TSN." We don't press for more details.

The trade-breakers (usually known as the insiders—everyone gets new names just for *TradeCentre*) have it tougher than the rest of us. They must relentlessly harass all their sources, to the point where they often spend the next few months mending fences. One year, Bob breaks Vinnie Damphousse being traded from Montreal to San Jose within seconds of the deal being agreed to. Imagine hanging up the phone with the other GM and TSN already has your trade up on the TV screen in front of you. "What the—?!?" The Canadiens are flying that day, and a reporter on the plane uses an air phone to call his desk. He hears about Bob's report and lets everyone on the plane know. The plane lands, everyone gets off except Vinnie, who heads back to Montreal to pack.

In 2014, Darren Dreger is working an Islanders source hard for where Thomas Vanek is going. At about the same time, Ray Ferraro is on The Panel, ripping the Islanders organization for, oh, just about everything. Dregs's source is watching the show while they talk. Now Dregs is getting screamed at for what Ray is saying 20 feet away. It's a delicate dance we perform every year.

But our best angry source story is the one about the Toronto executive who gives Gord Miller the scoop that the Leafs have signed Jeff Finger on Free Agent Frenzy day (*TradeCentre*'s twin brother) in 2008. Gord is on the line with the source, and we hear him say, "Okay, four years, $3.5 million. Sounds good. Thanks." And he hangs up. We're in commercial at the time, and a couple of analysts murmur, "Good job by the Leafs. Under a million a year. Decent signing." Then Bob says, "There's no chance that would be $3.5 million *per year*, right?" Silence and stares. Gord calls back just to make sure. "Hey, that Finger contract, it's $3.5 million total right, over four years?" The answer is so loud and angry, Gord has to pull the phone away from his ear: "NO, you #&*!! It's per YEAR!" Oh. Well that's … a lot. The Finger deal instantly becomes one of the all-time head-scratchers. He's in the minors two years later.

I don't make any effort to break trades, but occasionally, players I know will call me to tell me they've been dealt. On *TradeCentre* 2007, Aaron Ward (still a player for the New York Rangers, not yet an analyst) calls me while we're live on the air. I temporarily hand over control of the panel to Darren Pang (dangerous idea) and duck under the desk to take the call.

"I just got traded to Boston for Paul Mara," he tells me. I announce the trade on air a few seconds later, and we go to commercial. Bob McKenzie, the king of trade breaking and someone who always makes sure it's right before he reports it, says, "Are you sure about that Ward deal? Is your source good?"

"It's pretty good," I say. "It's Aaron Ward."

Darren Dutchyshen is hosting updates that day and hears all this. When we come back on air, he says, "How about Aaron Ward calling you to give you his own trade!" Few guys have better lines than Dutchy, but this one isn't helpful. Wardo calls back ten minutes later, fuming. "Did you say on air that I told you I got traded? The Rangers and Bruins didn't want it out yet! I'm getting killed!" It takes us a few weeks to make up. This is why I prefer leaving the trades to the other guys.

Wardo would have his own infamous *TradeCentre* moment in 2013. It is several nights before the deadline, and the belief is that Calgary is close to trading Jarome Iginla. Wardo has numerous

Bruins sources from his time playing there and is working the phones constantly. While we are doing a game that night, he gets a call saying Iginla is going to Boston. He even gets the names of the players going back. But he holds off reporting it, waiting for more confirmation. Bob and Darren Dreger are also in studio, but none of their sources are willing to confirm that a deal is done. They are both telling Wardo to be cautious. But his Boston people have given him several stories before and have never been wrong. While we are on air doing an intermission, Wardo gets a call and leaves the desk to take it. When he returns, he looks at me and nods, saying, "I have it." I say, "Are you sure?" He says, "Yes. It's done. Iginla is going to Boston." All of this happens live on TV. As soon as we go to break, there is nervous tension in the studio. Bob and Dregs still don't have confirmation. But it's out there now. Twitter has exploded.

"TSN is reporting Iginla to Boston is done."

And because of Bob, Dregs, and Pierre Lebrun's reputations, when TSN says something is done, it is pretty much gospel. But no confirmation comes from either team. Fifteen minutes go by. A half hour. An hour. By the time the Flames announce a major news conference, The Panel is extremely concerned. Fifteen minutes before the news conference, Dregs gets a call. We all can tell by the tone it isn't good. He hangs up.

"It's Pittsburgh."

You know that moment on *The Simpsons* when Lisa destroys lovestruck Ralph on *The Krusty the Clown Show*? Bart (pausing remote): "Look Lise, you can actually pinpoint the second when his heart rips in half!" That is Wardo the moment Dregs says Pittsburgh. He is shattered. He's not alone. TSN prides itself on being right above anything else. And this is a major wrong.

Except it turns out Wardo was technically right. Boston GM Peter Chiarelli explains a day later that Calgary did trade Iginla to Boston. The Bruins thought it was done, too. When Wardo got that call, the trade had been agreed to. Everyone in Boston believed

Iginla was coming. But at the last minute, Iggy changed his mind. The deal was off, and Jay Feaster was forced to make a trade with the Penguins instead. Nine hundred and ninety-nine out of one thousand times, Wardo's scoop would have been bang on. He just won the wrong kind of lottery.

He gets mocked on Twitter for weeks. Still is, occasionally. But self-deprecation goes a long way to healing. While filming our ridiculous skit *The Panel Hangover* (see Chapter 28) a few weeks later, Wardo has a scene where he walks into a hotel room (in a robe, shower cap, and clay mask) and greets us. Instead of doing the scripted line, he strolls in and says, "Hey, guys! Did you hear Iginla got traded to Boston? Confirmed!" We include it in the outtakes at the end of the piece. And this time, the hockey world laughs with Wardo.

Aaron Ward has broken several other stories since. "Iginla to Boston" is now just a punchline we use to break each other up. It's very effective.

While the insiders worry about breaking news and getting every detail right, my single-greatest challenge on *TradeCentre* is looking out for Number One. In other words, peeing. Our commercial breaks are typically two minutes. The bathroom is maybe a 30-second walk or 15-second sprint from my seat. That includes getting my microphone off. Don't want to have a Leslie Nielsen *Naked Gun* scene where the entire studio and control home get to hear my ... err ... live streaming. But to get to the stall, I have to go full Russell Wilson, deking out cameras, crew members, food tables, and Pierre Lebrun groupies just to get there. If it's occupied, I'm screwed. Thankfully, my floor director most years, Ellen Pfeffer, is a pit bull. She makes sure the stall is free, then clears a path like an all-pro pulling guard, screaming "COMING THROUGH!" the entire time. Ellen is always my MVP on *TradeCentre*.

But if I don't make it in time, it's no biggie. We break a lot of traditional TV rules on *TradeCentre*. People get up and leave the desk in the middle of a conversation if an important call comes in. We take the trades and analysis seriously, just not the show. It has really become a parody of itself—a bizarre piece of Canadiana. Twenty-five hockey commentators stuffed in a room for 12 hours, talking about Rob Flick. That's why we used to have Jay Onrait (before he was deported to America) doing live reports from his apartment in a bathrobe. Once he spent several minutes naming his plants: Bob Mckenz-tree, Jennifer Hedge-r. That's quality Canadian television right there. In 2013, I ask for a sound effects board to amuse myself during low points of the show. It has crickets for the quiet times (the crickets get used often), canned laughter for the corny jokes, and a loon just because I find the call of the loon soothing. In 2015, we bring llamas into the studio after CNN devoted a day's worth of coverage to a llama chase earlier that week. Fun fact: llamas smell worse than monkeys. This is the kind of valuable knowledge I've gathered over my career.

We've added music to the circus the last couple of years by bringing in Lester McLean, a TSN staffer and talented singer and musician. Lester and I have collaborated on songs for several TSN pieces in the past (the delay-of-game penalty ballad "Puck over Glass" being the best known). We write a handful of *TradeCentre*-related songs that he performs brilliantly throughout the show. When I lament the fact we haven't interviewed Brian Burke, Lester sings:

> *We need a Burkie interview*
> *We need a Burkie interview*
> *He's gonna yell at Duthie*
> *His tie's gonna be loose*

Our 2015 compilation includes the upbeat ditty "Dooby Dooby Doo," celebrating the success of Minnesota Wild goalie Devan Dubnyk, a journeyman turned MVP candidate.

Let's be very clear
The best trade of the year
Brought an unwanted child
To the home of the Wild

Dooby Dooby Doo
We should have never doubted you
Dooby Dooby Doo
There's just nothing getting through
Dooby Dooby Doo
Minny's new goalie guru
Dooby Dooby Doo
And for a 3rd rounder too

Yup. *TradeCentre* is slowly morphing into a Broadway musical. Sometimes it's a comedy, sometimes a tragedy. Either way, we'll keep singing and dancing our asses off. A few years back, I begged the bosses to start the show at noon, because trades rarely happen in the morning. It's four hours of talking heads guessing. Then they showed me the ratings, which are huge, even when nothing is going on. This makes me think you viewers watch just to see us squirm. Like rubberneckers at an accident scene. There are hockey fans across the country who call in sick every year (and then tweet us to brag about it) to watch a bunch of guys in suits talk about minor trades for depth defencemen. There may be no better example of Canada's obsession with hockey than *TradeCentre*. You are all sick freaks. And we love you for it.

chapter 24

CATTLE BRANDING CLAUDE JULIEN (AND OTHER RIDICULOUS SHORT FILMS)

The hardest part of making idiotic television is explaining the idiocy to those who are about to participate in the idiocy because, verbally, the idiocy makes little sense. Much like that sentence.

Case in point, I am standing in the office of Claude Julien, the head coach of the Montreal Canadiens. And I desperately need him to lean over his desk, lift his dress shirt, and show me some skin—preferably a meaty part of his back, just above his ass. It is late 2003, and the mockumentary-style reporting that I had abandoned after Vancouver to become a serious TSN broadcaster is back. In full force.

"So, Claude, here's the deal. The bit we're doing is about a fictional coach farm in the Ottawa Valley, which explains all the great coaches that have come from that area, you included. The coaches are raised like cattle, and all of them get branded with a C before they are shipped from the farm to the minor and junior leagues. So for this scene, you're going to say to me, 'Do you want to see it? I'll show it to you!' And then you are going to lift up your shirt just above your love handles, and we'll superimpose the brand in editing. Make sense?"

It does not make sense to Claude. Nor should it. But he's a great guy, and we go back a bit. A decade earlier, I was at a small news conference at a bar in Hull when he was announced as the new head coach of the Hull Olympiques junior team. And I'd interviewed him on the ice at the Robert Guertin Arena after his Olympiques won the Memorial Cup in 1997. So I figure he trusts me (a little). He gamely delivers the lines, bends over, and yanks his shirt halfway up his back. I am thinking this is Claude's first-ever money shot.

I had been cautious in my first few years at TSN. It's one thing to wear a pink bunny suit for a report on local news, especially when the audience in Vancouver in that first year amounted basically to friends and family members of the staff. (I believe they could measure them by name. "And the ratings for *VTV News* last night: Sean, Carl, and Heather. Also Heather's cat.") But national television is a different ball game. I don't want to push the envelope too far, too early. I figure I need to establish a little credibility as a broadcaster first. Besides, while there were some funny commentators on *SportsDesk*, I had never really seen any satirical (or stupid or moronic—choose your own word) features done on the network.

So while I try to throw a few light twists into my occasional reports for *SportsDesk*, I mostly keep the shtick locked away. The one exception is a piece in June of 1999, where I try out for the Toronto Argos, with Chris Schultz as my coach and trainer. The tryout goes (intentionally) horribly, of course, and when I get cut, I launch into a pretend, profanity-laced bleeped-out tirade ripping the organization. Strangely, there are no complaints after this airs. In fact, I get a couple of notes from higher-ups saying they enjoyed it. And so, the seed is planted. Maybe idiocy will fly on the "See It, Live It" network. Over the next few years, I do a series of pieces that get increasingly ridiculous. Here's a quick chronological synopsis of the most memorable (from my stand-point, anyway):

The Greatest Trade Ever

In 2003, I host my first Trade Deadline show. It is the year we expand from five hours to eight (we'd later go to 10). There is plenty of time to fill. I ask if I can do a feature poking fun at how we make every trade seem *soooo* important on deadline day. Let's face it, a deal that would barely be mentioned if it happened November 12 (e.g., Rob Flick for Maxime Sauve) can be talked about for hours on *TradeCentre*.

We dig through the record books to find the most obscure deadline trade we can. In 1996, the year Colorado wins its first Stanley Cup, the only deadline deal it makes is sending minor-leaguer Paxton Schulte to Calgary for fellow minor-leaguer Vesa Viitakoski. Perfect. I decide this deal will become, in our investigative *60 Minutes*–style documentary, the Greatest … Trade … *Everrrrrr*.

We interview former Colorado coach Marc Crawford (with the Canucks in 2003), who, with a little advance prepping, claims Viitakoski was *the* difference in Colorado's Cup run. Vesa never played a game with the Avs that season, but Crawford deadpans that just knowing he was in the organization gave them the confidence to push them over the top.

We find Viitakoski playing in Finland and send a camera crew to him for an interview. Problem is, Vesa only speaks Finnish. When the freelance Finnish crew asks what questions we want answered, we say, "Whatever you like." To this day, I have no idea what Vesa says in the interview. We just subtitle whatever we want him to say at the bottom of the screen (with his permission—Vesa gets the joke). I want to go to Finland just to shoot a stand-up (where the reporter talks to the camera) for the piece, but the bosses balk at sending me across the world for 20 seconds of silliness. So instead, the stand-up goes like this—delivered with Keith Morrison on *Dateline* dramatic pauses—with me standing in deep snow, between a few trees: "After a long investigation, we found Vesa Viitakoski playing right here … in his native Finland. Okay, this is not actually Finland. This is the TSN parking lot. But the wintery conditions and topography are … somewhat similar … to Finland."

We also find Paxton Schulte, playing in Belfast, Northern Ireland. He's a popular enforcer for the Belfast Giants. Paxton also plays along wonderfully. We interview our hockey historians Bob McKenzie and Dave Hodge for their take on how the deal changes the two franchises, and the game … [Keith Morrison pause] … forever. Dave's interview consists entirely of him mispronouncing the two names. "Veesa Vitakowplay?" "Paxton … Scooltay?" (At the 2011 World Juniors in Alberta, Paxton comes to visit our set with his young son. He tells me being in this farce of a story was one of the greatest things in his hockey career.)

And so, for five magical minutes of Trade Deadline 2003, we completely mock everything about our Trade Deadline coverage. And again, I don't get fired. So we get weirder.

The Trap

I feel for Steve Dryden. When he is hired to run hockey content for the *NHL on TSN*, he has the best of intentions. He continually delivers me story ideas that should make solid, serious journalistic pieces. And I continually warp them into idiocy. Perhaps the greatest example of this is The Trap.

In the fall of 2004, I'm going to Sweden to cover some of the Toronto Maple Leafs training camp trip. Steve wants me to do a piece on the originator of the trap, that suffocating system that has almost ruined the NHL game. Many believe it began with a Swedish coach named Ingvar "Putte" Carlsson.

I'm the opposite of keen. Just say the word *trap* and hockey fans start to nod off. A legitimate piece on its origins sounds like a five-minute cure for insomnia. So the story we end up doing is slightly different.

It begins with me having a nightmare about low-scoring trap hockey games. In the dream, I'm visited by a genie (Gino Reda in a genie hat) who demands I go on a quest to find the man who "built the trap." Genie Gino promises the man will have the answers on how to fix boring hockey. Then I wake up in a cold sweat, with Jennifer Hedger in bed next to me in a nightie (don't ever say I don't cast well). So begins four of the strangest minutes I've ever put together for television. It includes me running, bicycling, and rowing a rubber dinghy through Europe, being visited by another genie (Borje Salming), and dreaming about the Madonna–Brittney Spears make-out session at the 2004 MTV Awards. It also features the first of many musical collaborations between TSN colleague, friend, and musician Lester McLean and me. While editing the piece, I decide it could use a silly theme song. So I jot down a few lyrics and ask Lester if he could put them to music.

> *He's on a quest*
> *without a map*
> *to find the man*
> *who built the trap*
> *He's on a quest*
> *in a dinghy*
> *to find a way*
> *to fix hockey*

Take that, Bob Dylan. In a day, Lester has the perfect tune. And our first shtick with soundtrack airs on the *NHL on TSN*. These are the days before social media and viral videos, so generally, the only feedback I get is from people I run into. A couple of months later, I'm walking on Queen Street in downtown Toronto when I pass three young men. They say hello, and as they are walking away, they start singing in unison, "He's on a quest, without a map …" I believe I somehow got lucky enough to find the only three guys in the world who memorized the song, but whatever. It still amuses me greatly.

The Coach Farm

When we last left you, I had Claude Julien bent over his desk deep in the bowels of the Bell Centre. Wait, that didn't come out right … I mean, to show us his brand in our coach farm mockumentary. We shoot the exact same scene with Jacques Martin and Brian Kilrea, two other successful coaches from the Ottawa area. Killer does it on the bench, right before a game, which is extra-golden. Martin would become a semi-regular comedic actor for me, also doing a line for one of our Roberto Luongo farces (see Chapter 25). A few years later, Darren Dreger tells me that Martin always feels uneasy when I interview him, because he is never sure what lunacy I might be up to. This makes me strangely proud.

We hire an actor to portray our farmer, Delmer Campbell, "a third-generation coach farmer whose granddaddy raised the likes of Punch Imlach and Toe Blake." The piece is shot at a cattle farm at Angus Glen Golf Club, near my house north of Toronto. My pals, the golf pros at Angus Glen, play the roles of the coaching cattle, grazing in the fields until Delmer gathers them to train them how to coach.

I know. The whole thing is beyond ridiculous. Which is why it remains one of my favourites. I truly believe this kind of story-telling is an effective way to inform people. All we really wanted to let our audience know is how many great hockey coaches have come from the Ottawa Valley. Sure, we could have done that with four minutes of serious interviews and voice-overs. But this is way more fun.

In one scene, I ask Delmer if any of his "herd" ever get the "mad coach disease."

"Sure, once in a while, one of them goes a little squirrelly and we have to get out the tranquilizer gun," he responds casually. We then cut to a shot of one of the coaches trying to climb a fence and Delmer calmly raising his rifle and firing.

"You ... you shot me in the ass!" the coach yells as he falls down and passes out in his nylon warm-up suit. Delmer picks him up, throws him over his shoulder, and carries him back to the barn. Journalism.

The High Hockey Number Revolt

Hockey players are great to work with. But CFL players are on a whole other level. They will generally do anything to be on television. They are the single-best group of athletes I will ever work with in terms of accessibility, agreeability, and willingness to do dumb comedy.

During the mid-2000s, more and more NHL players are pulling a Gretzky/Lemieux/Jagr, using high numbers on their sweaters, from the 60s to 90s. This was unheard of in old-time hockey. But some teams have retired so many of the traditional numbers, players have no choice but to go high. This is hardly worthy of a story, unless of course it has enraged football linemen, who used to own high numbers all to themselves. It hasn't, of course, but it will in our story.

I convince Montreal Alouettes all-star lineman Bryan Chiu to go to a Canadiens practice and heckle goalie Jose Theodore (Number 60) angrily from the stands. Chiu does this so well, I believe security asks him to leave. Chris Schultz is interviewed and rips Mario Lemieux for stealing his number, 66. "Who is this guy, Lemminex?!?" Schultz scowls in mock anger. Three Toronto Argonauts agree to show up in front of the Air Canada Centre to stage a mock demonstration, for which we have provided placards for them to carry. They walk in a small circle, chanting, "Hey hey, ho ho, high hockey numbers have got to go!" The looks they get from passersby make the entire bit worthwhile.

Kerry Fraser's Hair Scare

When the NHL makes helmets mandatory for all officials in 2006, there is one man I think of. Kerry Fraser's perfect hair is as famous as Kerry Fraser. How will he possibly cope with the perils of helmet head? About three weeks after having that tiny thought, Kerry picks our entire crew up at the airport in Newark, New Jersey. Never in our history of silliness has a subject been so keen to help with a production. For the next 24 hours, he is our chauffeur, host (offering us the guest rooms of his suburban New Jersey home), and star of the cheesiest (and I say that lovingly) bit we've ever done. Fraser is actually out of action rehabbing a foot injury. But we pretend he's gone missing because he can't cope with the idea of messing up his trademark coif with a helmet. Fraser's acting is so over-the-top great, he should really be in soap operas. Or porn. My favourite scene is his confessional interview with me, where he admits, with sad dramatic music playing in the background, that the helmet rule has been devastating on his family: "Sometimes … sometimes I think … that I just should shave it. Shave it all! I want to take it all!" At this point, he grabs an electric razor and reaches towards his head. I dive into frame and tackle him, yelling, "No. Kerry, NO!"

Desperate, Fraser eventually consults then Flyer Simon Gagne, who advises him he has to train his hair to avoid helmet head. That leads to a *Rocky*-type montage, with another Lester McLean song as the soundtrack.

> *He's training his hair*
> *So it won't go anywhere*
> *Fraser won't be caught dead*
> *With bad helmet head*

The piece ends with Fraser climbing the *Rocky* stairs in Philadelphia (with his helmet on), leaping up and down with joy at the top, with Lester singing, "He looks fantastic! He looks fantastic! Hey, Fraser, two minutes for looking FAN … tastic."

I learn afterwards that the NHL is angry with Fraser for doing the story. They prefer their officials stay out of the spotlight. Which is the only thing dumber than the piece itself.

Puck over Glass

When you are stuck in the studio every night for six weeks—a phenomenon scientifically known as "playoffs"—you need to find ways to entertain yourself. One spring, there are a ridiculous number of too-many-men penalties. So we start a tote board, which we unveil on the big screen behind us every time another team gets penalized. The next year, the tote board is getting boring, so our terrific director Ben Zigelstein adds circus music to it. Then he adds explosions behind the number as it flashes. Pretty much any tacky '70s television effect available, we use.

The tote board reappears almost every playoff, but the trendy penalty changes constantly. And in the spring of 2013, the penalty of the moment is part of rule 63.2: delaying the game—puck over glass.

We are approaching 20 puck-over-glass penalties by the end of the second round, and we are long since out of lame effects for our tote board. Somebody says out loud, "We need to come up with something new for this puck-over-glass thing."

I can't read music or play an instrument. I played drums briefly as a kid, then gave it up after middle school because I sucked. (Playing "Pomp and Circumstance" at the Emily Carr Middle School graduation doesn't exactly get you prepared to tour with Van Halen.) But my father is an amazing musician. He plays piano, drums, and accordion, all by ear, and is still in a band at 83. The tiny piece of musical ability he passed on to me is that, occasionally, tunes pop into my head.

Driving home late that night, I start playing with those three words. Puck over glass. Puck over glass. Puck over glass. And before long, I have a simple rhyme that has the makings of a chorus. "Puck over glass. Hey ref, kiss my ass." (Though I realize I have to figure out how to sing it without actually saying "ass.")

As soon as I get home, I sit with a pencil and paper (old school), and start writing a song from the viewpoint of a player sick of that delay-of-game penalty. It comes oddly fast. When I used to write lyrics for a garage band (barely even that) my buddies and I had in our 20s, I would labour over verses for weeks. But "Puck over Glass" is done in 15 minutes. I record it in my iPhone voice memo folder and email it to Lester, my music magician.

> I worked so hard
> to make it to the league
> blood and sweat and a hernia
> a lockout stint in Slovenia
> now here I am
> playin' for the Cup
> but I keep getting caught in the ole sin bin
> cuz of this stupid rule that they made up
> puck over glass
> hey, ref, kiss my a-a-a ...
> ... another delay of game
> tarnishing my name
> we're tied at two in the third
> and the crowd is going nuts
> the puck's in my corner
> "I got it, Guy!"
> but I flick it a little too forcefully
> now his arm's in the air
> and I'm headed for the box
> the coach and the crowd are cursing my name
> they score on the power play
> we lose the game.
> puck over glass
> hey, ref, kiss my a-a-a
> ... another delay of game
> tarnishing my name

Lester takes the weekend to record it and does his usual brilliant job. But I figure it needs something more. Like say a ... gospel choir! I google "Toronto gospel choirs" and call a couple of them, trying to explain what I'm looking for. I really wish I'd recorded those conversations. Very similar to explaining the branding to Claude Julien. But before I can book anyone, Lester has rounded up several of his friends who sing in choirs to form the *NHL on TSN* Gospel Choir. He records a gospel chorus for the end, complete with a wild ad-lib high-pitched solo riff.

I call my boss, Mark Milliere, the next day to ask if I can do a music video to the song to air on our show. Mark trusts me and gives us the green light, though the night it is supposed to air, he sends me an email that says, "I'm more nervous about this one than anything you've done."

We decide Aaron Ward will be lead singer in The Panel Band. Lester will play guitar and sing backup in the video. I will fake-play a little pink electric guitar that I gave my 9-year-old daughter, Gracie, for Christmas that year. And Bob McKenzie will play keyboard. Although by the day of taping, we have added violin, tambourine, cowbell, and conch to Bob's repertoire.

I go back and forth on who should sing the gospel choir solo, until the only possible answer pops into my head: Vic Rauter. TSN legend. "Make the final!" Instantly, I know there is no other option. When Vic agrees, the band is set. We have an hour to shoot the video on a Sunday morning before a conference final game.

We shoot the "band" portion first, with Aaron lip-synching like a boss (the number of women who gush on Twitter later, believing he actually sang the song, terrifies me). The choir then takes over, recording live in studio with fancy equipment Lester and our audio crew have brought in. I find Vic alone in the green room, in his choir robe, practising his lines over and over again. Watching this, I instantly wish we would have filmed a *The Making of Puck over Glass*.

Vic's solo: "Oh no! Oh no! What have I done?! It went off my stick ... off the glass ... I didn't mean to do it! Oh no! What have I done! Ya! Ya! Ya! Ya Yaaaaaaaa! Puck over, puck over, puck over the glass!"

My go-to producer, the talented Jeremy McElhanney, edits it all together beautifully the next day, and *Puck over Glass* airs during Game 3 of the NHL's Western Conference final.

No comedy bit I have done, or will ever do, will match the permanence of that song. To this day, whenever a defenceman panics and fires one into the crowd in a key game, I'll get countless tweets reciting the lyrics.

"Hey, ref, kiss my a-a-a ... "

Perhaps the only thing missing from the song is a cameo from the man who has come to be known as my partner in TSN viral video idiocy. The Matt Damon of my Bournes. The Liam Neeson of my Takens. The Robert Pattinson of my Twilights (I really should have stopped after Neeson). A laconic goalie who goes by the pseudonym @Strombone1.

chapter 25

THE LUONGO FILMS

I am kneeling over the bloodied corpse of Anne Heche, trying desperately to reattach her severed arm, but distracted by her large penis.

Okay, that's the single-greatest sentence I will ever write. Really should have opened the book with that. Even just to terrify my mom.

Context: technically, it's not really Anne Heche. Though that would have been a *waaaay* better story. It is the dummy they used for Anne in some crappy horror movie. Which does not really explain the penis. Clearly this dummy has been around, playing other murdered actors who actually had penises (peni?), and it was all they could find for Anne's violent death scene. I'm sure it worked, despite the penis. What movie shows a dummy corpse full frontal? Zombie porn? These thoughts consume me as I try to reconnect dummy arm to dummy shoulder with duct tape. After all, when Roberto Luongo decapitates Cory Schneider in a few minutes, it has to look somewhat authentic.

Sequels generally suck. Aside from maybe the Godfather series, the Bourne movies, and *Air Bud* (that dog can play basketball, football, and soccer?!), I usually avoid them. But it's understandable why they're made. When you find a unique character you like, you want to see more of him. I happened to find one in a bowlegged Italian–French Canadian goalie named Roberto Luongo.

Luongo becomes my Sultan of Shtick by accident. During the 2005/06 season, Steve Dryden suggests doing a piece about what life is like for a true backup goaltender who only plays a dozen or so games a year. Steve has been in contact with Jamie "Noodles" McLennan, the backup to Luongo with the Florida Panthers. Noodles is both a great guy and a great character, the perfect combination for a feature like this. So Steve pitches the story to me: an informative feature about the ups and downs of life as a backup.

I take the assignment. And then, as per usual, I mutate Steve's solid feature idea into stupidity.

I figure it would be much more interesting to portray the little-used backup goalie as a slave to the starter. So along with my partner in crime, producer Jeremy McElhanney, we come up with several scenes where Noodles will do whatever Luongo asks—tying his skates, buying his groceries, spoon-feeding him lunch. My twist ending is that while Noodles outwardly accepts all of this, on the inside, he is seething. He fantasizes about offing Luongo so the job will be all his. Jeremy suggests Noodles run over Luongo with a Zamboni. This is why I love Jeremy. We are equally twisted. I turn it into a dream sequence, with Noodles laughing like a psycho the entire time. Jeremy rents a life-sized dummy from a movie prop guy in Florida for the murder-by-ice-cleaning-machine scene.

We fly to Florida, with Noodles only having a rough idea of our plan. Luongo knows nothing. I always believe it is easier to convince people to do ridiculous things face-to-face. But I'm uneasy about Luongo. I've never interviewed him before. And he seems very serious, even aloof, in most of his interviews I've watched over the years. Goalies are wild cards. They are usually the smartest, funniest, or strangest guys on the team. Sometimes all three. Unpredictable freaks. There's a reason Jason Voorhees wore a goalie mask.

These pieces are always guerilla filmmaking. We will have only a couple of hours from start to finish to shoot the entire piece after the Panthers practice ends. And because it happens on the ice, the climactic Zamboni hit-and-run will be shot first. So the very first conversation I have with Roberto Luongo in my life goes like this, as he steps off the ice.

"Hey, Roberto, James Duthie from TSN. Do you mind staying on for a few minutes? Hopefully, Noodles told you about the piece we're doing. Listen, we want to have him run you over with a Zamboni in a dream sequence at the end, so we need a couple of close-up shots of your terrified face as you are about to get crushed."

Long pause (okay probably not that long, but it feels like forever in the moment).

"No problem. Sounds great."

Well that went better than expected.

Not only does Luongo nail his "my backup is about to murder me!" face, he gets right into the piece. He suggests another scene, which shows him on the stationary bike, reading a magazine. When the camera tilts down, you see Noodles, lying on the floor exhausted, moving the foot pedals with his arms.

Luongo then invites us to his father-in-law's Italian restaurant for lunch, where we shoot Noodles hand-feeding him cannelloni. There is one more quick scene at a grocery store, and we're off to catch our flight home. Total shoot time: three hours. Budget (excluding our flights and the camera crew): 450 bucks for the dummy and his handler. (Dummy-handling degrees are offered at some of Florida's finest community colleges.)

The piece turns out great, if you like Complete Nonsensical Idiocy. If CNI is not your thing, well, you probably would have tossed this book 16 chapters ago, so never mind.

Noodles is excellent in it—a foreshadowing of the broadcasting career he'd launch a few years later. But the performance that gets the most attention is Luongo's. Few had seen this side of him before, deadpanning his real-life role as the starter who never wants to give up the net. Several people tell me it instantly changed their opinion of him. And if that is the only thing the bit achieved, I am more than content.

After we finish shooting that day in Florida, I barely see or speak to Roberto for two years. But in the fall of 2007, we do a sit-down interview in Vancouver before the season starts. It's mostly serious, though we do work in the Zamboni murder in a flashback scene and add one bit at the end poking fun at his infamous bathroom break in Anaheim during a playoff game. He delivers more quality acting (quality on the NHL-player acting scale—we aren't talking Pacino in his prime here), and as I'm leaving, he says, "We need to do a sequel to that Noodles bit someday." I promise him we will, but I'm not really sure I'll be true to my word. Comedy is hard. Sequels are harder. And there are only so many original gags you can do with a goalie.

So Roberto goes back to goaltending, having several good seasons in a row in Vancouver and winning gold with Canada in 2010. I go back to keeping The Panel in line. But in the fall of 2010, Jeremy—who knows I always need a push—is headed to Vancouver for another shoot and presses me to come up with something original we can do with Luongo on the same day. Problem is, whatever I come up with has to be shot in a short time, at the rink.

The only concept I come up with is that Bobby Lou is secretly a poet and has finally decided to share his art with the world. I'll write the poems; Luongo will recite them in Vancouver in the few minutes we have with him. Boom. High-quality sports television, while also contributing valuable work (cough) to the arts community. Win–win.

I write a quick poem about the Sedins and text Luongo the idea. He's in. His faith is encouraging, though misguided, since I really have no other ideas for poems. And I'm so busy with my regular job hosting hockey games that I still have none by the time I get on the plane for Vancouver a week later. But I always write better (or at least faster) under deadline. And by the time the plane lands in Vancouver, The Roberto Luongo Poetry Collection is complete.

The next day, Roberto meets us in an artfully lit luxury box after practice. Jeremy has picked up a cap, glasses, a scarf, and a pipe (do poets have pipes?) to give him that artsy look. Roberto has a quick look at the poems, shakes his head with a smile, gets into character, and nails basically every one in a single take.

This is the part where you should probably YouTube "Luongo Poetry" to get the full effect, but here are transcriptions, for all future classic early-twenty-first-century poetry collections.

Twins

Daniel, Henrik
Henrik, Daniel
Been four years now I bear witness to your art
And I still can't tell you dudes apart

Byfuglien

Human eclipse
Rhinoceros hips
Who will laugh last when I slash your calf?
Bring me peace
Make it cease
Get your big ass out of my crease

Backups

Cory Schneider, great guy
Andrew Raycroft, apple pie
I love all of my backups, oodles and oodles
Except Jamie McLennan. Noodles. Noodles.
First he fed me cannelloni
Then he ran me over with a Zamboni

Lou

Louuuuuuuuuuuuuuuuuuuuuuuuuuuuuuuuuuu!
(That's all. It's just beautiful on its own.)

Shootout

65 minutes, then a stupid gimmick
tarnishing my name, after a 48-save game
5 on 5? I'll keep you alive
4 on 4? You will not score
But … shootout. I despise you. I will not lie
Why can't we just end it in a tie?

Love Letter

Your golden glow makes me quiver
The way you feel on my skin, I shiver, I shiver
I lusted for you,
My dream come true
You belong to me
Eternally

At the end of the last one, he pulls his Olympic gold medal out of his sweater and grins like he's in a toothpaste commercial. Total shoot time: 10 minutes. Total budget: $30 for the cap and pipe.

There is one poem that didn't make the cut:

Green Men

I see you in my periphery
Giving me an epiphany
I appreciate you distractin'
Opponents with your actions
But how do you expect me to manage
When, dude, I can see your package

The poem (about the two guys in the green unitards who taunt opponents next to the penalty box in Vancouver) gets chopped because a couple of the bosses are worried about us using the word *package* in reference to a guy's, err, package. I fight this hard for a day, but figure resigning over my belief in the freedom to use male genitalia slang in a goofy poetry skit will not go over well at home when we have to sell the house. So "Green Men" gets cut. (We release it later on YouTube as *The Lost Luongo Poem*. Life rarely gets more ridiculous than this.)

The Poetry of Roberto Luongo airs during the intermission of a December Canucks–Blackhawks game. It goes viral (Canadian viral, anyway) quickly. My favourite comments online are from smitten teenage girls who write things like, "Lou's poetry is AMAZING. He's just so deep and … sensitive!<3<3<3"

I figure this is a good way to end our Luongo franchise. We have now shown the Zamboni scene in three separate pieces, if you count that 2007 interview. And though repetition is the key to dumb comedy, we've probably milked this baby dry. Or not.

Luongo and the Canucks go to the Stanley Cup final in the poetry season, and we all know the rest: one win short of a Cup, an upset loss to the Kings the next spring where he is benched in favour of Cory Schneider, months of endless trade talk interrupted only by a lockout, and finally a most uncomfortable Luongo–Schneider (Schneider–Luongo?) tandem for the shortened 2013 season. The Canucks choose Schneider as their guy. Except the other guy is still there.

It's a frustrating time for Roberto. So I'm a little surprised when I get a text from him a month into the season.

Luongo: "I have an idea for another bit. About me and Schneids and the whole who is Number 1 and who is Number 2 thing. You show us pretending to get along publicly, but behind the scenes we're at war."

Me: "Sounds good. Is Schneids good with this?"

Luongo: "I'll talk to him, but yeah, he's good."

So much for bitterness and tension in the Canucks locker room! I quickly get Jeremy on board and we come up with a few scenes. Roberto adds a couple of his own. And before long, we're in Columbus, Ohio, shooting the piece after practice on a Canucks off day before a game against the Blue Jackets.

It's a somewhat surreal shoot. Luongo and Schneider have been put in an incredibly awkward situation, a breeding ground for bitterness and animosity. Yet here they are, fake wrestling in full gear on the floor of the visitors' dressing room, giggling the entire time.

The scenes all involve the two goalies trying to one-up each other over who is the real Number 1.

Scene one: Schneider politely lets Luongo off the ice first, then two-hands him to the back of the calf.

Scene two: Luongo presents Schneider a gift, a Dr. Seuss Thing 2 shirt. Then he pulls off his jersey to reveal he's wearing the Thing 1 shirt.

Scene three: Luongo walks out of a bathroom stall, with Schneider waiting anxiously for him. Schneider says, "Number 2?" Luongo coolly replies, "Nope, Number 1."

We have discovered another silly-skit-acting gem in Schneider. Just like when I met Luongo for the first time in Florida, Schneider has brought along script ideas. He is a crossword puzzle junkie and comes up with a scene where he asks Luongo for a six-letter word for "opposite of to move forward." Luongo keenly answers, "Backup?" Schneider grins evilly. He also does a takeoff on the Luongo poetry bit for a dream sequence:

> *Lui, Lui*
> *Phooey, Phooey!*
> *There's a reason Cory rhymes with glory*
> *And Lou rhymes with number two*

(I am quickly realizing these bits sound even dumber in writing than they do on video, if that's possible.)

One thing I struggle with from the moment Luongo suggests the piece is the ending. Jeremy gets full credit for giving me the answer: "I think we should just go back to our roots. Cartoon violence."

And so the Zamboni is replaced by an arena golf cart. And seven years after he was run over by Jamie McLennan, Roberto Luongo runs over Cory Schneider, played by the Anne Heche dummy with the severed arm and penis. Apparently the head is also loose, as it flies off the second Luongo makes impact. Very Tarantino.

Total shoot time: 90 minutes. Total budget: $200 (for the Anne Heche dummy).

When the piece airs, everyone asks, "How the hell did you get those guys to do that in the midst of all this?" Simple answer: I didn't do anything. I just got lucky enough to find two great guys who were eager to laugh at their awkward situation.

But the piece doesn't help Luongo or Schneider get a fairy-tale ending. The Canucks surprise the hockey world at the 2013 draft when they trade Schneider to New Jersey and announce they are keeping Luongo. Roberto is in shock, believing he was finally going to get a fresh start somewhere else. He doesn't say anything publicly for almost two months, before telling me in an August interview from his Florida home, "It was like a divorce, except she wanted me back."

The divorce is finally complete in early 2014, when Luongo is traded back to the Florida Panthers. The Panthers are still rebuilding and miss the playoffs, allowing Luongo to make his first-ever appearance on The Panel ... and allowing us to make one last Luongo film. (Yes, I know we said that two films ago. If Neeson can make three Takens, we can make five Luongos.)

This one comes together in about two days. Luongo is only at TSN for a couple of playoff games, and we literally have

45 minutes between a Saturday doubleheader to shoot the entire piece. It's called *The Panel Intern*. The idea is that Luongo has joined TSN as an intern because his dream is to be on The Panel when he retires. But he'll have to intern under Jamie McLennan, his former Florida backup who ran him over nine years ago in Florida.

This is the first time I have virtually no script. We make it up as we go, Luongo now the slave to McLennan: doing his makeup, mopping his dressing room, and sucking up his excess cafeteria gravy with a straw. My favourite scene has Luongo getting a chance to practise on camera, while Noodles tries to distract him by yelling random chirps:

"Torts!"

"Eddie Lack!"

"My contract sucks!" (I will laugh every time I watch that, until the day I die.)

Luongo finally snaps when McLennan rips his goaltending on The Panel and takes him out with a jib camera. One last piece of Road Runner–Wile E. Coyote violence. And one last dummy flying through the air. This time, it wears one of my suits and a wad of duct tape coloured black with a Sharpie for hair. (We could really use an effects budget.)

With Noodles out of the way, Luongo struts onto the set in super slo-mo to music, taking his seat on The Panel and declaring, "Let the Luongo era begin!"

This is my favourite of the five Luongo films. Only because we did it so fast, with so little planning. It might also be the dumbest thing ever to air on our network. This makes me proud. (It features yet another flashback to the Zamboni scene, smashing the all-time record for milking one piece of silly video.)

Steve Dryden had no idea what he was starting when he sent Jeremy and me to Florida to do that serious feature on Jamie McLennan in 2005. The Luongo films will always be our one and only shtick franchise.

It's been fun to watch Roberto's reputation change over the
years. He's become far more popular, even as he went through
the worst time of his career those last two seasons in Vancouver.
Twitter is a large part of that. His self-deprecating tweets as
@Strombone1 helped people see him as one of the funniest players
in the NHL, maybe in all pro sports. Hopefully, our films added
to that rep.

I doubt we'll ever do another one. Though I have to admit,
when Florida acquired Al Montoya as their backup before the
2014/15 season, I did start to have Godfather ideas.

chapter 26

FANTASY ISLAND

Just behind the curtains onstage at the Lac-Leamy casino theatre in Gatineau, Quebec, three men are engaged in an extremely intense conversation. It is January 26, 2012, about five minutes before the start of the 2012 NHL All-Star Fantasy Draft.

There is Boston goalie Tim Thomas, the reigning Conn Smyth/Vezina/Stanley Cup winner. Earlier in the week, Thomas boycotted the Bruins White House visit, causing a major ... what's the proper English term here? ... shit-storm. I am planning on interviewing Thomas onstage after he is picked. But at this moment, he looks ready to go full Swayze in *Road House* and pull the throat out of anyone bearing the title Member of Media.

There is NHL commissioner Gary Bettman. He is clearly furious about Thomas's presidential snub and is concerned this one interview could single-handedly ruin All-Star Weekend.

And there is ... me. Trying to convince both of them (and myself) that I know exactly how to handle this.

Bettman is worried. Thomas is angry. I am hungry (hadn't eaten since breakfast). Oh, and also mildly concerned, seeing that I was the one who fought for this interview, and now I figure there is a chance it could get me fired.

It's all Brendan Shanahan's fault. The former NHL star turned league executive (soon to turn Toronto Maple Leafs president) came up with the idea of a draft to jazz up All-Star Weekend. The league had tried a variety of formats over the years for the game—Campbell vs. Wales, North America vs. the world, East vs. West. Shanahan figured why not just let the players choose their own teams, like we all did on the local rinks and streets when we were kids.

I like it. Nobody really cares who wins the All-Star Game anyway. In fact, nobody really cares about the All-Star Game, period, except kids mainly. And they just want to see the stars dangle. The new format adds a twist and creates a ton of buzz leading up to its debut at the 2011 All-Star Weekend in Raleigh, North Carolina.

We find out a couple of months before the event that TSN will be doing the All-Star Fantasy Draft show. I am keen, but cautious. This hasn't been done before in any sport and has the potential to really … suck. The majority of NHL players are genuinely good, humble guys. But that can also be a tragic flaw, especially when you are trying to do a show that will succeed or fail based almost entirely on their personalities.

Brass from the NHL and TSN hold countless meetings to figure out the format of the show. They debate everything, from who should be captains and how many there should be, to what rounds you have to pick goalies and defencemen by and whether the players should put on sweaters after they're selected, like they do at the draft. In fact, the most intense argument I hear in my two years of All-Star Drafts is one between two executives over what colour shoes the hot models who bring the players their sweaters onstage should wear.

But the most contentious topic that first year in Carolina is how the show should end. There is concern, especially from the NHL Players' Association, about the final player picked being embarrassed. It's every kid's worst nightmare to be the last guy chosen for the after-school pickup game. And for proud All-Stars who had never been the last guy picked for anything, it could be a massive ego blow. Especially on national TV. There is talk they might not even leave a last guy, instead leaving two players or four and just dividing them up randomly, to spare them the embarrassment. Lame. TSN brass and the NHL want that money shot: the last man standing. And to the NHLPA's credit, it agrees. The players want the show to be a hit as much as anyone else.

The only thing I really don't get is the name. The NHL calls it the All-Star Fantasy Draft. My response to them is, "Uhh ... what's the fantasy part? This is an actual draft."

A few hours before airtime in Carolina, it is clear this is different from any hockey show I've done before at the network. One of the great things about TSN is that they trust you and leave you alone. There is little to no interference from the guys upstairs. But this is a new species. In the hours leading up to the show, I am pulled aside by a dozen different suits, mostly from the NHL and NHLPA, giving me instructions on how I should "do" this show.

"Make sure you say it EXACTLY this way ..."

"The tone is crucial ... keep it light but not too light."

"What do you think of the models' shoes?" (Okay, they don't consult with me on the last one. But for the record, I would have gone with stilettos instead of wedges.)

Then there are the logistics.

"Okay, James, you have to stand on this exact spot to announce the pick, then move exactly three steps to your right, take the sweater from the model with your left hand, fill 10 seconds while the player gets to the stage, give the sweater to the player with your right hand, then fill 15 seconds while you walk backwards to the right of the stage, pause for three seconds, then ask the other captain to make the next pick. Oh! And make sure you keep track of exactly how many forwards, d-men, and goalies each team has picked so the captains don't screw up the draft!"

Got it. Sure you don't want me to juggle fire at the same time? But I'm not too concerned about missing my mark by a step. We are doing an all-star hockey draft, not choreographing a Lady Gaga concert.

About two hours before showtime, everything is smooth, except for one tiny detail: several players are missing. There are weather issues in the east, causing numerous flight delays. Some players are just arriving at the airport and have to be whisked right to the convention centre. And no one can find Mike Green, one of the assistant captains for the draft, and Alexander Ovechkin, the biggest star of the show. (Sidney Crosby is injured and not coming.)

I have Green's number and text him. "Are you with Ovie? Where are you guys?" He answers a couple minutes later: "Airport in Wash. Lounge bar."

Oh. That's probably … not good. I have visions of Ovie with nine shots lined up on the bar, his flight already 10,000 feet in the air. But it turns out they are just delayed. I text Green back: "You gonna make it? The NHL guys are freaking out a little." He responds: "Understandably. Our flight is supposed to leave in a half hour. We'll do everything we can, but it'll be tight."

It is tight. They sprint in about five minutes before showtime.

Brendan Shanahan has me address the players just before they go onstage. I tell them to try to have fun, joke around, and promise I won't do anything to embarrass anyone. Still, they look apprehensive (apprehensive or bored—players are tough to read sometimes).

It is, as expected, tough to get personality out of many of them. But some are terrific. Cam Ward, picked first overall by his teammate Eric Staal, deadpans in our interview that he is clearly "the best player available." The Sedins, chosen to play on separate teams for the first time ever, rip each other. Team captain Staal makes his brother Marc sweat it out for several rounds. Marc then deadpans how "classless" Eric is when I interview him. And Patrick Kane, an assistant captain on Nick Lidstrom's team, keeps passing on Jonathan Toews, leading to several camera shots of Toews looking angry in the crowd. (He is joking, too, though most of the audience thinks Captain Serious is Captain Furious.)

Toronto's Phil Kessel is picked last. The plan is for me to interview him onstage, then surprise him with a new car. Except Phil makes a beeline for his seat in our makeshift bleachers, leading to the most awkward moment of the show for me, as I attempt to get his attention for about 20 straight seconds without success. Rough transcription: "Phil, come on down here. Phil? Phil? Phil, if we could get you back down here, just a couple of questions. Hey, Phil! Phil? Phil, can you hear me? Phil? PHILLLL!!!!!"

Kessel looks embarrassed as he comes back down to the stage. It gets worse when Ovechkin snaps photos of him sitting alone before he is announced as the last pick. But backstage after, he is classy, saying he doesn't mind at all (whether that is honesty or politeness, I'm not sure—like I say, they are tough to read sometimes). Brian Burke does mind, though. The Leafs general manager is furious his player was put in that position and complains to the NHL. A year later, the last two players left (Dallas's Jamie Benn and San Jose's Logan Couture) share the stage so there can't be a repeat of the Kessel shot, one player all by his lonesome.

I have mixed feelings about doing the so-called fantasy draft the next year in Ottawa. To me, it is a gimmick with a short shelf life. But the ratings were massive in Carolina, and I knew it was coming back.

The Tim Thomas story dominates that week's news coverage leading up to All-Star Weekend. I'd always liked Thomas. I'd written a piece a couple of years earlier on his unlikely rise to greatness after a journeyman career, and his fiery competitiveness. His family had little money growing up, and Thomas had used just one goalie stick for his entire youth. Then he was invited to the U.S. equivalent of a World Junior tryout camp and given a dozen new sticks. He couldn't believe it—he was over the moon. During the tryout intra-squad games, Thomas felt he was the best goalie on the ice, giving up just one goal, where all the other goalies gave up several. But he was cut from the team. So he stormed into the dressing room and smashed every one of his new sticks. God, I love that story.

Thomas had never mentioned his political views in any of our previous conversations. But the Obama/White House snub makes it clear this goaltender is really a hardcore right-winger at heart. Many of his Boston teammates are furious with their goalie—and the dressing room tension is widely reported, much to Thomas's chagrin.

The morning of the draft show, one of my bosses calls to tell me we can't interview Thomas. The NHL wants this story dead and fears he will say something else controversial and ruin the entire All-Star Weekend.

I'm not happy. This is the biggest story in hockey right now, and Thomas hasn't commented on it since releasing a statement when it happened. I understand this is a fun draft show—not the right platform to go all Mike Wallace on him. But if we ignore it completely, we will look like idiots. We have to at least acknowledge it.

Steve Dryden agrees and we are able to convince TSN senior VP Mark Milliere that I have to bring it up with Thomas during the show. Mark has terrific TV instincts, and though I'm sure he's getting significant pressure from the league to drop the interview, he tells the NHL we're doing it. Though he is a little anxious.

"If this blows up and he says something to ruin the show, it's on you," Mark tells me. He has a dry sense of humour, so I'm not sure if "it's on you" means we wouldn't be going for beers later, or that I'll be fired. Could go either way, I figure.

We decide on something simple, like, "Did you ever expect your decision not to go to the White House to get so much attention?" A fairly soft and fair way to acknowledge the story without it derailing the show. I agree to speak with Tim before the show to make sure he won't use the question as a platform for his political views to stir up more controversy.

The players arrive at the theatre just minutes before showtime, and I immediately pull Tim aside right behind the stage. By coincidence (at least, I think it is coincidence) Gary Bettman is standing nearby and immediately jumps into the conversation.

So here, roughly, is what is said. These quotes obviously aren't word-for-word accurate, but I jot them down in my BlackBerry right after the show, figuring they are too good to forget.

Me: Tim, I have to ask you about the White House thing. We'll look stupid if we don't.

Thomas: I've said all I have to say.

Me: What if I just ask, "Did you expect this thing to get so big?"

Thomas (face turning red): Okay. Ask me that. Then I'll say, "No I didn't expect the media to tell lies and try to drive a wedge between my teammates and I."

Bettman: No, No, No, No, No!

Me: I get that's how you feel, Tim, but that probably wouldn't go over too well.

Bettman: Here's what you need to say. You need to apologize. Say, "I'm sorry for the controversy this has caused—"

Thomas: I'm not sorry and I'm not apologizing for anything.

Gary then gives him another option that also sounds like an apology and is too long and flowery for me to even attempt to remember. By this time, we are about one minute to air, and I have to cut him off.

Me: Sorry, Gary ... the show is starting. Tim, we can't tell you what to say, but why don't you just deflect. Say you've said all you have to say and you'd rather focus on the game.

Thomas: Okay. I can do that.

So, I've not only told an interview subject my question, but I've also told him his answer (my old journalism professors would be thrilled with this approach). Oh, and I've also basically told the NHL commissioner to shut the f*%& up.

There is always a chance Thomas will change the script and go on a political or anti-media rant, but I'm not betting on it. I get the sense he wants this over as much as the league does. We don't have to wait long to find out. He is picked third overall by his teammate, team captain Zdeno Chara.

As he puts on his all-star sweater and I step forward for the interview, I figure I better attempt to lighten the mood.

"Pretty uneventful week for you, Tim." He laughs and says, "Yeah, no problems."

I ask the question almost exactly as promised. "Did you expect this whole thing to get so big?"

He says, "I followed my conscience. I'm extremely grateful for all the support I got from my teammates, fans, and friends. I said in my statement, that is the only time I will be addressing that topic. We're here in Ottawa to celebrate the game of hockey, and I'm really excited to be a part of that."

Stick save and a beauty by Thomas. The crowd applauds. Somewhere, the execs in the suits exhale.

The rest of the show goes smoothly. Logan Couture goes last, and again, wins a car. One of the models in her fancy new shoes hands me a ridiculous, giant two-foot-long fake key that I am supposed to give Couture, and I can't help myself.

"This looks like the actual key for Chara's car."

The crowd likes it. But I glance over at Big Z and he isn't laughing. I send an internal memo to myself: avoid lines about guys who could crush you with their baby toe. I run into Chara later at the after-party.

"Hey, Z, hope you didn't mind that line about the key."

He gives me the Chara death-stare, a look that has made the toughest NHL players back away from fights with him. I quickly translate it to mean, "I am about to crush you with my baby toe." He holds the look for about five (eternal) seconds, then busts into a wide smile. "That was a pretty good one."

chapter 27

NAKED MEN IN BATHROOMS
AND OTHER INSPIRATIONAL
OLYMPIC MOMENTS

I am 10 years old, lying in the dark in the back bunk room of our cottage in Arden, Ontario, shaking. A Canadian high jumper named Greg Joy has a chance to win a medal at the 1976 Olympic Games in Montreal. But I won't see it. I have left the room because I'm too nervous to watch.

With the Games taking place in my country, I have instantly become a full-fledged Olympic geek. When I hear the rest of my family's happy freak-out, I scramble out back to the TV to see Joy celebrating his silver. (Years later, as a news reporter in Ottawa, I run into Greg working at the Ottawa Food Bank and tell him he gave me one of the best moments of my sports-viewing childhood. Even though I was too much of a wuss to actually watch it.)

From that age on, I worship the Olympics. Horst Bulau, a teenager from Gloucester where I live, becomes a world-champion ski jumper. I proceed to build a four-foot jump on the hill near my house and spend every day after school flying (okay, that's a stretch) off it on the five-dollar cross-country skis my dad buys me at some used exchange. I really needed to meet girls.

This is why Vancouver meant so much. And why I opened the book with it. I could work 20 more Games and never match those 17 remarkable days. But 2010 is not my only Olympic adventure.

My road to Vancouver actually starts in July of 2003 in Prague, Czech Republic. The International Olympic Committee (IOC) is meeting to decide who will host the 2010 Winter Olympics. Vancouver/Whistler, Salzburg, and Pyeongchang are the three cities in the running.

Prague is my first IOC meeting and it is an eye-opener. I have long heard the stories of corruption and vote buying. I just never expected it to be so blatant. The day of the presentations from the bid cities, officials from Pyeongchang are swarming IOC delegates begging for their support. I hear several say, right out in the open, "We will do whatever it takes to get your vote!"

I sit down in a hotel lobby next to a voting IOC delegate from Africa. He only speaks French, so my years of French immersion at Emily Carr Middle School and Gloucester High come in handy. I tell him I am from Canada and he starts asking me questions about Vancouver. Keep in mind, this is one day before the final vote to decide who gets the 2010 Olympic Games.

"So, is Vancouver near Toronto?" he asks me in French. I chuckle, then quickly realize he is dead serious.

"No, it is on the West Coast, sir. On the Pacific Ocean."

"Are there mountains there for the skiing?"

What the? Yes. I believe there are mountains in British Columbia … for the skiing. Unreal. An IOC delegate has shown up in Prague with ZERO knowledge of at least one of the cities he is about to vote on (not to mention questionable geographical skills in general). I politely tell him he should pay attention to Vancouver's presentation to help him make a decision. But I figure there is a decent chance his vote has already been paid for.

I am covering the announcement live for CTV. Brian Williams will cover it for CBC. This is rather daunting, as Brian is the king of Olympic broadcasting in Canada, having done about a dozen Games already. Meanwhile, my Olympic resume to this point includes once pretending I was Horst Bulau on the hill behind my house. Minor mismatch.

We are outside the theatre when IOC president Jacques Rogge announces that the Olympics are indeed coming back to Canada. We can hear the Vancouver delegation's joyful screams through the closed doors. Then it's mayhem. My main assignment is to get Prime Minister Jean Chrétien before CBC and anyone else. I am on CTV live as he approaches, and we make eye contact, but he is caught up in a swarm of humanity just a few feet away. I try to grab him, but the wire that attaches my earpiece to our audio cable is about two feet too short. So I'm stuck. I quickly throw it back to Lloyd Robertson in our Toronto studio and unplug my cord. I reach over two guys and grab our prime minister by the shoulder, yanking him towards me. It is essentially assault. But le petit gars de Shawinigan is tough and doesn't seem bothered a bit.

The Vancouver victory party that night ends right on time (we even celebrate politely), and I end up at the Salzburg defeat party with Canadian Olympic hero Catriona LeMay Doan and a few other media pals. Seems one of the leaders of the Austrian contingent is infatuated with Catriona. Her ability to dodge him the entire evening is as impressive as her speed skating. I have to hand it to the Austrians, though. They party all night after losing the chance to host the Olympics. Remind me to be there when they win.

A year later, TSN lends me to the CBC to call a couple of lower-profile events at the 2004 Athens Games, but an illness in the family forces me to cancel last minute. So my first real Olympic gig is Turin in 2006.

The semi-friendly Olympic partnership between TSN and CBC gets a little ugly in Italy. Though TSN shows some of the events through a sub-licensing agreement, CBC controls the rights and the accreditations. Since we are competitors most of the hockey season, someone at the CBC decides they don't want TSN's hockey crew anywhere near the venues. So Bob McKenzie, Gord Miller, and I aren't allowed credentials. We head to Italy with no way to get into the games. We end up covering the Olympic hockey tournament by sitting in the stands with tickets

Gord buys from a scalper named Smiley. Once again, lessons not taught in journalism school.

One afternoon, while Gord is off making ticket deals in back alleys, Bob and I decide to go to a Chinese restaurant for lunch. Why we choose Chinese in the middle of Italy I have no idea. As we're waiting for our food, I excuse myself to use the men's room. I open the door, and standing directly in front of me is a completely naked Chinese man. I mean head to toe. Not even socks. He does not move. He just stares. I scream. Okay, I only scream on the inside. But really really loud. I take two very slow steps backwards, shut the door, walk back to the table, and sit down. Bob can see it on my face.

"That was fast. What's wrong? You look like you've seen a ghost."

"I just ... I ... he was ... we have to go ... now."

I'm still scarred. Can't unsee him. I have spent years trying to figure it out. Best I can come up with is that it was a chef changing before or after his shift. That's what I'm going with, anyway. Any other explanation is a place too dark for my mind to venture.

When you have no credentials for the Olympics, and you are only really covering Canada's hockey team, there is a fair amount of down time. Which is dangerous. One night Bob and Gord head back to the apartment we have rented. I stay later, sharing beverages with a few crew members who are staying in a different part of the city. Around 3:30 A.M., they finally kick us out of the bar, and I wander to the main taxi stand. Jumping in the cab, I say to the driver, "Please to take me to ... [long pause]." Oh crap. I have no idea where I live.

Gord has been making fun of my sense of direction the entire trip. Which is unfair, because he is some sort of freakish human Google map who can walk through a city once and know every shortcut and secret cobblestone path instantly. I just never pay attention in places I'll probably never come back to. But now, it's caught up with me. I neglected to put the address in my phone.

Ditto the phone number of our apartment. I remember the street starts with "Saint." But apparently, this is not a unique first word in Italian street names. The impatient cabbie curses and kicks me out.

So here I am. 4 A.M. in the middle of my first Olympic Games. Homeless. I figure I have three options:

1. Go to the police station and report myself missing.
2. Wait until morning, show up at the Canadian Embassy, and declare, "I'm a lost Canadian broadcaster. Also, an idiot."
3. Pretend to have been kidnapped and sold into the sex trade. Then call Liam Neeson.

After a half hour weighing the pros and cons of each, I decide to try one more cabbie. This guy is friendlier, and spends 10 minutes slowly repeating every Saint street he knows in Turin. "… Joseph, Francesca, George, Dominica, Antoine …"

"Yes! Antoine! I live there! Take me there!"

Salvation. And now I can keep this story to myself for eternity, and no one will ever know how dumb I … Oh. Right. Dang. (Publisher, please remove this section in editing.)

We all act like fools in foreign countries. Nothing makes me laugh more during our two weeks in Turin than my pal and producer, Bill Dodson, trying to give directions to our Italian driver, who speaks no English. Bill does what pretty much every North American tourist does in the same situation: he starts speaking English really slowly with an Italian accent, believing that will somehow work better.

"We-a need-a … to go-a … to the speed-a skating … oval-la." Gold.

Unlike the Canadian men's hockey team, which never sniffed gold. The Canadians lose in the quarter-final to Russia. With no credentials and no other stories to cover, we head home early with the team. It's an odd Olympic debut for me. One naked Chinese man, one almost fake kidnapping, zero hockey glory.

It makes the magic of Vancouver four years later all the more memorable.

We are still basking in Vancouver's glow when we head to London in 2012 for the Summer Games. I am partnered with the terrific Jennifer Hedger for Olympic daytime (prime-time hours in London). It's a great shift, as most of the main medal events are held while we are on the air.

One afternoon, princes William and Harry visit our studio. They seem very kind and friendly. It is my first meeting with a royal, if you don't count George Brett, who I saw once as a kid at spring training. Brian Williams interviews them on set, then they pose for a photograph with our entire crew. As soon as the photographer gets his pic, I put my arm around Prince William's shoulder and give it a good hard guy-pat. You know, those firm buddy-buddy smacks guys do to acknowledge kinship. After all, we've just posed for a photo together and briefly said hello to each other.

"What up, Will?"

"Yo, James. Sup?" (Something like that.)

Bestie status. The Prince of Wales doesn't seem to mind my man-love, grinning his royal grin and giving me a little nod. It's the British secret service guy standing a few feet away who doesn't look happy. As the princes leave and the crowd scatters, he leans in to me and whispers sternly, "You aren't supposed to touch the royals." Whatever. Wills and I will most likely be going for beers tonight and probably to Vegas for a guys' weekend soon. So back off.

Cheryl and the kids arrive in London for the second week of the Games. Everyone assumes when you host an Olympics, you can get tickets to anything. Reality is, there is nothing. You have to buy tickets online like everyone else. I waited until the last minute (disorganization is another character flaw) and all I could get was a one-day afternoon ticket for track and field. But the family will get to see the great Oscar Pistorius run for South Africa in the 4 x 400 metre heats. When I get the tickets a week before they arrive in London, I tell my kids to read as much as they can about Pistorius, the double-amputee "Blade Runner" who has become an inspiration worldwide, and one of the big stories of these Games.

"You guys are so lucky!" I keep telling them. "You are going to watch the Blade Runner run! You are going to witness history!" (Accurate, though I may be overcompensating a little for the fact I couldn't get them tickets to see Usain Bolt or Michael Phelps race for actual medals.)

By the time we get to Olympic Stadium that day, my kids are jacked. "Where's Oscar?" "When is Oscar running?" It's all we hear for the three hours leading up to his race. Finally, the big moment arrives. They are standing and cheering for their new hero as the gun goes to start the race. Pistorius will run the third leg for South Africa. But as the second leg South African runner makes the turn directly in front of our seats, another runner bumps him, and he goes down hard. He doesn't move.

"Get up!" my kids scream, part encouragement, part anger. And by "my kids," I mean me. He isn't getting up. Down the track a few metres, Oscar stands with his hands on his head in disbelief, waiting for a baton he will never get.

"Dad, what's happening?" my youngest daughter, Gracie, asks, mild panic in her voice.

"Umm, yeah … well … Oscar isn't going to get to run today, kids. But hey, the decathlon discus preliminaries are coming right up!"

We're all bummed, but we get over it quickly. A year later, Pistorius is arrested for killing his girlfriend, which is much harder to explain to the kids than the 4 x 400 wipeout.

Cheryl and the kids do the London tourist thing while I work the rest of the Olympics. Hosting a Games from studio is a blast, but not quite as glamorous as it may seem. You get up, take a series of tubes and buses to the broadcast centre, prep and write for several hours, host your show for another five, and then get on the same tubes and buses back home.

My highlight most days is the cafeteria, which we share with NBC. At one point, I'm in line at the salad bar with Jimmy Fallon, Bob Costas, and Bruce Jenner (three years pre-Caitlyn). I say, "Love your show" to Fallon, but Jenner thinks I'm talking to him and says, "Thanks!" I have never enjoyed any show involving a Kardashian, but I'm too Canadian-polite to tell Bruce the compliment was meant for Jimmy. So I just load up on beets and skulk away shamefully.

The last night of the Games, I pack up my suits to get shipped home. I leave one out for the closing ceremony, which Jennifer and I will host. As we're heading over to the stadium, I bend over to pick something up and ... *riiiiiiip*. My suit pants tear from my belt line at the back to my boys at the front (about an inch below the zipper). Apparently I spent more time at the dessert bar than the salad bar. My only saving grace is that the suit is navy and the underwear is black. (If I had chosen my Super Friends boxers, we would have really had an issue.)

We only have to do one on-camera before the ceremony. Jennifer looks like a billion dollars, as always. And I am standing next to her with a fully vented ass. It's liberating, frankly. Fortunately, the several million people watching across Canada only see me from the front, waist up.

The Spice Girls dance around a lot, Paul McCartney sings "Hey Jude," the evening breeze flows gently through my crotch, and another terrific Games comes to an end. I'm eternally grateful and honoured for the opportunity to host events like this. I still shake my head at the lunacy of it. How in the heck did that weird little kid from 1976, the one who loved the Olympics so much he almost threw up watching Canadians compete, get to actually cover all these Games?

Like the naked guy in the Chinese restaurant, I'll never understand it.

chapter 28

THE PANEL HANGOVER

Mary Hart's husband is screaming at me. Not 12-year-old-girls-at-a-One-Direction-concert screams, more like angry senior citizen screams. He's well into his 70s. And though he is not carrying a cane, if he were, there is no question he would be shaking it at me, or maybe whacking me with it, like Joe Kapp on Angelo Mosca.

But Mary is cool. She still looks basically the same as she did when she was on my family room TV every night hosting *Entertainment Tonight*. And when a camera is pointed at her, as ours is now, she nails that Hollywood smile like the all-pro she is. She doesn't seem too concerned about her hubby's desire to go geriatric Chris Brown all over my ass.

This is totally my fault. As it usually is. We find Mary and her sugar granddaddy (actual and most appropriate name ever: Burt Sugarman) in the stands at a Kings game. I approach to explain my odd request.

"Hey, Mary! Big fan. Show hasn't been the same since you and Tesh left. So anyway, my name is James and I'm a hockey broadcaster from Canada, but we also do some weird, uhh, goofy spoofs sometimes, and tonight we're shooting a parody of *The Hangover* starring some of the Kings. And you know during the credits when they show those still shots of what happened during the night when they were hammered? Well, would you like to be in one with me? I will wear a funny hat and we could be, I dunno, pretending to make out or something?"

Now, if I were Mary, I would have screamed for security. But Mary just smiles. Which makes me love her more. Though she doesn't go for the whole "pretend making out" thing, she does say yes to the pic. Even Burt seems okay with it at this point. Mary asks me to wait for her at the intermission down in the tunnel beneath her front-row seats.

The period ends, Mary shows up, we get ready to shoot the photo. Then I decide to push my luck.

"Hey, Mary, do you think for the photo you could put on this T-shirt with my colleague Bob McKenzie's face on it? I know you don't know Bob, but he's a big deal, and it would be funny to the folks back in Canada. Oh, and I'm going to put on this fur panda bear hat we picked up on Venice Beach today just … because."

It is at this moment, as I put on the hat and get the T-shirt ready to slip on Mary's head, that Burt loses it. (When you read this next quote, try to do it in your scratchiest, angriest Abe Simpson voice.)

"Nooooo! Don't put that on, Mary! We don't know who the hell that Bob guy on the shirt is! He could be some kind of criminal! Let's get the hell outta here!"

But Mary, gamer that she is, ignores Sugargrump again and, though she won't put it on, holds the T-shirt in front of her and makes a perfect what-the-hell-is-going-on-here face. Money.

Of all the comedy bits we've done at TSN, the one I get asked about the most is *The Panel Hangover*. Ideas for these kinds of pieces come from different places. Full credit for this one goes to a buddy's beard. Richard Hodgson is a producer at TSN. When Aaron Ward or Jeff O'Neill wants a piece of video for an intermission, it is Richard who puts it together with his team in an edit suite. He is one of the backbones of our show and a main reason our intermissions run smoothly. But more importantly (for this chapter, anyway), when he grows a beard, he is a dead ringer for Alan from *The Hangover* movies (Zach Galifianakis).

NHL on TSN producer Bill Dodson sees me one day in early 2013 and says, "We were just talking about Richard's beard. You should do some kind of *Hangover* parody with the LA Kings and their Stanley Cup hangover, and use Rick as Alan."

I smile and say, "Great idea!" Like I always do when people give me suggestions for pieces. But I can't see this ever happening. We can get cheap laughs by running dummies dressed in goalie gear over with Zambonis (and replay it over and over and over), but we can't pull off a movie parody.

And yet Bill's suggestion attaches to some small part of my brain, like gum on the bottom of a chair. Those little ideas that gnaw at you are usually the best ones. (Unless you have been thinking a lot about robbing a convenience store to help buy a pet boa constrictor. That is an awful idea. Let it go.) Every couple of weeks, when I'm bored during the hour at the rink before my boy's hockey game or daughter's swim practices, I start pondering how a Panel Hangover would work. Aaron Ward makes sense playing Bradley Cooper's character. He's got the looks and stubble. I could probably pull off Ed Helms's dentist. (In fact, some people have started to tell me I look like Ed Helms. I used to get Ben Stiller. Then Seth Myers. Now Ed Helms. This is not trending well. If I start getting, "Hey, it's Steve Buscemi," I'm retiring.) We would have to lose someone in our Hangover, just like the real movie. The first guy that pops into my mind is Darren Pang. It would be easy to lose Panger. He's like a toddler.

The closest thing to a screenplay I come up with is that The Panel goes to LA, somehow gets roofied, loses Panger, and uses the LA Kings to help sober up and find him. "You got over your Stanley Cup hangover, help us get over ours." So corny. I'm lukewarm with the idea, and am guessing there's a 95 percent chance it dies. Too many plot holes, too hard to get everyone to LA with conflicting schedules, unlikely to get the Kings on board with some silly acting skit, and little chance TSN will agree to let us run around LA like drugged-up idiots for a feature. It's a 50 to 1 shot.

A month goes by, and now it's mid-winter. I've been too busy covering games to think any more about the idea. Matt Cade, another of our brilliant young producers, calls me, saying *NHL on TSN* content guru Steve Dryden really needs a Kings feature for a pre-game show in late March. Matt is wondering if there is any chance we can still pull off *The Panel Hangover*. So we start tossing around ideas again, trying to figure out if it's worth pursuing. The problem with a full parody is that you actually need a plot, and an ending. Most of my other skits have just been a bunch of gags strung together. We need to have a payoff at the end where we reveal who drugged our drinks. Bob McKenzie? Bob could pull off evil, but that makes no sense because he is on The Panel. Torts? Now that would be fun. But he is busy coaching the Rangers. Plus if he hated The Quiz, he will loathe this. Then it hits me. LA Kings coach Darryl Sutter. Sutter's one-word-answer news conferences and general distaste for the media are legendary. Plus, we could make it work with our story. Alas, like Torts, no shot he would ever agree to it. Yet for the next couple of weeks, I can't get the idea of Darryl Sutter, smiling like Dr. Evil as he slips something in our drinks, out of my head.

It's March now, and the Kings are life and death to make the playoffs. Most teams shut down feature requests about now, let alone something like this. I'm not even sure how to ask. *Hey, Darryl, we're doing a parody of* The Hangover *where The Panel gets drugged and runs around LA looking like hammered idiots. Could you be the guy who drugs us?* The pitch is always so awkward.

But Mike Altieri, the Kings vice-president of communications, is a really good guy who has always been very helpful. So I write him a long note explaining our idea, and asking for Darryl and a few Kings to be involved. I text Anze Kopitar asking if he'll play a key role in the piece. "For sure," he says. That part was simple. I have known Kopy since his rookie season. He is one of the most easygoing guys in the league. Sutter, I figure, is the anti-Kopy.

I'm surprised when Altieri agrees to try. "I just need to ask him at the right time," he says. "Maybe I'll try at the White House when we visit. He'll be in a good mood then." Perfect. And getting him really drunk so he won't remember being asked would help too. Or maybe ask him at gunpoint. Wait, he's a Sutter. That wouldn't faze him.

While we wait on Darryl, Matt and I try to figure out the rest of the cast and script for *The Panel Hangover*. My original plan quickly falls apart. Our only window to shoot is two days in April, when the Kings have a home game and then a day off. Darren Pang is busy on the road elsewhere with the St. Louis Blues, the team he regularly does TV analysis for. Aaron Ward, my Bradley Cooper, has an event with one of his kids he can't miss. Bob can't go either. So all we have is … me. Oh, and Rick, the producer who looks like Alan, who has been growing his beard just in case. My last hope is a guy who is one of my best and most dependable friends, but is surely way too busy to give up two days to fly to California and act like a fool. But he's all I've got.

"Hey, Dregs, how would you like to spend a couple of days away in LA? We have to shoot a couple of scenes for this silly thing I'm doing, but it'll be just a couple of quick lines for you. You can go to the beach or hang by the pool the rest of the day." (This is a total fabrication. This shoot will take every second we have in LA and Dregs will now be the star.)

"Sounds good," Dregs responds, naively.

(Here's another valuable lesson and takeaway from this book, kids. When you really *really* need your friends to help you, lie to them. You can always suck up and apologize later.)

I decide Aaron Ward will now be the panelist who gets lost. We only need him for one scene at the end, and we can film that later in Toronto. The Kings confirm Kopitar, Jared Stoll, Dustin Penner, and Dustin Brown for the shoot. *The Panel*

Hangover is on. (Still no word on Sutter. And without him, we have no ending.)

A few days before the shoot, Mike sends an email. "You better make alternate plans for the ending. I've asked Darryl a couple of times, but no response." Yup, that's about how I figured Darryl would respond: by deeming it not even worthy of responding to. We're screwed.

Then, the same day we're flying to LA, another email pops up on the phone. One simple, shocking sentence from Mike:

"Darryl is in."

Turns out he has seen the Luongo–Schneider piece we did earlier that season, and loved it. I'm shocked. And thrilled. But mostly shocked.

Now we have a cast and a great twist ending. But zero script. I scratch out some ideas, Matt adds a few scenes, and we arrive in LA a few hours before a Kings–Avalanche game. We plan on trying to find celebrities at the game for random cameos. Then we'll drive around LA all night shooting the party scenes (tough assignment). The next day, we'll shoot our bits with the Kings and Darryl. We have 24 hours to be done and on our way back to Canada with some semblance of a movie parody.

The Kings game is a series of absurdities. Rick (the Alan look-a-like) is wearing the exact outfit Zach Galifianakis wore in *The Hangover*. Same T-shirt. Same pants. Same satchel. And as we walk the concourse, everyone is freaking out and taking photos, believing he actually is Zach Galifianakis. Which is hilarious, because if Zach is going to go watch a Kings game, that would surely be his choice of wardrobe—to dress exactly as his best-known movie character.

We find Matthew Perry's suite, and the *Friends* star (and good Canadian boy) is kind enough to agree to shoot a scene with us. I know exactly what I want Matthew to say in the scene, but I'm not sure how to ask him. I want to be hanging off him, completely out of it, yelling, "Hey, everyone, look, it's Joey from *Friends*!" Perry, of course, played Chandler on *Friends*. Matt Leblanc played Joey. That is why this line amuses me. It would be the exact worst thing a drunken buffoon could say to Matthew Perry. But I figure he is sick of *Friends*, and if I suggest we use it in the skit, he'll walk out. So I play dumb.

"So Matthew, I think it would be funny if I was a really drunk obnoxious fan. What could I say to you in this scene that would be the most annoying thing anyone could say to you?"

Perry, without skipping a beat, responds, "Just say, 'Are you the guy from *Friends*?'" I love it when a plan comes together.

"Amazing idea! Hey, how about if I take it further and call you Joey from *Friends*? Just to be even a bigger jerk!"

"Perfect!" he says. I own you, Chandler Bing.

Perry is great. He nails the angry-movie-star-being-harassed-by-a-hammered-stranger look, and we have our first scene.

We shoot some other stills with Dregs on Luc Robitaille's lap, and with actors Eric Stonestreet from *Modern Family* and Kevin Powell from *30 Rock*. Then we find Mary Hart, and the mayhem described at the opening of the chapter ensues. We sprint off before Mary's hubby can have us removed by security.

The rest of the night is spent driving around LA, acting like, well, the guys from *The Hangover* are supposed to act during the parts you don't see until the still photos and phone videos at the end. We pay the doorman to get in at some trendy club, then have to bob and weave our way around the dance floor to avoid several angry bouncers who want to confiscate our cameras. (Didn't really have time to get the old "permission to film" thing you apparently need everywhere in LA.) We act like fools on the dance floor, much to the confusion of the 18- to 25-year-olds who make up the rest of the dance floor. We hang out with celebrity-imitators and cross-dressers in West Hollywood, get chased by a cop on a Segway, and yell the most ridiculous things that drugged-up hockey commentators could yell. The very last thing we shoot on our way home ends up being my favourite line in the entire video.

I get Dregs to hang out the window as we cruise down Hollywood Boulevard and scream at the top of his lungs, "Luongo has still not been traded!"

To this day, people ask how ripped we were filming those scenes. We were stone sober. Idiocy comes naturally.

We shoot Darryl the next day before practice. It's the final scene of the movie, a flashback to the night before to reveal who slipped the drugs in our drinks. We tape it in the Kings offices, done up like a club for the scene. Dregs and I stand by a table, dancing like typical Canadian white guys would in a club (heavy overbite). We pretend to notice Zach Galifianakis across the bar and try to hang out with him (explaining Richard's presence in the rest of the film). Darryl is classic. He just wants to talk hockey. Then when we finally say, "Ah, we better get this done, your practice is starting," he proceeds to deliver it perfectly for three straight takes:

SCENE: Los Angeles bar. Tight shot of two drinks on a table. A hand comes in and empties drugs into the drinks (sugar packets from the Kings coffee room—we have a limited props budget). Camera slowly tilts up to reveal Darryl Sutter, with an evil grin. Sutter looks towards the departed Duthie and Dreger and says, "That's what you get for picking the Canucks last year."

We shoot our scenes with the Kings players right afterwards. Jarret Stoll looks like a movie star, so he's a natural. Dustin Penner is predictably fantastic, berating a passed-out Dregs with expletives ("You're an embarrassment! Wake the f@#% up!"). Colin Fraser is a last-minute replacement for Dustin Brown, who forgot about the shoot and went home. (I'm guessing this doesn't happen to Scorsese.) And Kopitar is exactly what we'd hoped for. The Slovenian superstar will never be Daniel Day-Lewis, but he delivers every line in the exact cheesy B-movie (okay, C-movie … maybe F) way we wrote them.

Our final location is Hermosa Beach. We shoot a replica of the opening scene of the original *Hangover*. I'm on the phone calling Kopy, telling him we've lost Aaron Ward just hours before we're supposed to do The Panel for a Kings game.

Two quick notes on the cost of doing business: First, I watch the opening scene of *The Hangover* a hundred times that day on my phone to make sure we get as many details as possible correct. I neglect to get a data plan before I leave, and am informed the next month that my phone bill is nearly $5,000, almost all of it from those 24 hours in LA. Fortunately, we have a wonderful production manager named Nicole Anderson who bails me out with the bosses at Bell. Second, we need to shoot a scene with Dregs sitting in the sand leaning up against a play structure, yelling random things at the sky. But there is a young mother with her kids playing. She doesn't speak English and refuses to move when we politely ask her to. So we do what any good movie producer would. We pay her $20 to get lost for 10 minutes.

Dregs on the beach is my other favourite scene in the piece. The premise is that he is out of it, gonzo, "babbling incoherently at seagulls." As I told you earlier, though most know Darren only as a very serious TSN insider, he's hilarious. Maybe the most satis-fying part of the entire production is that the world gets to see that twisted side of Dregs. He sits in the sand for 10 minutes, yelling things like, "Sources say, you're a bird!" I've rarely laughed harder in my life.

The exhausted crew goes to dinner at The Strand, my favourite LA restaurant, right on the water in Manhattan Beach. It's a classy place. I am wearing a dress shirt and nice jeans. But everyone in the restaurant is staring. And the waitress is acting odd. Then I realize I haven't taken off the Mike Tyson face tattoo I have worn the entire day for the shoot (the same one Ed Helms gets in Bangkok in *The Hangover Part II*). Closest to badass I will ever get.

We shoot the last scene a week later in Toronto, with the Westin Harbour Castle doubling as our LA hotel. Wardo strolls into our room the morning after, in bathrobe, shower cap, and face clay, not lost at all.

"Don't you guys remember? I stayed in last night. Had to get ready for my spa day!"

Matt Cade puts the piece together perfectly and it airs on our playoff preview show. *The Panel Hangover* gets more reaction than anything we've ever done. It later gets nominated for a Canadian Screen Award for Best Feature, up against a series of serious issue-oriented documentaries. The fact that our six minutes of lunacy is grouped with these important pieces of journalism still makes me giggle. Alas, *The Panel Hangover* doesn't win. There really needs to be a category for Best Idiotic Film Parody Involving Drugged Hockey Panelists. We would own that.

chapter 29

BLACK MONDAY

It is right about when Jennifer Lawrence is shooting some good-looking adversary from District 7 with a bow and arrow that I get the text that changes everything.

I feel my phone vibrate, but no chance I'm looking. I'm a loyal follower of the no-check-phone-in-theatre code. Plus, this is date night with my daughters, Darian and Gracie. And there is no text important enough to distract us from seeing JLawr survive for part three of *The Hunger Games*.

But when we get in the car afterwards and I check, the text from my pal Bob McKenzie is a punch in the pants. "Text Phil King for me. I'm hearing we may have lost the NHL rights."

Oh. That's a … problem.

It is late November, 2013. Negotiations for the NHL's Canadian TV rights have been ongoing for several months. As the talks move along, most believe TSN is going to get a much better package of games for Wednesdays and the playoffs, perhaps even taking over events like the All-Star Game. CBC is expected to hold on to *Hockey Night in Canada*, and Rogers would emerge with a new Sunday night national game. I realize throughout that rights talks are tricky, and the outcomes can be surprising. But I never for a second ponder a scenario where we would be shut out.

Bob's text is an hour old when I get it, so before I text Phil, CTV's president, I respond to Bob first.

"I'll ask, but is that plausible?"

Bob responds within seconds.

"You don't need to text him. I already confirmed it. We're out."

Okay then. Is there an opening for a table tennis host in Malaysia?

When I get home, I park myself in front of *Monday Night Football* and spend several hours texting back and forth with Bob and Dregs, all of us trying to figure out how this could have happened and what it means. Bob wrestles with what to do with the information. It's a strange story to break—that the national hockey show you have worked on for 12 years is going to be gone at season's end. But breaking news is what Bob does. So late in the evening, he sends out a tweet. "Pains me to report this, but NHL closing in on landmark CDN TV deal with two CDN networks. Many years (10+), many billions. #overandout."

He follows it a short while later with the hammer: "Official announcement expected Tuesday by NHL: CBC and Rogers have exclusive English-language NHL rights deal. Believed to be 12-year deal."

And with that, Twitter and all of our phones blow up.

I turn mine off, and go to bed. But I don't sleep much. There are a million things swirling around my head. How will this affect our network, everyone who works there? And selfishly, how will it affect me?

I am angry, mostly with the NHL. I have no details at this point as to what really happened, except that Bell had made the original giant offer. Gary Bettman liked most of it, but not all. So he took it to Rogers, and asked them to fix the things he didn't like. Rogers agreed, then made their own "bully-bid," meaning take it or leave it. Bettman and the NHL took it. And we were out.

What bothers me the most in those first few hours (days … weeks) is that I truly feel we'd done a good job with the *NHL on*

TSN. We had come so far from the puppetry of year one. I'm immensely proud to work on that show every night. We have so many people, in front of and behind the cameras, who truly care about broadcasting hockey the right way. I know the people at CBC's *Hockey Night in Canada* feel the same. They have 60 years of tradition, and are also suddenly out in the cold, too. Hockey would still be shown on Saturday nights on CBC, but will be controlled completely by Rogers.

The only difference is the CBC has financial issues and saw this possibility coming. TSN did not. No one had promoted and covered the game in the last dozen years like we had. And I just can't figure out why the NHL would turn its back on that relationship.

I am not bitter with Rogers. It is a helluva play by them. Keith Pelley, the guy who hired me 15 years earlier, has pulled off one of the biggest moves in the history of Canadian broadcasting. They hold a news conference the next day that I watch for a few minutes, but then turn off.

By the end of Tuesday, speculation is in full swing on what will happen to the commentators at the various networks. I don't want to go anywhere. But I have no idea what I'm going to be doing if I stay. My mind is foggy. And I'm too busy to clear it. We have games all week, then we're heading to Ottawa to broadcast Daniel Alfredsson's return with the Detroit Red Wings on Sunday. I'm scheduled to speak to journalism students at Carleton on the Friday night before. It is only my second trip back to the school since I graduated in 1989. So I spend the rest of the week working, prepping, and trying to avoid phone calls, because they are all questions I can't answer.

Mom: Are you going to lose your job?

Buddy #1: Are you going to Rogers?

Mom (again): Are you sure you still have a job?

Buddy #2: Are you going to the States?

Mom (she really cares): Can you go back to Ottawa and be an anchor there again?

Buddy #3 (smartass): So are you going to do darts now? One hundred and ... EIGHTY!

I have no clue. But Bob does. He has already sprung into action. He only wants to work another five years or so, so he has no intention of going anywhere. But he's making it clear to the executives that he doesn't want to stay unless the rest of us do. And Bob has the ability to be very direct when he says, "You better make sure that happens."

I arrive in Ottawa Friday evening. I'm staying at the Westin by the Rideau Canal, and I'm already late for my speaking engagement at Carleton. As I jump in my rental car, my phone rings. It's Cheryl.

"Gracie ran away," she says, not panicked, but clearly exasperated. Gracie is my youngest, 10 at the time. She lights up the world, a personality roughly the size of Greenland. Which means she occasionally gets a bit theatrical. So after a little fight with Mom, she packs up her pink suitcase and walks out the front door. As Cheryl and I are talking (we're not really worried—it's unusually warm out and she can see Gracie 20 yards away walking in circles on our court), my phone buzzes again. It's Phil King, the president of CTV.

"Honey, I'll call you right back. Just go out and tell her to get back inside."

Phil wants to know how I'm doing. I ask him the same. It's been a rough week all around. Phil has been great to me since I arrived at TSN when he was the head of accounting. Then someone realized he was a genius at programming, and he quickly climbed the ladder, to where he is now running Canada's largest television network.

"We want you to stay," Phil says. "Tell us what you want to do, and we'll try to make it happen."

Right around that moment, the phone buzzes again. Cheryl.

"Sorry, Phil, could you hold on? I really have to take this." (HOLD and ANSWER)

"Did she come home?"

"Sort of," Cheryl says. "She walked in, walked to the kitchen, grabbed a knife for protection, and left again."

Now, I know the right parental reaction is to be terrified. But instead, we both break out laughing. Gracie should have been in movies years ago. Within a couple of minutes, she's home, quietly slipping the knife back in the drawer, giving up on the idea of "living on the railway" for a while.

Back to Phil.

"Listen, we are going to tear up your contracts, and Mark Milliere and Stewart Johnston are flying to Ottawa tomorrow to present offers to you, Bob, and Darren …"

As Phil is talking, another call comes through from a number I don't recognize. I let it go to voicemail, thank Phil for the call, and rush in to Carleton to speak.

The students make my night. When it comes time to ask questions after I speak, one after another, they say how much they love the *NHL on TSN*, and how bitter they are that the NHL shut us out. It means more than they know.

The next day, I'm about to walk across the street to the Château Laurier to meet with Mark and Stewart, and receive a new contract offer. As I'm leaving my room, I remember the call the night before and check my voicemail.

Before we go any further, this is the part of the book I laboured with the longest. There is a story to tell. But it's best told over a beer when I'm 93, and long since kicked out of my TV anchor chair. So this will be the part of the FBI file that gets blacked out before they release it. There are certain things I believe in. One is loyalty. Another is that conversations that are labelled "between us" when they begin should remain that way after they are over. If not, your word isn't worth much.

The *Toronto Star* and some other outlets figure I am headed to NBC. *The Globe and Mail* reports a few weeks later that I was contacted by Rogers to become their main hockey host. I will only say that it was a very strange, confusing few days.

TSN makes me a very generous offer on Saturday afternoon. It involves changing my role to one similar to what Bob Costas does at NBC, hosting most of the major events on the network. The chance to go back to doing the Grey Cup, the Super Bowl, The Masters, and more is very appealing. But I tell them I need a couple of days to figure things out.

The TSN crew goes out for dinner in Ottawa on Saturday night. Bob looks defeated at dinner. The week has taken a toll. No one has done more to build the hockey brand at TSN than Bob McKenzie. And now we have lost the national rights, and he believes I will leave and a bunch of others will follow. It crushes me to see him like that. We all stay out late and have a few, trying to forget the last few days happened.

Mark Milliere calls me Sunday morning. I've had a thousand phone calls with Mark in my career. This may be the only one I'll always remember. He knows the stress I'm under, and tells me to think of this not as a problem but as a wonderful opportunity. He calls it a once-in-a-lifetime chance to control what I want to do with my life. And he tells me he'll understand whatever I decide. (Though I figure if I leave, I'll be dead to him. He bleeds TSN.)

Watching Alfredsson that night return as a Red Wing is bizarre. He is the first player I covered as a sportscaster. My very first NHL feature was on Alfredsson as a rookie, living in a downtown Ottawa hotel filled with Abba CDs and Pop-Tarts.

Eight years later, in 2003, I brought a box of Pop-Tarts with me when I went to interview Alfredsson at his Kanata home for an *NHL on TSN* feature. It was a (relatively lame) prop to give him at the end of the interview for old times' sake. Alfredsson agreed to do the interview on the players' only full day off that month. We had promised the Senators PR staff we would be in and out in an hour. TSN had broadcasted a game the night before, so I would fly in that morning and go straight to his Kanata home. But winter in Canada being … winter in Canada, there was some weather. Which meant delays and de-icing, and by the time I arrived in Ottawa, I was almost three hours late. The camera crew had been at Alfredsson's house since 9 A.M. Now it was noon, and the guy who was supposed to ask the questions was still nowhere to be seen. I sprinted through the airport, only to find a taxi line about 50 people deep. Panicked, I looked around and saw a white super-stretch limo, with the driver leaned up against the side, waiting for … I dunno … R. Kelly? Matchbox 20? Clay Aiken? I mean, it's 2003 Ottawa. Who grabs a white super-stretch at the Ottawa airport? Me, apparently. Desperate, I ask him if he's free to take me, and he obliges, seemingly shocked he's found a sucker to spend $100 to go to Kanata.

And thus, in quite possibly the most egomaniacal-looking (yet actually humiliating) moment of my career, TV boy pulled up to the humble Ottawa captain's very modest suburban home—on the captain's one day off—three and a half hours late. In a white super-stretch limo.

Of course, Alfredsson just laughed and asked if I needed lunch after the long travel day. And he laughed again when I gave him the Pop-Tarts. Even though he was surely long since sick of seeing that clip.

And now, another decade later, I'm back covering Alfredsson's return to Ottawa as a Red Wing. Between that, visiting my old school, and this big career decision ahead of me, the entire weekend feels like some bizarre circle-of-life moment. And it freaks me out a little. The game coverage goes well, though my head is elsewhere. I need time to think.

But I don't have any. I'm on an 8 A.M. flight back to Toronto, where I am going to interview Will Ferrell at the CTV headquarters at 299 Queen St. West for a half-hour special we are doing on him. It's intimidating interviewing one of the funniest men on the planet and a guy whose movies I have quoted for pretty much every intro in my career.

Ferrell is exhausted. He has been touring non-stop promoting *Anchorman 2*, and was in Winnipeg the night before doing curling with Vic Rauter. We chat for about 10 minutes before the shoot. He is, as I expected, a really nice guy. The curse of the comedian is that people expect them to be funny 24/7. Which is impossible. Will and I talk about kids and hockey. He does not make a single joke or funny face. The interview goes well, but anyone expecting Frank the Tank or Ricky Bobby to show up might be disappointed.

Afterwards, I spend an hour in Phil King's office trying to figure what my life at TSN and CTV will be like after the national rights are gone.

That night I have a long talk with my trusted agent Rand Simon, and a longer one with Cheryl before bed. I finally sleep well. And when I wake up, I know I'm staying at TSN. I just have too many good friends and good feelings to leave. I let Phil, Stewart, and Mark Milliere know that I will sign a long-term contract that day. Bob and Darren do the same.

As I get out of the shower that afternoon, just before heading into work, my phone rings.

"Hey, James, it's Peter Mansbridge."

I have been a long-time admirer of the CBC news anchor, but have never met or talked to him. But our industry is small. Peter apparently knows people who are intimately aware of what has been going on the last few days and has called just to lend his support and offer advice, if I need it.

Standing naked in my bathroom (sorry for the visual) talking to Peter Mansbridge about my future is right up there on the

TSN Top-10 Strange Moments of My Life list. It is very kind of him, and I won't forget it. But I don't need advice anymore. I sign a 10-year contract that night to stay with TSN and CTV.

It feels right.

And in an odd way, it feels like I'm starting a whole new career.

chapter 30

WELCOME TO THE NEW AGE

The Russian teenager sitting next to me looks like he is about to hyperventilate.

"Oh my God. Oh my God. Oh my God," he says over and over just as I'm about to interview him on air. Nikita Scherbak is a messy mix of joy, relief, and "holy crap, this really happened!" Moments ago, he was drafted late in the first round by the Montreal Canadiens. He had been a long shot. The third-last player taken in the junior import draft. Now he is about to give the most heartfelt, funniest, broken-English interview of the 2014 NHL draft in Philadelphia.

Nikita: It's amazink heemotions. My hand eetz shakink right now. Eetz crazy day!

Me: Having Russians like Markov and Emelin should help your transition …

Nikita: Yes, but I speak a little French. Bonjour. Comment ca va?

Me: Assez bien. Et vous?

Nikita: I don't know. Only know easy words.

Me: I heard you watched TSN back in Moscow.

Nikita: No. But I watch before. American football. NHL, leettle bit.

Me: You ever watch curling with Vic Rauter?

Nikita: Curl ... ink?

Me: Yes.

Nikita: It's my favoureet sport!

It ends up being my last interview of the draft. And thus perhaps my last interview on the draft stage ever. This is our final event as national NHL rights holder. And I will miss hosting it more than any other thing we've lost.

The games go on. We have regional rights for the Leafs, Senators, and Jets. We'll be broadcasting as many hockey games as we always have during the regular season. The Panel is eternal. But the draft is different. Special. Every year, there are 30 champions. Thirty kids wrapped in new suits and hair product, all beaming as they finally put on that NHL jersey and hat, their moms weeping in the crowd. And getting to interview them a minute after hearing their name called is as good as it gets for me.

Just before Nikita, we have P.K., Malcolm, and brand-new Vancouver Canuck Jordan Subban on the stage together. It is the completion of a remarkable brotherly hat trick. Malcolm wipes the tears away. Then his brothers rib each other about who has the sharpest suit. These are some of my favourite moments in this job. And on this day, it is hitting me how much I will miss them.

We sign off by wishing Rogers luck when they take over next year. And that's it. Fade to black. Drinks, wings, and reminiscing follow in some basement bar in Philly until the early morning. Then it's time to start over.

I figure the best way to explain my new job definition at TSN is to give you a chronological play-by-play of my first year, post–national rights holder.

July 20, Ottawa

Part of my new TSN gig is to co-host the CFL playoffs and Grey Cup with Rod Smith. I'll also do the odd marquee game during the summer. No better place to start than the stadium where I sat with Mom and Dad watching the Riders get pounded 52–10 every week. It is the Ottawa Redblacks home opener. Their first game in the league. Everyone is there. My sisters and their families, and of course my mom and dad, now in their 80s—still as passionate as ever about Ottawa football. I have my son, Jared, with me, and bring Mom and Dad down on the field before the game to get a photo of the four of us. I well up a bit. Damn, I'm soft when it comes to family stuff. (And football. I cry a lot over football.)

The first autograph I ever got was from Tony Gabriel, the legendary Rough Rider tight end. I was 11. I stood in line at the bookstore at St. Laurent Centre for a half hour to get him to sign a copy of *Double Trouble*, his autobiography. I bring it along on the trip, thinking I might use it as a prop on TV. Turns out Gabriel is there for the pre-game ceremony. When I show him the book, his smile is wider than mine was when he signed it. And then he asks if he can get a photo with me. Life is weird.

The Redblacks win, which doesn't jibe at all with my childhood memories of this place. The second the game ends, Henry Burris yells into the TSN broadcast camera, "Where's Duthie? I told you, Duthie! You didn't believe! I told you! This ain't hockey!" I believe this has something to do with Jock Climie and I saying a day earlier on *SportsCentre* that winning six games would be a successful first season for Ottawa. Henry clearly doesn't agree. (They'd go 2–16.) But I love Hank. He was a rookie QB my rookie year of hosting CFL at TSN. And the fact his first thought after his team wins its inaugural home game is to taunt me makes me feel welcome again in the CFL.

September 11, Manhattan Beach, California

Darryl Sutter won't stop talking. This may be a shock to those who only know the LA Kings coach from his news conferences, where three words is a run-on sentence. Earlier in the day, we play a game called Darryl Sutter: Win or Lose? with his players. We show them post-game clips from Darryl in the playoffs and ask them if it was after a win or a loss. They mostly fail. Miserably. Darryl is equally grumpy, no matter what the result.

But here in his home in Manhattan Beach, away from the cameras and obvious questions he can't stand, you see the real Darryl. We do a long interview with him for our NHL season-preview show. He then asks (demands) the entire crew to come to his favourite pub for dinner and drinks. Now it's five hours and multiple beers later, and Darryl is still telling stories. Stories about his playing days. Stories about his brothers. Stories about his farm in Viking, Alberta. Like the day the Cup came there, buckled into the passenger seat of a Gator four-wheeler driven by Sutter's son Chris, who has Down syndrome. Darryl smiles ear to ear as he describes Chris, driving Lord Stanley's mug through the fields, hootin' and hollerin' the whole way.

Sutter should really have a talk show on Oprah's network: *Darryl!*

September 21, Toronto

It's an hour before the start of *The Amazing Race* after-show and former ballet dancer Rex Harrington is throwing a diva fit. Rex can't stand another team from the show, twin brothers Pierre and Michel from Quebec. So he decides to walk out. Thus begins my life on the other side of television. When I decide to stay at TSN/CTV, we talk about crossing over to do some non-sports shows. *After the Race* is the first. I've been a fan of the American version for years, so I'm up for it. But now the dancer has bailed, the producers are freaking a little, and I'm realizing this will be different from asking Jonathan Toews about the Hawks forecheck.

They eventually track down Rex in a nearby bar, and coax him back. He quietly sulks most of the show, until the end, when the French brothers go on a rant about how the program was edited to make them look bad. Rex decides to pipe up and call them motherf#$%ers. Fortunately, the guy manning the six-second-delay button catches it in time and the nation never hears it. Besides that, the show is a blast. And the motherf#$%er comment makes me feel at home. It's an angry hockey player favourite.

November 30, Vancouver

Henry Burris isn't mad at me anymore. I know this because we are rapping onstage together at the CFL awards. I've mutated Naughty by Nature's "O.P.P." to introduce the MOP (Most Outstanding Player Award). Rapping is a secret talent. Don't giggle. When I was in grade 7, I memorized every word of the extended version of The Sugarhill Gang's "Rapper's Delight," the first rap song to cross over to mainstream. When The Sugarhill Gang visits my pal James Cybulski's studio on his radio show to promote a documentary, James remembers this fact. (I believe I may have done it for him once as I have no shame.) He calls me at home and puts me on the air. And I perform "Rapper's Delight" with the guys who actually did "Rapper's Delight." I lied about the Vancouver Olympics. THIS is the single-greatest moment of my career.

On Grey Cup Sunday, I get to introduce the halftime act, Imagine Dragons, to the crowd. This has always been a dream—to be that guy who grabs the mic and screams in an AC/DC voice: "Hello Vancouver! Are you ready to rock?!?" My bosses don't let me do that at the Grey Cup. Sadly. Instead, I just get to say something boring and straight like, "Please welcome international recording artists Imagine Dragons." I leave my set and go watch the show for a few minutes. During their hit "Radioactive," as they belt out "Welcome to the new age," I think to myself, that would be a really cheesy title for the chapter on my job change. Even I'd never stoop that hokey. Wait. Oh.

December 4, Toronto

I have never felt smaller. Not in an ashamed, humiliated way. I've had plenty of those (see most every chapter). I mean, literally. I am sitting on a stage next to Charles Barkley, Dikembe Mutombo, and Magic Johnson. I look like a pre-schooler. I want my booster seat. Toronto Raptors GM Masai Ujiri had asked me to host this panel at his fundraiser, Giants of Africa, commemorating the one-year anniversary of Nelson Mandela's death. It's a mildly intimidating gig, for a couple of reasons. First, I don't want to let Masai down, as I know how important the event is to him. Mandela was his hero. Second, George Cope, the head of Bell, thus my boss's boss's boss, is standing directly in my line of sight. And though he has been extremely nice to me in all of our chats, my vivid imagination has him making a throat-slashing gesture if I screw up. But the panel goes smoothly. Charles is hilarious, as always. Masai is thrilled. George Cope is smiling. I live to work another day. The moment I say goodnight, I jump off the stage, out the door, and into a cab to the airport. My flight leaves in 25 minutes for Ottawa.

December 5, Gatineau, Quebec

My first soccer gig at TSN is hosting the draw for the Women's World Cup. Soccer was the sport I played the most growing up. Until I got cut from the Gloucester Hornets top junior team at 17, threw out my cleats over the hedge in my backyard, and swore I'd never play again. (I didn't handle rejection well.)

Canada draws China in its first game. Though I've been researching, I brain-cramp and can't remember a single player on China. I cover up by referring to them as the "always dangerous Chinese." Veteran move. Thankfully my analysts Jason deVos and Kara Lang know everything. TV Rule 27: Good analysts make it easy to be a good host.

January 5, Toronto

My wife texts me from her seat across the Air Canada Centre.

"WHAT IS HAPPENING???" (She enjoys the all-caps in dramatic moments.)

Cheryl isn't a big hockey fan, but her question is fair and pertinent. Canada had been up 5–1 on Russia in the gold medal game of the 2015 World Junior Hockey Championship. Now it's 5–4, and the entire nation is having horrific flashbacks to Buffalo in 2011, when Canada blew a 3–0 lead to Russia in the third and lost 5–3.

The World Juniors ruin every Christmas for our family. And I wouldn't trade it for anything. The 2015 tourney has been one of my favourites. It's right up there with 2009 in Ottawa, when my parents sat with me in our suite for the semi-final against Russia. With about two minutes left and the Russians ahead, I suggest they might want to leave early to beat the brutal traffic out of Kanata. They leave. Eberle. Oops. They remove me from the will the next day.

No one leaves early this time. Canada plays a perfect defensive third and holds on to win, ending the five-year gold medal drought. Hours later, as the players celebrate with their families, assistant coach Dave Lowry is taking a family photo with the trophy and his wife asks me to be in it. Which feels ... awkward. But hey, that's Canada: where everyone gets to be an honorary uncle or cousin when gold is won.

January 27, Phoenix

The last Super Bowl Media Day I covered was in Jacksonville in 2005. My lasting memory is of that Mexican reporter from Azteca Deportes who asked questions with a hand puppet. I arrive at Media Day in Phoenix and the first person I run into is the same reporter, now with a sidekick and two new hand puppets. I quietly wonder if the original puppet got a better offer and jumped to Telemundo.

The problem with Media Day is that half the "reporters" don't seem to actually work in the media. There must be radio stations who hand out passes to contest winners. There are a couple of guys in the Rob Gronkowski scrum filming with their iPhones and asking probing questions like, "Gronk, why are you so awesome?"

Though that is actually better than many of the questions real media asked.

I am standing with Seattle punter and Canadian boy Jon Ryan when a reporter sticks his mic in and asks:

Reporter: You are Canadian, right?

Ryan: Yes.

Reporter: Do you like pontoon?

Ryan: What?

Reporter: Do you like pontoon?

Ryan: Poutine?

Reporter: Yes, poutine.

January 31, Scottsdale

I am standing in the bleachers behind the sixteenth hole at the Phoenix Open, the craziest golf tournament the planet has ever known. It's my brief recess from Super Bowl coverage. The most fruitless job in sport belongs to the volunteers who ask the crowd for silence before players hit their tee-shots on 16. The fans scream, cheer, boo, chant, and mostly drink through every shot. You hit one tight, it's a football stadium celebrating a game-winning touchdown for the home team. You miss the green, it's the same crowd after the ref called the touchdown back. Jon Rahm wears an Arizona State football jersey for his tee-shot. The crowd goes ballistic. Then he hits it long to the back of the green, and they boo him relentlessly. The 16 Bleacher Creatures also perform every chant ever used in American sport. Examples:

- "USA! USA!" for every American player, and some Euros who they believe are American because they have had 17 Budweisers.
- The Atlanta Braves Tomahawk Chop chant. For no explicable reason.
- "Bald spot! Bald spot!" As Phil Michelson strolls towards the green.

You need to put the bleachers at 16 on your bucket list. Just don't bring the kids. The tournament is basically the world's largest nightclub. Except it opens at 7 A.M. Women show up in heels and cocktail dresses. And stumble out covered in mud. There are more than one hundred thousand people on the course the day I'm there. I figure about ten thousand are watching golf. Always thought the Phoenix Waste Management Open was a terrible sponsor name. But in my three hours there, I see two fights, a couple of guys throwing up, and one young lady (in heels) passed out in a hazard. The sponsor name, in retrospect, is perfect.

I eat dinner with my CTV colleague Anju King and her sister Azalea at Lo-Lo's Chicken & Waffles in Scottsdale, highly recommended by Deion Sanders on Twitter. I assume the name means waffles for breakfast, and chicken as a specialty for dinner. I am wrong. It means fried chicken and waffles, together, for every meal. Broccoli is not allowed within 10 miles of the place. It is a bylaw, I believe. I order the Tre-Tre because it sounds like it gives me street cred. It has two drumsticks and one giant waffle with an ice cream–sized scoop of butter. It is spectacular. I have no regrets.

Later that night, Phoenix

Have quadruple bypass surgery.

February 1, Phoenix

Game day. I'm in the auxiliary press box in the nosebleed section of University of Phoenix Stadium, missing Andy Rooney a little. I'm a mile from the stage for the halftime show. In fact, from my vantage point, it almost looks like Katy Perry is dancing with sharks! Lol. As if. No choreographer would be that drunk. Unless they were at the Phoenix Open all weekend. The game is spectacular. Once again, we watch the end from the bowels of the building, in a Disney ride–like lineup to get on the field. I have never seen a group of jaded media types gasp the way they did when the Seahawks threw an interception on that last play instead of handing the ball to Marshawn Lynch.

Even the hand puppets said "Holy Shit!" (In Spanish.)

February 15, Paraguay

Covering the Super Bowl is not my favourite football moment of the year. That comes in a poor village in Limpio, Paraguay, when I present a TSN football to a five-year-old boy who has never seen a football. He acts like it is the single-greatest gift in the history of humanity. Jose is the little boy my family sponsors. This is my first trip with Christian Children's Fund of Canada, an aid agency I'm working with. Jose lives in a tin shack the size of your en suite bathroom with his mom and seven brothers and sisters. They have nothing. And yet running with that football, he looks like he has everything he needs. Jose does his best DeMarco Murray on me, even though he has no clue who DeMarco Murray is. Every time he gets by, he finishes by throwing the ball into the tree at the back of his yard. I don't bother to get the translator to explain the rules. Though I have this vision that he will grow up and teach his nation that this is how you score in football. I will return someday and find the Paraguayan Professional Football League, where running backs bust one for 75 yards and then throw the ball into the goal post.

My son, Jared, is with me on the trip. My plan is take each of my children to a country CCFC does work in. It's a life-changer for a 15-year-old who has never wanted for anything. We see poverty he could never have imagined. And we also visit the schools and medical centres that donations have built. Jared wants to do more. Wants to figure out other ways to help. As he sleeps on my shoulder on the long flight home, I think to myself, we raised a good kid. I'm pretty certain Jared, Darian, and Gracie will do much more important things in life than talking about sports on TV.

March 2, Toronto

There are llamas in our studio. We get sued by Toronto Maple Leafs Joffrey Lupul, Dion Phaneuf, and his wife, Elisha Cuthbert, for an offensive tweet that inadvertently scrolls on the bottom of our screen. I tell Chris Stewart he has been traded to Minnesota live on the air. Just another ho-hum day on *TradeCentre*.

March 8, Toronto

"I'm gonna need some Seacrest from you now," says the producer. Oh God. What have I signed up for?

A few weeks earlier, CTV president Phil King calls me, asking if I want to audition to host a new Mark Burnett (*Survivor, Shark Tank*) show that is going to be co-produced by CTV. It's called *Dream Funded*, a combination of *Dragon's Den* and *American Idol*, where aspiring entrepreneurs will try to win over a crowd and a pair of business experts in order to fund their invention. I have no time, and limited interest, but I respect Phil a ton, so the next day, I'm standing on my mark in a casting office, in front of a row of executives, producers, and a camera to record the carnage.

"Let's just start by you doing some of your lines from the script," one says.

"Script? Oh. Umm. Yeah. I didn't read that," I respond.

There is semi-stunned silence for a moment. Apparently, you are expected to read the script they email you before the audition. Who knew? Inexplicably they don't have security escort me out, and instead I spend the next two hours winging intros and auditioning with would-be entrepreneurs and experts. Most of them are extremely nervous. I could not be less nervous. One of the producers has already told me they'll likely be going with a female host. So I'm as relaxed as a nap, thinking mostly about the hockey game that night.

A week later, the phone rings. "You got the job! Mark Burnett loved you." Life is really weird.

We tape the pilot on a weekend in the CBC studios in downtown Toronto. In fact, the *Dream Funded* studio is right next to the new *Hockey Night in Canada* studio. I briefly contemplate busting in and tackling my friend George Strombolopolous live on the air, screaming madly, "Mine! This should have been all MINE!" Would have been funny. Career-ending. But still funny.

Hosting the show ends up being a lot of fun. It's much more positive than *Dragon's Den*. No one gets ripped for their ideas. But there are Idol-type eliminations, where I am told to summon my inner Seacrest, and pause for what feels like an eternity at every dramatic moment.

"Mike … … … … I'm sorry, you're in the bottom three."

But it's hard to argue against cheese when you have done the bits I've done on TSN. By the way, here's the least real thing about reality TV: it takes us 18 hours to shoot a 41-minute show. By the end, I'm so loopy, I ask one of the entrepreneurs if they have any trades to report.

April 10, Augusta, Georgia

Jordan Spieth was eight the last time I covered The Masters. This week, at 21, he plays like Nicklaus in his prime, and speaks with the wisdom of Nicklaus … now. I've never seen a younger star with an older soul. I stroll alongside him as he leaves the eighteenth green Friday after shooting the lowest 36-hole total in tournament history. He calmly shrugs to his agent and all he says is, "I could use a sandwich."

Spieth goes on to win his first green jacket handily. As we get set to tape our post-show on Sunday evening, I make a pit stop in the men's bathroom in the International Media Center. Former

PGA star turned analyst Paul Azinger steps up to a urinal down the row (I'm in the middle one, obviously) and says, "Man, this water is cold." It's a way-old male endowment line, but I still chuckle, because it's the polite Canadian thing to do. Thirteen years after Tiger Woods made a cute pee joke at the urinal next to me, I get this Azinger-zinger. In my head, I hear Jim Nantz's voice: "Famous golfer urinal jokes at The Masters. A tradition like no other."

June 11, Edmonton

For the first time in my career, our panel has been pre-empted by God. Or Mother Nature. Or someone up there with anger issues. I am hosting the Women's World Cup, and an apocalyptic thunderstorm has hit just as our pre-game show for Canada vs. New Zealand is about to start. Former Canadian star Kara Lang, ace analyst Kristian Jack, and I are drenched, despite the efforts of lighting guru Slobodan Marin and his crew to put tarps up to shield us from the storm. We do the entire show without appearing on camera, huddled in front of the desk. I carry on despite the fact my supposed "firm hold" moulding paste isn't holding firmly. Heroic. Kara is pregnant, so as the wind and rain howl around us, I yell in mock Bill Paxton disaster-movie voice, "Forget me. Just save the baby dammit!" The soccer panel has learned quickly what the hockey panel has known forever. Its host is an idiot.

July 7, Toronto

It's my last day before summer vacation after a long, strange, great year. I am on the set of the film *Goon: Last of the Enforcers*, shooting a couple of scenes in the role of a hockey panel host (typecasting continues to plague my acting career). I joked to writer/actor/director/great guy Jay Baruchel at an awards show a couple of years ago that *The Panel* should be in his *Goon* sequel. I figured he was drunk when he said, "Good idea."

My character's name in the original script is Michael Leroy. They later change it to James Duthie, thus making it official. I am no longer real. I am a fictional character.

chapter 31

VIEWER MAIL

Whoops. I only really had two goals in writing this book. One was simply to share some stories, before I forgot them. The other was to answer the most common questions I get asked. That way, whenever someone asks one from now on, I can just glare at them and say, "Buy the book, sucker." And then fist-bump my bodyguards, and get back to making it rain.*

*Note of clarification for my future grandkids if they read this. The Urban Dictionary defines "making it rain" as throwing large wads of cash in the air at strip clubs. Your grandpa never made it rain. For a long time, he believed "making it rain" involved causing actual rainfall, and he couldn't figure out why rappers wanted to do that. Gramps was a nerd.

But here we are in Chapter 31, and there are still more unanswered questions than a Marshawn Lynch scrum. So instead of rewriting the entire book to eloquently weave in the knowledge you seek (way too much work), I'll just answer them here. Like Letterman's old Viewer Mail segment. Except not as funny. But more heartfelt. Maybe.

Your questions:

Which NHL team do you cheer for?

I am frequently labelled as an Ottawa Senators fan, mostly because I am from there, and will always defend my hometown. My mom and dad cheer hard for the Sens, so it would make me happy to see them win, just to give my folks a thrill. But I don't root for the Senators or any team. That's one of the few regrets of this job. It sucks the fan out of you. I grew up a Chicago Blackhawks lover, then switched to the New York Islanders when Potvin, Trottier, and Bossy took over the league. (I could jump bandwagons with the best of them.) But now I only cheer for the teams that can help me out in life. Case in point: Jared is set to graduate from grade 8 on the night Game 7 of the 2013 Stanley Cup final is scheduled. So as I watch Game 6, I'm begging for a Blackhawks victory. If Chicago wins, they take the Cup and I make it home for the graduation. Boston wins, and I have to call my boy to tell him I won't be there. With the Bruins up 2–1 late in the third, I'm saying all kinds of curse words involving Tuukka Rask under my breath. Then the Hawks score two goals in the last two minutes to win. The rule is "no cheering in the press box," but I am doing internal cartwheels. As a fan, I would have loved a Game 7 in Chicago. But as a dad, I needed it over. Same thing happens a few years earlier when Detroit loses a Cup-clinching game and costs me seeing my daughter Darian's first soccer goal. I am sour at Nik Lidstrom for months.

This is basically the way I look at sports now. Whatever result will screw my family the least is the one I hope for. I still love the games. I will never take for granted being at events that I know many of you would sell a kidney to attend. Those of us who get to cover them for a living are beyond spoiled. But mostly, I cheer for people instead of teams—guys I've gotten to know like Roberto Luongo, Jordan Eberle, Anze Kopitar. Hockey has plenty of really good guys worth rooting for. I just don't care what logo they have on.

Do you have a nickname?

You mean besides Thor? Not really. Standard stuff: JD, Jimmy, Forbes (my middle name), Monkey-Boy (damn you, Maggie). There are few great nicknames anymore in sports. I once asked NHLer Kris Versteeg if he had a favourite nickname. He had just won the Stanley Cup with the Blackhawks and people were calling him Verstud and Verbeauty. He preferred those to the nickname he had in Bantam AAA. Versteeg complained a lot, so the manager gave him the handle Bitch. It stuck. One night, they were losing 1–0 and Versteeg was struggling. His grandmother was in the stands, and she started yelling, "Skate, Bitch, skate!"

What is the strangest thing a player has ever said to you?

If we expand the category to unintentional voicemail, it's no contest. One day, I see Eric Staal's name on my missed call list. When I check the voicemail, it is muffled and hard to understand, but I can make out a male voice that sounds like Eric's, saying, "Grrrr! Grrrr! Look at the big bear! Grrrr! Grrrr!" I am doing a corporate event with Eric and his brothers a few weeks later, and when I ask him about the call, he gets a sheepish grin on his face.

"I was wondering what was on that voicemail," he says with a chuckle. "I took my young son to the dump in Thunder Bay to see the bears. I was trying to get him into it, making these bear noises, and later noticed I pocket dialed you. I was kinda hoping it wasn't at that moment."

I love that story. Any time an NHL star inadvertently leaves cute baby talk animal sounds on your voicemail, you know you have an odd existence.

Who is your favourite interview?

I enjoy every Brian Burke interview, especially the ones where he just scowls at me. So ... all of them. But the interview I am most proud of is the one we did with Brian and his son, Brendan. It was Brendan's first appearance since he came out in a John Buccigross ESPN.com print piece. He was the manager for the Miami University hockey team, and became the first openly gay man at any high level of hockey. I am honoured that the Burke family trusted me to handle it properly. And I am proud we were able to tackle an issue bigger than the Leafs penalty kill on our show. Brendan died less than two months later in a car accident. It was a tragedy in so many different ways. He would have made a great spokesperson for gay people in sport. In his memory, his brother Patrick founded You Can Play. It is a wonderful legacy for Brendan.

What's your biggest screw-up on air?

The time I was on drugs on radio. Wait, that came out wrong. The 2013 World Juniors in Ufa, Russia, is one of the most challenging events I've ever done from a sleep perspective. Bob and I stay in Toronto for the tournament. With the time change, we are doing pre-game shows at 3 A.M. I am not a great sleeper anyway, so trying to go to bed at 7 P.M. and get up at midnight isn't working for me. My trusted Panel producer and buddy Sean "Puffy" Cameron tells me to try NyQuil to knock myself out. It doesn't really work, so I decide to triple the dose. I take three plastic shot glasses' worth at 6 P.M. one night before a Canada game. Small problem. I forget I have a radio interview to do with a Saskatchewan station at 8 P.M. The phone rings in my hotel, and it takes me a solid minute to figure out

- where I am
- who I am
- why there is a unicorn in Cooperalls doing the *Running Man* on my bed. (It was a lot of NyQuil.)

I finally answer, and I'm so drugged, I can barely speak. When they call you for radio interviews, there is no long lead-up. It's basically, "Hey, James, Phil from WKTC ... you're on with Mike and The Badger in 10 seconds, enjoy!" So there is no time to back out. I attempt to answer questions for a few minutes, speaking in some form of super slo-mo language (think Frank the Tank in *Old School* when he takes the tranquilizer to the jugular). They mercifully cut me off early, sensing I am out of it. Time for another valuable book takeaway: kids, say no to drugs—in particular, say no to chugging sedatives right before you do radio interviews in Saskatchewan.

What is your most memorable celebrity encounter?

You mean besides dating Madonna briefly in the 80s when I was a dancer on the Like a Virgin Tour? Well, there was the time Kid Rock and John Cusack almost make me miss introducing Brendan Shanahan into the Hockey Hall of Fame. They are there to see their Malibu pal Chris Chelios get inducted. While Gary Bettman is speaking, the pair comes backstage to smoke a cigar. We chat for a minute and I get them to pose for a pic with me. While we're taking it, I realize the crowd is politely clapping. Bettman is done, and I'm supposed to be onstage introducing Shanahan to the Hall. But I can't bail mid-pic on the American Badass and my adolescent movie hero Lloyd Dobler. So there is an empty stage and awkward silence for several seconds before I sprint out to give Shanny his moment.

My true favourite comes more than a decade earlier. It is pure Canadiana. I am sitting in the dark in some hall in downtown Toronto watching the premiere of musician, writer, and filmmaker Dave Bidini's *The Hockey Nomad*. When the lights come up, I quickly congratulate Dave on the film, which was great, and head for the exit, when I get a tap on my shoulder. I turn around to see Gord Downie smiling at me.

"I just wanted to say I watch you all the time and really enjoy your work," Gord says.

"Uhhhh ... ditto," is about all I can get out in response.

I don't get star-struck often. But The Tragically Hip has been the soundtrack of my life for the past 15 years. I have seen them around 20 times live. (No, I'm not one of those Springsteen freaks who counts every show and ranks them—"No way, bro! Philly '99 can't hold a candle to Dayton 2003!") Outside of Cheryl and my parents, I have heard more of Gord's words than any other human. And he might be first, because Mom and Cheryl aren't on replay in my headphones. This is the moment where I say to myself, "This is now officially the best life you could have ever imagined."

How can I get a job like yours?

I get this question not only from high school and broadcasting students, but from 40-year-old computer programmers with two kids and a mortgage who want to give up their jobs and go back to school to chase their dream of being on TSN. I'm never sure what to say. I prefer dream-chasing over dream-crushing. But it's a long shot. It took me four years of journalism school, eight years of local news and sports, and several more working my way up at TSN to get to be The Guy on the Left. And so much of it was luck. The list of "what ifs" that fell my way is just silly.

What if I hadn't had that last second change of heart and had gone to McGill instead of Carleton? Would I have been happy teaching kids how to climb the rope in some middle school gym class? (I think I probably would have, but not this level of happy.) What if Guy Lepage hadn't broken that rib skiing the weekend after my apprenticeship at CJOH? Would I have gotten another job in the business (when there weren't many around) or just given up and joined the RCMP, following in my dad's massive footsteps? What if Max Keeping hadn't given me a chance to do sports? What if Keith Pelley didn't like the fact I was wearing jeans in that tape I sent TSN? What if Linda Freeman loved hosting hockey and TSN loved her back? What if I hadn't said, "No, I'm happily married, leave me alone!" when Kate Upton tried to whisk me away to Bora Bora that night? Wait, what?

You wearing your rubber boots tonight?

Yes. The blue ones with polka dots.

What's the best part of your job?

That one requires one final chapter.

chapter 32

THE JUICE

When I move to Vancouver in 1997 to do news, I believe I am The Man—the LeBron of local news reporting. No one could milk a-minute-thirty out of a city council debate on dog parks like me. Before the station goes to air, VTV hires a consultant named Scott Rensberger to help reporters with storytelling. I believe I already know everything about storytelling. So I'm barely paying attention during Scott's seminar. Until he pops one of my stories into his VHS machine (Old Guy Reference #421). *Here we go kids. Watch the king and learn.* It's a fluffy feature I did in Ottawa about an estate auction—part of a series on saving money that won an International Edward R. Murrow Award. So I figure it's pretty much the greatest thing that has ever aired on a local newscast. I rented a tux and went to LA to accept the Murrow. So in my head, I'm basically George Clooney now (if George Clooney looked like my odd combination of Ben Stiller, Ed Helms, Seth Meyers, and the drug-addicted brother from *Blossom*). Rensberger shows my piece to all the reporters and producers in the room, compliments a couple of things about it, then starts ripping it apart.

"Where's the juice?!?" he yells.

The basis of Scott's teaching is that reporters need to find the "juice" of a story. What's the part that really matters? What gets the viewer's attention? What will they remember? It could be a key character, a piece of information, a sound bite, or maybe one single telling shot. It's the heart of the story. And while my Murrow winner has some smart writing and editing, it apparently is juice free.

"WHERE'S THE FREAKIN' JUICE?!" he yells again, as I slide further down my chair. And I realize, he's right. My big international award winner has no soul. Scott not only teaches me a crucial reporting (and humility) lesson that day, but gives me a new way to look at life. Your job, your hobbies, your relationships … finding the juice in them is what we try to do every day. And if there's none, it's probably time to move on.

In those early years, I get my work juice from doing a good TV story or writing a column people enjoy. At TSN, it's covering a big game, or getting tapped on the shoulder by Gord Downie, or convincing goalies to be run over by Zambonis. When you get married and have kids, most of your juice comes from them. First step, first word, first Niners shirt (have to teach them early). Nowadays, it's when I watch Gracie onstage in a musical—the place she is happiest in the world. Or when Darian scores three touchdowns for her school's flag football team. (Okay, I might have been coaching and gave her the ball a lot, but still … juice.)

And then sometimes you get one of those perfect days when it just flows. The last NHL lockout ends at some crazy hour of a January Sunday morning. When I get the news, I feel like Andy Dufresne in *Shawshank* when he comes out of that "five hundred yards of shit smelling foulness I can't even imagine." I have rarely been so jacked coming in to work. Especially at 5 A.M. There is nothing I despised more in my career than those years waiting for hockey to come back. We're on the air as soon as I get in. I am texting every player I know to come on the show because we have hours to fill. And one after another, we get them—Stamkos, Giroux, Luongo, Crosby—all thrilled that hockey is back. With Dregs, Wardo, and Pierre Lebrun reporting live from New York, and Bob and I in studio, we're all over it. Few things get the blood (and juice) flowing like covering a major breaking-news story. But I have a problem. Jared is playing in the final of a big hockey tournament at noon. We're supposed to be off the air by 9, but we get extended to 10, then 11, then 12. All I can think about is that I'm going to miss my boy's game. We finally do get off at noon, and I race up Highway 404, arriving just in time to see our Aurora Tigers blow a 3–1 lead in the final minute and head to overtime. On the first shift of OT, Jared takes a perfect pass from his pal Jack and one-times the winner. It's probably his single-greatest moment in hockey. And mine as a hockey dad. Tournament over … lockout over … your kid looking up at you in the stands with that giant mouth guard grin and MVP trophy in his hand. JUICE. 7/11 Big Gulp size.

So back to that question from the end of the last chapter. *What is the best thing about your job?*

I still get plenty of juice working at TSN—covering big events like the World Juniors, the Grey Cup, the Super Bowl, The Masters. They will never ever get old. But the single-best part of my job is that it occasionally allows me to meet remarkable people, who teach you more than any Ph.D. could.

On the first night of November, 2014, I get an email from my sister Merydee, with a link to a story in the *Ottawa Citizen*. "One of the most heart-wrenching things I've ever read. In the end, he talks about wanting to be a sportscaster—I'm wondering if TSN could do anything for him. It's unimaginable what he endures."

The story is about a 14-year-old boy from Russell, Ontario, named Jonathan Pitre. Jonathan is a "butterfly child," the name for the few who suffer from a rare genetic disease called Epidermolysis bullosa (EB). It causes almost every inch of his skin to constantly blister and tear off. Jonathan's body must be wrapped in gauze from neck to toe to protect it. He has been in pain every second of his life. *Citizen* reporter Andrew Duffy does a wonderful job describing Jonathan's condition and his life in the piece. Google it if you have a few minutes. And prepare to be heartbroken. And inspired.

Jonathan's positive attitude and courage are astonishing. I write Andrew as soon as I'm finished reading and ask if I can contact Jonathan and his mother, Tina Boileau. Within a day, Tina and I are talking and planning a visit to TSN for Jonathan. A month later, he is sitting on The Panel, analyzing the Senators play ... being a sportscaster. Living the dream.

Jonathan's story touches everyone who reads it. He appears on several hockey broadcasts. The Senators sign him to be a scout for a day. TSN producer Ross Rheaume crafts a long documentary about him for *SportsCentre* that goes viral and is watched by millions around the world. Jonathan agrees to do it all, not because he wants the attention. He's the opposite of that. He does it so people can learn about his condition. So the next kid with EB doesn't get the stares and comments he's had to live with. So money can be raised to search for a cure. At 14, he has found his calling.

In late 2014, I text Toronto Raptors GM Masai Ujiri and tell him Jonathan's story. Two months later, Jonathan and Tina attend their first Raptors game. Masai invites them to be his guests. They are treated like VIPs. Before the game, Masai wheels Jonathan to centre court to present an All-Star jersey to Raptors star Kyle Lowry. Jonathan's eyes are saucers.

The Raptors win on a DeMar DeRozan bucket in the final 10 seconds. Jonathan, who is often too weak to stand, pulls himself out of his wheelchair and pumps his arm to the sky. For a kid who rarely shows emotion, a calm old-soul, it is beautiful to watch.

There's probably some guilt involved in the dynamic of my friendship with Jonathan. Here are two people who shared the exact same dream: to have a life in sports—if not as an athlete, then as a sportscaster. Everything fell my way, and Jonathan gets this massive brick wall stuck in front of him, blocking his path from the second he's born. Before he can even dare to dream it.

He knows the facts. Knows kids with EB rarely see 30. But every day, he gives the finger to the impossibility of his situation, vowing to change the world while he's here.

After the Raptors game, I walk Jonathan and Tina back to their hotel. I give him a gentle hug, the only kind his frail body can take, and he whispers, "Thanks for everything you've done for me." He has no idea it is the other way around.

What's the best thing about your job?

It is that moment right there. In front of a hotel elevator with a kid who is braver and better than you will ever be. He's looking up at you from his wheelchair, exhausted, but smiling, and saying the most sincere thank-you you've ever heard.

That. That is the juice.

acknowledgments

If it takes a village to raise a child, it takes a country to raise a sportscaster/author. We are a LOT of work (and that's just hair and makeup).

It takes two parents who love you unconditionally, and let you know from the time you are cruising the sidewalk on your Big Wheel that you can be anything you want to be, and they will be behind you through all of it. Jim and Sheila Duthie are all of that and more. I owe everything to them.

It takes two older sisters who are so much smarter and well-rounded than you, it terrifies you to be the one that will fall on your face behind them. That fear pushes you to where you are now. They used to torture me every Christmas by making me search for hours for my present (once submerging it in our cottage lake in the fall with a buoy attached so I had to pick-axe through a foot of ice on Christmas Day to get it), but besides that, Merydee Duthie and Kristy Brundage are pretty freaking fantastic. Not to mention their husbands and kids.

It takes childhood friends, who become lifelong friends, who are all funnier than you and somehow their idiocy seeps into your skin over time. Ward, Tad, Scoot, Harv, Shaw, Jimmy, Rick, Miller, Roch, Darryl, Mike, Laz, Vaz … I don't see you enough anymore, but you are all my brothers. And you all bear responsibility for the silliness I've forced on the nation on television and in this book.

It always takes at least one person, early in your career, to truly believe in you. To give you that shot. For me, that was Max Keeping. He saw something in me when, frankly, I don't think there was that much to see. He basically gave me my career. He would tear me apart if my story intro was poorly written in those early news days at CJOH in Ottawa. I can still hear him when I mail one in now. So I quickly hit delete and start fresh. And now, as I watch him fight the ugliest of cancers, I wish he could do the same to that disease.

It takes risk-takers like Keith Pelley, who plucked me out of local news to host his big football show on TSN. And then, along with Rick Chisholm, put me in countless other positions where I really could have screwed up the network. That kind of faith you never forget. You are supposed to dislike your bosses. Isn't that the first commandment of work? But that has never happened for me at TSN/CTV. Phil King runs the biggest TV network in the country in CTV, and yet he is the opposite of a corporate suit— just a great guy who you love having a beer with. Stewart Johnston personifies all the good things about TSN: hard work, integrity, and class. Mark Milliere has been my direct boss for more than a decade. He is the one who calls to tell me my agent is asking for too much or that he doesn't like my brown suit (he hates brown suits). He also is the guy who surrounds me with tremendous talent, hands me countless amazing opportunities, and always has my back when it matters most.

No one has taken more abuse from me than Steve Dryden. The Panel's favourite pastime is harassing its CEO. We avoid at all costs telling him the truth—that he is the backbone of our show. If you have ever enjoyed a segment or interview I've done, thank Steve. The ideas and questions are usually his. And since every book should have a big reveal at the end, Steve is The Evil Quizmaster.

It would take a phone book to name all the great colleagues and crews I've had at TSN, CJOH, and VTV. A sincere thank-you to every co-host, panelist, camera operator, producer, director, technical producer, editor, audio tech, lighting director, public relations person, makeup artist ... and any position I've forgotten ... that I've worked with. Quick story: Cameraman Marc Malette and I fly to Sweden one fall to do a story on the hockey factory that is Örnsköldsvik, Sweden. It is the home of the Sedins, Peter Forsberg, Victor Hedman, and numerous other NHLers. The town's club team, Modo, has arranged a day at the rink for us to get video of hockey players of all ages. The organizer tells us the city is very excited about a "big TSN crew" coming to town. But Marc gets sick on the plane and is bedridden for two days. So imagine the reaction from the folks in O-vik when the "big TSN crew" turns out to be ... me. Alone. I try to use Marc's equipment, but it's a disaster. My footage is shaky, blue (forgot to white-balance), and out of focus. Point is, my job is easy. The people behind the scenes do the real work.

TSN is just a helluva team. That's not a lame sports metaphor. It's true. Once, while we were on our set outside at a Cup final in Pittsburgh, a drunken fan threw a beer and hit Bob. In about a second, producer Bill Dodson had jumped out of the production truck to chase the guy. Bill, by the way, had a broken ankle in a cast. So the chase didn't go so well. But damn ... the spirit of a teammate.

It takes a pestering book agent like Brian Wood, who keeps calling every couple of months after you wrote two books in one year and swore you'd never write another one, because the whole publishing industry frustrated you. But Brian planted that seed. And I'm glad he did. And it takes an editor like Nick Garrison from Penguin to understand that you hate writing about yourself, and would rather toss it and just do TV. So he's patient and understanding when you miss deadlines and a huge help cutting out the really lame lines. (I know. He didn't get them all.)

It takes friends and colleagues who helped me with all the finishing details of the book (details ... not a strength). Production editor David Ross and copy editor Catherine Dorton had to cope with my generally horrendous punctuation issues"?! Photographer Darren Goldstein shot the cover photo. Renee Rouse, Greg McIsaac, and their TSN PR team helped find old photos. And a big thanks to the odd mix of family and friends who read the book for me (for feedback and lawsuit prevention): Mom (who didn't like the swear words and any stories where I was drinking), Merydee, Brian Wood, Sean Cameron, Corrie Moore, and Brad Fritsch (professional golfer/proofreader ... odd combo).

Most of all, it takes a family willing to put up with you being away a lot for TV, then constantly writing during your free time at home. It takes kids who would sometimes have to ask Dad five times to watch the dance they learned or read the essay they wrote ... before he finally tuned in and looked up from his keyboard. I hate that I was like that. I'm blessed they understood. Jared, Darian, and Gracie are the greatest gifts of my life. And I won the Stanley Cup of life finding Cheryl. From the moment we met, she was willing to sacrifice everything for my career. Give up her job and move across the country? Sure. Move back 10 months later, even though she loved it in Vancouver and really never wanted to leave? Yes. Without hesitation. Take care of three young kids while you are away livin' the dream at the Stanley Cup Final, Super Bowl, Masters, Olympics, etc.? Never a single word of complaint. You need a partner that selfless to let you do something as selfish as write a book.

And finally, it takes all you guys ... for watching all these years and spending your hard-earned cash to read this. (Unless you cheaped out and borrowed it from your roommate Kevin. But thanks for reading anyway.)

JAMES DUTHIE hosts TSN's hockey coverage along with major events like the Grey Cup, the Super Bowl, and The Masters. He has also hosted the Olympics, *SportsCentre*, and CFL and NBA coverage for TSN and CTV. Duthie has received three Gemini Awards and a Canadian Screen Award for Best Sportscaster.